GYNOGRAPHS

"L'esprit agit aussi bien que le corps, il a besoin de nourriture"
["The spirit acts as does the body; it needs nourishment"]. Unsigned.
Frontispiece, *Les femmes savantes ou bibliothèque des dames*
(Amsterdam: Michel Charles Le Cene, 1718).

Joan Hinde Stewart

Gynographs

FRENCH NOVELS BY

WOMEN OF THE

LATE EIGHTEENTH

CENTURY

University of Nebraska Press

Lincoln & London

Acknowledgments
for the use of previously published
materials appear on pp.x–xii.

Manufactured in the United States of America
The paper in this book
meets the minimum requirements of the American
National Standard for Information
Sciences—Permanence of Paper for Printed Library
Materials, ANSI Z39.48–1984.

Library of Congress Cataloging-in-Publication Data
Stewart, Joan Hinde.
GYNOGRAPHS: French novels by women of the late
eighteenth century /
Joan Hinde Stewart. p. cm. Includes bibliographical references and index.
ISBN 0-8032-4227-1 1. French fiction – Women
authors – History and
criticism. 2. Women and literature – France –
History – 18th century.
3. French fiction – 19th century – History
and criticism. I. Title.
PQ648.S66 1993 843'.5099287–dc20
92-33052 CIP

To Philip Stewart
&
To Dorothy LaRose
&
Mary McShea

CONTENTS

ILLUSTRATIONS

PREFACE

My subject is the complex conjunction of language, etiquette, ethos, and eros that is translated into character and plot in late eighteenth-century French novels by women. Chapter 1 introduces and situates this largely forgotten body of literature, and chapter 2 begins with a polemical exploration of men's prerogatives and women's capacities and of the relation of both sexes to speech and writing. The remainder of chapter 2 and the following chapters are readings of works by eight francophone novelists whose major publications began appearing between 1750 and 1800 and who were among the most popular and acclaimed writers of that era, even if many of them thereafter slipped into critical oblivion: Isabelle de Charrière, Sophie Cottin, Anne Louise Elie de Beaumont, Félicité de Genlis, Jeanne Le Prince de Beaumont, Isabelle de Montolieu, Marie Jeanne Riccoboni, and Adélaïde de Souza.

The multiformity of their novels is reflected in the asymmetrical structure of my chapters. At times, I find it useful to treat several novels by one author together. At others, I prefer to concentrate on a single work, or to discuss novels by different authors in tandem. In devoting my three central chapters to Riccoboni and Charrière, I mean to focus with some precision on their writing, for the psychological depth and the concision of their best stories epitomize the period's finest work. By the favor she enjoyed and the classical qualities of her style, Riccoboni dominates the third quarter of the eighteenth century, while Charrière is now gaining widespread recognition as one of the most original writers of its last quarter, and even of the entire century. Since context is essential to the story I wish to tell I provide some biographical detail; but on the whole I am less interested in biography than in the larger cultural concerns of a historical moment.

For the most part, eighteenth-century novels that did not find a place in the canon have not been reissued for well over a century and are therefore available mainly in private collections and major research libraries. A paradoxical index of the popularity of French novels by women of the period in question is that they are more difficult to find along the quays and in the rare book stores of Paris than those by men: I suspect that they were literally read to pieces.

In retrospect, I can locate the starting point of this project in a couple of incidents: a telephone call from Mary Ann Witt, who had spotted the beautiful 1786 illustrated edition of Riccoboni's complete works for sale in an unlikely shop in Pigalle, and Robert Dawson's suggestion that I take a look at some new acquisitions of his, including rare editions of several novels by women. Today the works of Riccoboni, Charrière, and a few others are appearing in modern editions; several years ago, undertaking this kind of study would have been inconceivable without attentive friends and windfalls like these.

I wish to acknowledge my immense debt to Robert Dawson for his kindness in calling my attention to pertinent works, for sending me countless original and sometimes unique books and issues from his collection, and for sharing his bibliographical expertise. Without him this study would simply not have been possible. James Rolleston has been, since the project's inception, an indispensable reader, generous and demanding. Alice Kaplan's speculations on several early essays helped me to imagine a framework for the book, and she has continued over the years to give encouragement, while conversations with Patricia Spacks have been exhilarating occasions for trying out ideas. Philip Lewis and Georges May have provided crucial support. Cathey Baker, Alex De-Grand, Michèle Farrell, Rona Goffen, Susan Jackson, Elizabeth Mac-Arthur, Gilbert Smith, Samia Spencer, Linda Stillman, Jean Vaché, Janet Whatley, and the members of the Triangle French Studies Seminar have

Preface

given generously of their time and expertise to read and comment on portions of the manuscript. Susan Marston provided editorial assistance and made judicious suggestions. I am deeply grateful to all of them. To Philip Stewart, for his constant help and patient (re)readings, I am especially indebted.

I am also grateful for leaves from North Carolina State University, fellowships at the National Humanities Center and at the Center for the Humanities at Wesleyan University, and a fellowship from the National Endowment for the Humanities. Publication was supported by a grant from the College of Humanities and Social Sciences at North Carolina State University.

This book has been a long time in the writing. Since the introduction and key chapters were drafted, a number of studies and anthologies have been published, indicating the simultaneous preoccupation of other scholars with questions about the role and significance of the work of early modern women writers. In some cases (I think for instance of Joan DeJean's *Tender Geographies,* on the writing of seventeenth-century Frenchwomen) work has appeared too recently for me to enter as extensively into dialogue with it as I would have liked.

Portions of chapter 1 were included in more schematic form in "The Novelists and their Fictions," in *French Women and the Age of Enlightenment,* ed. Samia I. Spencer (Bloomington: Indiana University Press, 1984): 197–211. Chapter 3 was published in different form as "A Wife for the Marquis," in *Dilemmes du roman: Essays in Honor of Georges May,* ed. Catherine Lafarge (Saratoga, CA: Anma Libri, 1990): 57–69, and chapter 6 as "Sex, Text and Exchange: *Lettres neuchâteloises* and *Lettres de Milady Juliette Catesby,*" in *Isabelle de Charrière/Belle van Zuylen,* ed. Beatrice Fink, special issue of *Eighteenth-Century Life* 13, no.1 (February 1989): 60–68. Permission of the publishers to use these essays is gratefully acknowledged.

An earlier version of part of chapter 2 appeared as "Allegories of Difference," in *Romanic Review* 75, no.3 (May 1984): 283–93. Reprinted by permission. Copyright by the Trustees of Columbia University in the City of New York.

xi

My appendix of the eighteenth-century novels by women that are discussed in this book gives original bibliographical information as well as indications of editions referenced. The bibliography indicates other original and secondary sources that were especially useful to me. For full information on abbreviated references appearing parenthetically in the text, the reader should consult these two lists. I have used modern spelling in all quotations. Three unspaced dots in a quotation represent *points de suspension* appearing in the original text. Translations are my own.

CHAPTER I

VOCATION & PROVOCATION

Si le mariage avait un noviciat, on n'y verrait guère de professes. [If there were a novitiate for marriage, very few would enter the order.]
—*Lettres de Madame du Montier*

J'ai vu beaucoup d'hymens, aucuns d'eux ne me tentent. [I've seen a lot of marriages; not one of them tempts me.]—La Fontaine, *Le mal marié*; epigraph to *Lettres de Mistriss Henley*

Se marier, cela est si sérieux, si triste! [Getting married is so serious, so sad!]—*Lettres de Madame de Sancerre*

In homage to the covert female rebellion that this book seeks to bring into the open, I am subversively borrowing—or rather reclaiming—my title from Restif de la Bretonne, who was acutely interested in analyzing and regulating women's verbal acts. His reform treatise, *Les gynographes,* appeared in 1777, subtitled *Idées de deux honnêtes femmes sur un projet de règlement proposé à toute l'Europe pour mettre les femmes à leur place et opérer le bonheur des deux sexes* [Ideas of two honest women regarding statutes proposed to all of Europe for putting women in their place and bringing about the happiness of both sexes].[1] Articles emanating from the pen of Restif's eponymous "honest women" bear titles like "Sequestration," "Clothing," "Girls," "Pretty Girls," and "Ugly Girls," and articulate an obsessive preoccupation with female sexual identity, while giving voice to one of the most frighteningly restrictive views of women imaginable, even for that era.

Restif focuses on the need for strict surveillance of girls and women of all classes and demands their complete submission to men, from whom they derive their very raison d'être. Baby girls, therefore, unlike boys, should be swaddled, "les mouvements de la fille devant être retenus et contraints dès le premier instant de sa vie" ["since the girl's movements should be restrained and constrained from the first instant of her life"] (*Oeuvres* 3: 92), and the education women subsequently receive must differ "absolutely" from that of men, for they should learn only useful skills and acquire only ideas likely to solidify a taste for service and subordination. Graduated and degrading punishments are to be meted out by whorls of parish committees in cases of sins against industriousness, economy, and hygiene, and especially against modesty and chastity. Infidelity in wives is punishable by torture. Woman is to man, Restif explains, as man is to God.

An underlying theme of *Les gynographes* is the need for both physical containment and the suppression of woman's fantasy life. Restif would regulate every routine, every activity, and every leisure minute so that no freedom of thought, let alone action, is possible. Specifically, all casual writing would be excluded, for Restif insists that while women of the merchant classes may be taught to read and write just well enough to conduct business, those of the upper classes should by no means learn how to write:

> Les filles de condition, et opulentes, n'apprendront jamais à écrire sous quelque prétexte qu'on puisse alléguer; si quelqu'une d'elles était convaincue d'avoir violé cette défense, elle sera punie sévèrement. (3: 108)

> [Girls of quality and wealthy girls will never learn to write under any pretext that may be advanced; if one of them is convicted of having violated this injunction, she will be severely punished.]

The novelists examined here, more or less Restif's contemporaries, have precisely this in common: an interest in exploring, through writing, the life of fantasy. It seems therefore paradoxically fitting to appropriate Restif's title and to restore gynography to its legitimate place in literary history.[2]

Restif deplored the usurpation of authority by "le second sexe." "Une femme savante, ou seulement pensante," says a character in one of his novels, "est toujours laide, je vous en avertis sérieusement, et surtout une femme auteur. . . . Une femme autrice sort des bornes de la modestie prescrite à son sexe" ["a learned woman, or merely a thinking one, is always ugly—I warn you solemnly—and especially a woman author. . . . An authoress transgresses the limits of modesty prescribed for her sex"] (*Paysanne* 354). But women were hardly deterred by such reactionary injunctions, and in the advancing eighteenth century—particularly in its last few decades—there was a distinct increase in the number of prominent women novelists. They produced a body of works whose significance, vast and pervasive, derives partly from the range and depth of what they wrote and partly from its critical mass during a period crucial to the genre's evolution. Starting around the mid-eighteenth century, one begins to see a steady current of literary production by women—testimony to their inventiveness and resilience.

In fact, as the century wore on, more and more commentators were admiring the style and psychological depth of women's writing and encouraging them to believe that their talents were peculiarly fitted to novels. The marquis de Sade, for one, in his *Idée sur les romans*, describes the female sex as "naturellement plus délicat, plus fait pour écrire le roman" ["naturally more delicate, better suited to novel-writing"] than men (44). Around the same time—the 1780s—in his correspondence with Marie Jeanne Riccoboni and especially in his review of Frances Burney's *Cecilia*, Choderlos de Laclos is suggesting the same thing (449, 757–68). Poetaster Claude Joseph Dorat likewise maintains that women are emotionally more versatile than men and better at plot development (38–39).

By the last quarter of the eighteenth century in France (Restif's sinister reform project notwithstanding), the idea that women are virtually made to write novels has become something of a critical commonplace—an insight essential to an understanding of the history of the French novel.

There is, of course, a degree of condescension in remarks like these.[3] But large numbers of women writers were all the same finding an increasingly supportive environment.

Women writers of the eighteenth century constitute one of the earliest significant groups to attempt to earn a living by the exercise of their creative talents in a domain that led to wide recognition. George Eliot pays generous tribute to women of seventeenth- and eighteenth-century France when she asserts that "in France alone woman has had a vital influence on the development of literature; in France alone the mind of woman has passed like an electric current through the language, making crisp and definite what is elsewhere heavy and blurred; in France alone, if the writings of women were swept away, a serious gap would be made in the national history" (59).

But Eliot's related vision of a leisured female class gracefully engaging in an enjoyable pastime—"They were not trying to make a career for themselves; they thought little, in many cases not at all, of the public" (59)—while it may be apt for some of the letter-writers of an earlier era, holds little validity for the period under consideration here. These novelists did not for the most part write just to while away idle hours: they were often independent, they sometimes lived far from Paris, and they wrote for the market. As Jeanne Le Prince de Beaumont, the aristocratic resonances of her name notwithstanding, succinctly explained after the nullification of her marriage in 1745: "Quant à moi, je dois gagner ma vie" ["As for me, I have to earn my living"] (Reynaud 122). Another case in point is Adélaïde de Souza, who, in an effort to support herself and her son during their years of exile in the mid-1790s, tried her hand at hatmaking and fiction writing.

"The journey of a text from an author's mind into print was one fraught with perils and frustrations," Robert Dawson tells us, adducing the dizzying complications and innumerable pitfalls of the European book trade (*French Booktrade* 3). Correspondences provide eloquent testimony to the obstacles women faced in their business dealings with the literary establishment. Marie Jeanne Riccoboni alludes repeatedly to the problems she encountered in getting paid by her English publisher, even though translations of her works were successful in Britain; at the same time, pirated French editions of her novels vexed her:

> L'indulgence que [mes productions] éprouvèrent pouvait me procurer une fortune honnête, si la piraterie tolérée, même encouragée dans la librairie, n'avait dérangé mes projets; j'ai enrichi des fripons et tiré peu d'avantages de mes travaux littéraires.[4]

> [The reception with which my works met would have procured me an honest income, if literary piracy, which is not just tolerated but even encouraged, had not derailed my projects; I enriched rogues and drew little profit from my literary labors.]

Isabelle de Charrière had comparable problems. Disappointed at her work's reception in Switzerland, she sent her brother in Holland several hundred copies of her novels in the spring of 1784, specifying that if he sold her *Lettres neuchâteloises* [Letters from Neuchâtel] to a bookseller at ten sous each she would break even with the costs of shipping and printing. But the Dutch bookseller, finding the volumes rather slender, offered eight sous instead of ten (*Oeuvres* 8: 42). A letter of May 1798 from Sophie Cottin to her cousin alludes to negotiations with her bookseller over her first novel:

> Maradan ne voulait donner que 240 frs.; on n'a pu obtenir que 300 frs., mais il a fait le plus grand éloge de l'ouvrage. . . . Si cet ouvrage réussit, je deviendrai plus difficile pour celui que je vais faire. (Sykes 399)

> [Maradan wanted to pay only 240 francs; I was finally able to get only 300 francs, but he praised the work very highly. . . . If this work is successful, I'll drive a harder bargain next time.]

Men, too, of course, experienced difficulties in arranging for administrative permissions, printing, publications, and sales; but because of women's social status and economic inferiority, their professional problems were more intense. In January 1793, shortly after the death of Riccoboni, her companion, Thérèse Biancolelli, described her difficulties with the book trade in a letter to La Harpe: "Dès qu'elle fut connue, on lui disputa ses ouvrages; c'est la règle surtout à l'égard des femmes" ["As soon as she became known, her works were attributed to others; that is the norm, especially where women are concerned"] (La Harpe, *Oeuvres* 15: 524).

Isabelle de Montolieu, a phenomenally productive Swiss author who lived in Lausanne and who, after the death of her second husband in 1800, supported herself in part by her translations, wrote continually to the editors of the *Mercure de France,* imploring them to send payment for the stories they accepted for publication. "Le métier d'auteur, de traducteur," she complained, "ne convient pas à une femme éloignée de Paris et qui n'y a personne pour veiller à ses intérêts!" ["The trade of author, of translator, does not suit a woman far from Paris and who has no one there to look after her interests!"] (Berthoud 326).

We should not expect to find in the novels these women wrote any direct expression of the kind of professional problems I have just evoked. But, on the other hand, we should not assume, as one commentator does, that "the reality of their own lives had no bearing on what they wrote."[5] If the difficult conditions under which eighteenth-century women lived and wrote are not immediately evident in their novels, it should be remembered that protest in the novel is masked and mediated. We must therefore look beyond the stylized formulas and the apparent moral conservatism to appreciate the varied and sometimes subversive use to which women put the novel in a period when there were few autobiographies or memoirs and little notable lyric poetry.

During this era, the novel was evolving rapidly on many fronts and in ways that may seem more contradictory than complementary. After the publication of Samuel Richardson's novels in French in the 1740s and 1750s, *sensibilité,* with the artifices and the cult of pathos that it entailed, soon reached its apogee in the French novel. But at the same time the novel itself, especially the epistolary form which women writers most often adopted, was increasingly recognized as a privileged means of representing not only morality and sentiment but also social reality (Ouellet 1218).

Novels translated historical and psychic realities into the ordered codes of fiction, and the self-conscious and ironic use of the conventions of society and of writing sometimes accounts for a subtle play between conformism and contestation. Hence the subversiveness of texts whose style and surface often appear orthodox. None of the novels discussed in this study may be handily categorized as a "typical" novel of sensibility, for although the novels participate extensively in the conventions of such literature, they often revise or subvert those conventions. A close reading suggests that women organized their understanding of the ambivalence of their status around the concept of *sensibilité,* which they seemingly adopted but routinely undercut. That is to say, the superficial sentimentality that novels extolled and exalted sometimes masked other, less admissible tendencies. If women writers helped glorify *sensibilité,* they also made legible its symbiosis with oppression.

While underscoring the distinctively literary qualities of my chosen texts, the chapters that follow explore the ways in which, under the pen of women writers, crucial words like "virtue," "beauty," "reason," and "happiness" slip from their accustomed places, acquiring new functions and unwonted nuances.

Certainly, many novels are convention-bound in the extreme. Mademoiselle Motte's highly formulaic *Célide* (1775), about young love triumphing over economic prejudice, exhibits no spark of originality: things seem to happen here for no other reason than that they routinely do in this kind of fiction. Françoise Albine Benoist's *Les erreurs d'une jolie femme* (1781), where the caricaturish "pretty woman" passes from the hands of one man to the next, has little more to recommend it: the protagonist's affairs are as monotonous as her sentiments.[6] In a popular novel by Cornélie Vasse, *Les aveux d'une femme galante* [Confessions of a woman of easy virtue] (1782), the title character, in the course of reforming her life, utters the predictable pieties—declaring, for example, that virtue is a woman's finest adornment.

But other novels—including others by Benoist that I shall discuss shortly—reveal a richer engagement with fictional protocols; even where language seems most sex-neutral and convention-bound, a woman's point of view may emerge. If we read Robert Mauzi's wide-ranging *L'idée du bonheur dans la littérature et la pensée françaises au dix-huitième siècle*, with its careful elucidations of connections among Enlightenment notions of happiness, reason, and virtue, against women's novels, a slippage of referents is sometimes apparent. When the heroine of Charrière's *Lettres de Mistriss Henley* (1784) writes, "Ma situation est triste, ou bien je suis un être sans raison et sans vertus" ["My condition is sad, or else I am a being without reason and without virtue"] (119), her operative terms are so drenched in the specificity of female experience that her assertion reveals the dubiousness of the alliance between the concepts of reasonable living and virtuous conduct so dear to the century's moral and philosophical thought. Mistress Henley's letters show how the supremacy of "reason" can make a "virtuous" woman virtually suicidal. In a certain female lexicon, then, "virtue" is positioned at the other extreme from "happiness."

Opposition to traditional notions that support oppressive social systems may also be expressed by means of lumbering irony. Benoist's *Célianne ou les amants séduits par leurs vertus* [Célianne or the lovers seduced by their virtues] (1766), which assiduously presages, then barely averts, adultery in a swift and edifying conclusion, proclaims itself a narrative of lofty feeling, but is replete with examples of double entendre. Here "virtue" defines women restrictively yet teasingly, beginning with a title that parodically juxtaposes virtues and seduction. In the discourse of the protagonists, the effects of "virtue" are similar to those of erotic attraction: shortly before Célianne's admirer, Mozime, attempts to make love with her while she half sleeps, he asks rhetorically, "Pourquoi faut-il hélas que la vive contemplation de votre vertu, en élevant mon âme au-dessus de moi-même, égare mes sens?" ["Why, alas, must the eager contemplation of your virtue, by exalting my soul, lead my senses astray?"] (107–8).

Approaching the question of virtue in ways vastly less sober than Charrière's, Benoist covers the formalized neutrality of the vocabulary she inherits with gaudy graffiti. Célianne aspires to being a prodigy of virtue but behaves not altogether unlike a seductress. Despite an artificially decorous ending, the May 1766 *Correspondance littéraire* at least had no

"Que de choses leurs coeurs éprouvèrent!" ["What a lot of feelings
were aroused within their hearts!"]. Unsigned. Frontispiece,
Françoise Albine Benoist, *Célianne ou les amants séduits par leurs
vertus* (Amsterdam and Paris: Lacombe, 1766).

trouble "translating" the superficial virtuousness of plot: "sous une plume moins délicate que celle de madame Benoist, c'est la tendre et vertueuse Célianne prête à faire son mari cocu en faveur du vertueux Mozime" ["a less delicate pen than Madame Benoist's would declare the tender and virtuous Célianne ready to cuckold her husband with the virtuous Mozime"] (part 1, 5: 226).

Benoist published other novels and several comedies, mostly during the 1760s and 1770s, which, despite extravagant story lines, sometimes compel interest for their treatment of the intersections of virtue and desire. In *Elisabeth,* a much longer novel than *Célianne* dating from the same year, Benoist makes explicit the danger of believing too blindly in the prophylactic value of virtue: "l'enthousiasme de la vertu égare plus d'amants que la volupté n'en séduit, parce que nulle défiance ne les garantit du péril" ["more lovers are led astray by virtue than are seduced by sensuality, because their very self-assurance exposes them to danger"] (1: 56–57).

Even the words "marriage" and "charm" were subject to covert revision. In Marguerite Daubenton's lengthy *Zélie dans le désert* (1786), the heroine is shipwrecked on Sumatra; for years, she steadfastly guards her virginity, holding her fiancé at bay. But eventually she recognizes that he can no longer stand it, and with the same practical good sense that impels her to raise chickens and plant crops, she agrees to a "private marriage" which, to all appearances, simply means asking God's blessing on irregular cohabitation. Meanwhile, Zélie's adopted daughter Ninette makes clear that the appeal of the man she loves has more than a little to do with *masculine* "charms." She evokes Monsieur Spring's exquisite reticence and the alluring informality of his hair and clothing in terms cu ͜omarily applied to women:

Ah! maman, qu'il était bien dans ce déshabillé galant qu'il paraissait avoir honte de porter devant moi! . . . Ses cheveux étaient négligemment relevés par un ruban; sur sa tête était un bonnet de la même étoffe que la robe, et fait de manière de turban. (2: 125–26)

[Ah, mother, how fine he looked in that gallant dishabille that he seemed ashamed to wear in front of me! . . . His hair was casually pulled back with a ribbon, and on his head there was a bonnet of the same fabric as the dress, and made like a turban.]

The uncivilized, "desert" setting of *Zélie dans le désert* allows its heroines the freedom to use familiar terms in original ways.

During that most "rational" of ages, novelists like Charrière, Benoist, and Daubenton, with different degrees of polish and subtlety, were destabilizing the givens of reason, elliptically suggesting new affiliations of words, and forming new networks of meaning and intertexts. In making linguistic space for themselves, they were also attempting to carve out social space by commenting obliquely or directly on institutions and traditions affecting women's lives most closely. The focal point of the majority of novels was, of course, just as it had been in earlier periods, marriage. In *Les gynographes,* Restif features marriage and motherhood as the biological and moral destiny of every woman, the events that give her life civil and Christian meaning. In his version of utopia, good girls are rewarded with husbands and bad girls denied them (although to a woman Restif's ideal marriage more nearly resembles punishment than reward). A long pivotal article lavishes particular attention on the content of the marriage contract, specifying in detail the duties of a wife while those of a husband are dispatched in a few lines. The model wife of Restif's treatise can look forward to life as an automaton: there are hours for rising, working, eating, and retiring, so that the performance of marriage becomes as ritualized as the marriage ceremony. His restraining codification emphasizes the institutionalized enslavement to which the contracting bride is made to assent.

Novelists frequently portrayed that enslavement in their fiction: poor Suzanne Chomper in Madeleine de Puisieux's *Mémoires d'un homme de bien* [Memoirs of a good man] (1768), for example, docilely accepts the bilious and miserly husband proposed by her father and becomes in just a few days "l'*épouse* de l'Ecriture, c'est-à-dire, la servante très humble de son mari" ["the *biblical wife,* that is to say, her husband's very humble servant"] (1: 6). She lives an unhappy life and dies unfulfilled.[7]

Other contemporary women novelists emphasize the fragility of the consent that many women were forced to give to arranged marriages.

Mademoiselle de Lascy in *Anecdotes de la cour et du règne d'Edouard II, roi d'Angleterre* [Anecdotes of the court and the reign of Edward II, king of England] (1776, begun by Claudine de Tencin, completed by Anne Louise Elie de Beaumont), is "frozen with fear" at the altar and capable of responding at the decisive moment only with a silence that is hastily interpreted as a "yes" (196). In the case of other heroines, the word "yes" itself, as often as not, means "no." During her wedding to a man she despises, the heroine of Adèle de Souza's *Emilie et Alphonse* (1799) has to be asked twice by the priest for her formal consent, only to answer with "un *oui* à peine articulé, un *oui* qui a expiré sur ses lèvres, et qui cependant l'engageait pour jamais" ["a barely articulated *yes*, a *yes* that died on her lips and which nonetheless bound her forever"] (431).

The protagonist of Anne Mérard de Saint-Just's *Mon journal d'un an* [My diary of a year] (1788), dragged to the altar against her will, writes: "J'étais à demi morte; j'ignore si je dis ce OUI fatal, qui dans tant de bouches est un non positif" ["I was half dead; I'm not certain whether I pronounced that fatal YES, which in so many mouths is a positive no"] (100). One of the protagonists of Louise d'Epinay's *Histoire de Madame de Montbrillant* refers to her new husband as a dark little man "à qui j'ai toujours dit *non* au fond de mon coeur" ["to whom I always said *no* in the bottom of my heart"] (184).[8] Many women writers view marriage as an inevitable economic and emotional goal, while they also develop its ambiguities and imagine ways of averting the *mariage de raison* which was then widely in force and which Restif's *Les gynographes* implicitly exalts.[9]

They wrote at a time when preadolescent French girls of the middle and upper classes were generally sent to a convent for an education and married as soon as they returned home—sometimes before they had reached sexual maturity—to someone chosen by the family. He was often at least several years older than the bride—possibly even much older. Through marriage the young woman was simultaneously reabsorbed into her family and introduced into society (Darrow 45–46). Marriage was thereby burdened with a heavy weight of tradition and meaning. It was also often the only road to economic survival.

In general, however, even a married woman was not in a strong civil or economic position, whatever social influence she might acquire. Contracts could not be entered into without the husband's consent, and it was he who was charged with official responsibility for all decisions regarding the children. Robert Joseph Pothier, a noted contemporary legal commentator, remarks in the first sentence of his *Traité de la puissance du mari* [Treatise on the power of the husband] (1770) that marriage creates a society composed of husband and wife where the former has power over both the person and possessions of the latter, and he explains a couple of pages later that a wife's dependence is such that she can undertake no legally valid action without her husband's authorization (3).[10]

Divorce did not exist in France until 1792. During the Ancien Régime it was possible, albeit difficult, to obtain a separation: a woman seeking one would have to prove her husband guilty of excessive brutality or defamation of character. In this system, a woman's adultery, if socially or economically expedient for the couple, might be indulged, but under other conditions it could draw severe sanctions. While a man's adultery was legally inconsequential, his wife's could be considered of the utmost gravity, because it could cast doubt on paternity and thereby have important economic consequences (Darrow 47; Portemer 457). A woman suspected of adultery might be locked up in a convent.[11] Contemporary treatises like Fournel's 495-page *Traité de l'adultère* [Treatise on adultery] make it clear that only women could be guilty of adultery and that the decision for punishment resided squarely with the husband, who was the legally constituted guardian of his wife's morals (1). Among the other questions that Fournel examines is the issue of a man's right to kill his wife if he discovers her in an adulterous act. Specific laws varied from region to region and were not necessarily enforced, but their very existence is a chilling commentary on the ultimate place of authority.[12]

In a preface to *Célianne,* Benoist specifies the social arrangements relating to marriage that form the background of numerous stories of marital dissatisfaction and infidelity:

> Le plus grand nombre des femmes, je veux dire celles que les parents marient par des vues d'intérêt ou de convenance, n'aiment point celui à qui on les unit, et sont trop jeunes pour avoir jamais

connu l'amour. De sorte que, si, ce qui n'arrive que trop souvent, elles ne prennent du goût pour leur mari, il vient un moment où l'indifférence est pour elles un fardeau insupportable; et le vide du coeur leur fait rechercher, à leur insu, un objet propre à l'affecter. (ix–x)

[Most women, I mean those who are married by their parents for self-serving or social reasons, do not love the man to whom they are joined and are too young ever to have known love. So if, as happens all too often, they do not come to love their husband, at some point their indifference becomes an insufferable burden; and the emptiness of their hearts makes them look about, even without design, for an object that can move them.]

The narrator of *Mon journal d'un an*, Mérard de Saint-Just's novel about a fourteen-year-old girl forced by her stepmother to marry a man she loathes, sounds the same theme. She contends that there would be fewer adulterous women and abandoned wives if marriage arrangements took into account the preferences of the bride:

Hélas! si les parents consultaient plus nos goûts dans le choix d'un mari, il existerait bien plus de bons ménages: la femme serait attachée au mortel dont elle prendrait le nom; elle serait attachée à ses devoirs, à sa maison, à ses enfants; et jamais elle ne cesserait de se respecter, et de respecter les lois de la société. (73)

[Alas! if parents inquired more into our taste in the choice of a husband, there would be far more good marriages: the wife would cling to the mortal man whose name she took; she would cling to her duties, her home, her children; and she would never cease to respect herself and to respect society's laws.]

A character in Riccoboni's *Lettres de Mylord Rivers* (1777) tersely highlights the irony of standard procedures and the falseness of ostensible goals: the two people whose "happiness" is supposed to be at issue see the marriage contract only at the moment when they are made to affix their signatures to this "voluntary" pledge of their troth (349).[13]

There were countless stories like these of marrying, remarrying, and unmarrying (*démarier,* as Le Prince de Beaumont puts it) through separations, annulments, and widowhood, and women novelists who expanded on marital arrangements and on the related subjects of authority, oppression, obligation, happiness, and adultery (usually virtual or putative rather than real) enjoyed enormous favor. But despite the sheer numbers and contemporary prominence of the writers, these stories have on the whole slipped into the penumbra of near nonexistence that has been the lot of so much female productivity.

I am not the first to note that eighteenth-century literary history is highly canonical, and that critics have focused on a few giant male writers (cf. DeJean and Miller, *Displacements*). Even a revisionist effort like *Femmes d'hier et d'aujourd'hui,* a popularizing monograph published in 1966, leaps from *La princesse de Clèves* (1678) to Germaine de Staël and George Sand, women who published mostly in the nineteenth century. Eighteenth-century novelists are passed over without a word.[14]

This neglect, combined with three other factors—eighteenth-century conventions of naming and signing; the problematic social status of women during the eighteenth century and, perhaps even more, during the early nineteenth when the canon that excluded them was being established; and the ambiguous status and whimsical protocols of the novel itself during the period when they wrote—has so obscured women that it is sometimes difficult or impossible even to ascertain their complete names.[15]

Authors of innumerable novels are designated on title pages only by a single name preceded by the word "Monsieur" or "Madame." In the case of women, that name is generally a husband's. The usual reference sources, both contemporary and modern, fail to indicate, for example, the given names of the marquise de Belvo (alternately spelled Belvaux) or of Madame Beccary, author of *Mémoires de Fanny Spingler* (1781). The latter is also spelled "Beccari": Laurent Versini remarks that she called herself "Mrs. Beccary" to take advantage of the vogue for English novels (*Laclos* 185),[16] but it must also be kept in mind that the letters "i" and "y" were in fluctuation during the eighteenth century, and people often failed to adhere to a single spelling for their own names.

The author of *Les gynographes,* for example, early opted to spell his name "Restif" and used that spelling until reverting to "Rétif" in the signature of his last work; his father, however, used "Retif," without an accent (Testud 1–2). Many of his contemporaries were still more arbitrary about spelling their names. Even booksellers, from whom one might reasonably expect standard spellings of the family name that identified the business, frequently used variant spellings on title pages of the books they published.

The status of women and the conventions and politics of signing in the eighteenth century considerably complicate questions of authorship.[17] In a probing article on female authorship in France, Carla Hesse investigates the "legal contingencies of both the identity of the female author and her relation to her work" (487), analyzing in particular why eighteenth- and nineteenth-century Frenchwomen wrote pseudonymously. She adduces legal pressures for publication under a male pseudonym but also, concomitantly, "repeated gestures of self-distancing from the name of the father or the spouse" (486).

It is quite true that countless books were signed "Monsieur" or "Madame" followed by one or several initials and asterisks or dots. The first edition of *La jardinière de Vincennes* (Gabrielle de Villeneuve, 1753) bears the signature "Madame de V***." The title page of the first edition of Riccoboni's *Histoire de M. le marquis de Cressy* (1758) indicates that the volume is translated from the English by "Mme de ***," while later publications are signed with only slightly more precision "Marie de M***" (for "Mézières," one of the names Ricccoboni used). In the case of Elie de Beaumont's *Lettres du marquis de Roselle* (1764), the first edition is signed "Madame ***," while some later editions, including the Cellot 1770 edition which I cite, are signed "Madame E. D. B." Mérard de Saint-Just, on the other hand, sometimes signed with *all* her initials: the title page of her *Histoire de la baronne d'Alvigny* (1788) says that it is by "Mad. D. M. S. J. N. A. J. F. d'O" (Madame de Mérard Saint-Just, née Anne Jeanne Félicité d'Ormoy). Le Prince de Beaumont makes fun of the use of asterisks in *La nouvelle Clarice* (1767) when Hariote, the confidante, writes in jest that she is tempted to publish Clarice's story "incog-

nito": "l'auteur sera Madame de trois étoiles" ["the author will be Madame three asterisks"] (2: 29). But at the same time it should be stressed
that many women did in fact sign with their patronymics or, more precisely, those of their husbands. If women took assumed names, these too
were usually feminine: Riccoboni's first novel was signed "Adélaïde de
Varançai"; the George Sands, like the George Eliots, are of a later age.

The question of naming authors which Hesse raises is one that has
preoccupied me during the writing of this book. On the one hand, it is
sometimes difficult, as I have indicated, to identify fully a woman author,
or even to know with certainty whether a given novel is the work of a
woman or a man. But what strikes me about women of the Ancien
Régime and the years right after the Revolution is that, from a late
twentieth-century point of view, there is less a "distancing" (in Hesse's
term) from the names of father or spouse than a symbolic burial under
them.

People frequently bore a profusion of names that renders somewhat
awkward the feminist and human gesture of designation by full names (as
opposed to the standard "Madame Such-and-Such"). For their names are
complicated by compound and sometimes hyphenated given names,
multiple patronymics, legitimate titles, assumed names and titles, the
vagaries of spelling, and, in the case of women, changes of name through
marriage and remarriage. Take for example the case of Marie Jeanne de
Heurles de Laboras de Mézières Riccoboni. Her mother was a member
of the Parisian middle class; her father, Christophe de Heurles, from
Champagne, was a bigamist. Her marriage act designates her by her
father's assumed name, here spelled "de La Boras." When she became an
actress, she took another name, Mézières, which is variously spelled—a
May 1767 letter to Robert Liston is signed "Marie de Meisière," and a
letter to David Garrick six months later is signed "Marie de Meizière
Riccoboni" (*Letters* 110, 120). She eventually began signing the family
name of the actor-husband from whom she was estranged, although
biographers have sometimes confused her with her mother-in-law, just as
they have confused her husband with his father.[18]

There is little unanimity among literary critics and historians about how to identify and reference women writers. Jeanne Le Prince de Beaumont was born Le Prince (also spelled Leprince), and her husband's name was Beaumont, while in the case of Anne Louise Elie de Beaumont, all but "Anne Louise" came from her husband. These two writers, who bore the apparently homonymic names of their husbands, have been confused in studies as influential as Servais Etienne's *Le genre romanesque en France,* which attributes Elie de Beaumont's *Lettres du marquis de Roselle* to Le Prince de Beaumont. Other allusions to them are hidden in various volumes, both contemporary and modern, under a handful of letters of the alphabet, and commentators are wont to reference one or both interchangeably as "Madame de Beaumont."

Allusions to the Swiss writer who was born Isabelle de Polier de Bottens may be found under the names of both her husbands, Crousaz and Montolieu. The novels of Adélaïde Filleul are indexed under Flahaut (the name of her first husband) almost as often as under Souza (the name of her second), and sometimes in the same volume. In *Le roman féminin,* Michel Mercier first calls her Madame de "Flahaut," then Madame de "Souza (comtesse de Flahaut)," and finally, in the index, lists her as Madame de "Flahaut-Souza." The catalog of the Bibliothèque Nationale cross-references her; but under "Flahaut" she appears as "Adèle Filleul, comtesse de Flahaut, puis baronne de Souza," whereas under "Souza" the name is "Adelaïde [sic]-Marie-Emilie Filleul" and her title is "marquise" de Souza rather than "baronne."

In the case of Riccoboni, whose work has recently been attracting substantial attention, it is also revealing to note the considerable number of modern references to her as "Madame *de* Riccoboni." The gratuitous inclusion of the seemingly ennobling particle signals not only the lingering obscurity of her identity, but also the enduring stereotype of the woman writer as leisured aristocrat. In recognition of the complications of naming women, the complete works of another recently rediscovered writer have been issued under a double indication of authorship which nicely incorporates given name, nickname, the French version of the patronymic, and married name: Isabelle de Charrière/Belle de Zuylen.

Given the failures of standardization and the elusive nature of copies of early noncanonical novels, it is not surprising that there has been relatively little available in the way of modern analysis of novels by women, except for a few of the better-known writers. Versini's groundbreaking *Laclos et la tradition* (1968) examines how novelists preceding Laclos used the epistolary form, and Pierre Fauchery's erudite tome, *La destinée féminine dans le roman européen du dix-huitième siècle* (1972), also organizes and interprets aspects of hundreds of eighteenth-century novels in illuminating ways. I am pleased to recognize my debt to these studies. However, while they feature numerous passing references to the novels of, for example, Jeanne Le Prince de Beaumont, we are hard put to locate more than two successive sentences about her work.

Like Le Prince de Beaumont, other French women novelists have until recently been catalogued but not studied. Their major role is seen as vulgarization. Fauchery is persuaded that the determining myths were of masculine invention and were adopted without alteration by women novelists; in his book on "female destiny," only 20 pages out of 900 treat the woman writer specifically. For him, female novelists are verbose, gauche, most comfortable writing short fiction, consistently prone to betray the "'moraliste' de naissance" ["born 'moralist'"] lurking beneath the "romancière d'occasion" ["part-time novelist"], and inevitably inclined to autobiography: the heroine imagined by the woman novelist is "encore et toujours elle-même" ["forever and eternally herself"] (94, 111).[19]

In fact, earlier generations of critics were sometimes even more condescending in their determination to identify and implicitly discredit the autobiographical impulse. The only study before the present one to treat early modern women novelists in French as a group was published by Anne Louis Anton Mooij in 1949. Mooij emphasizes not only the autobiographical, but also the supposedly accidental or "occasional" nature of the writing of women who, as I have said, often tried to supplement resources by proceeds from the sales of their writings. He, too, compares "hommes de lettres" and "romancières d'occasion," although he subsequently promotes the latter to "dames de lettres" (64, 107).

At the same time, he confuses biography and fiction, qualifying Charrière's husband, without benefit of quotation marks, as a "mari de roman" ["story-book husband"] (39)—a phrase she uses to describe one of her own protagonists. Servais Etienne tells us that Riccoboni could think of only a single story to write and rewrite—her own (106). In *Mémoires et souvenirs de comédiennes (XVIIIe siècle)* (1914), Paul Ginisty unabashedly calls Riccoboni's novels her "memoirs" (e.g., 57, 115), viewing her whole fictional corpus as a single autobiographical act, one continuous rememoration of her love affairs.

The publication history of Louise d'Epinay's lengthy *Histoire de Madame de Montbrillant* is a particularly compelling example of the lengths to which readers and editors have been led by the prejudice that the woman novelist's heroine is "eternally herself."[20] Composed during the second half of the eighteenth century, the work was first published in 1818 in an abridged and extensively modified form as d'Epinay's "memoirs"; it was labeled "pseudo-memoirs" in the mid-twentieth century, and only recently recognized as imaginative fiction.

Fauchery's very phrase, "forever and eternally herself," ignores the fact that current concepts of representation take for granted that there is no such thing as unmediated, uninventive transcription of the real, let alone the self. This supposed paucity of invention, moreover, is viewed as a defect only when applied to women. Has anyone contended that *A la recherche du temps perdu* is minor because Proust and his narrator share countless experiences and sensations? Proust is just as much "eternally himself."

At various points in the chapters that follow I shall engage judgments like those I have just cited. I recognize, of course, that only in recent years have new critical perspectives made it possible to read women's work in new ways, and I am interested in contrasting my readings with those of earlier generations, including contemporaries who were alternately inclined to criticize violations of fictional codes and to refuse to acknowledge any encroachment on the proprieties. Indeed, there is a fundamental contradiction vitiating these traditional critical perspectives, one that enables us to include that tradition within our readings of the original texts. For if women writers are "merely" autobiographical, how can they also be "merely" vehicles for conventional versions of *sensibilité*?

The only meaningful way to make both these claims at once would be to say that women "lived" the conventions of the age with an intensity that transformed those supposedly public notions into something wholly personal. And in fact my readings point in this direction. The cluster of values surrounding marriage permeated women's lives so thoroughly that the standard adventures which traditionally defined the texture of a novel became, in their hands, the vicissitudes of conventional values as such. And since the question of ethics and identity was moving, thanks to Kant, Rousseau, and others, to the very center of public discussion, the historical moment was right for the political to mesh with the personal. These women helped make it happen. As we overcome the amnesia that blocked the posthumous reception of their work, we can begin to see the web of connections between private and public, sex and class, silence and speech, the rigidities of convention and the dreams of freedom.

Let me stress that the period in question was not exactly characterized by a clear division between popular and elite novels: the audience reading Richardson and Rousseau was also reading Riccoboni and Elie de Beaumont; the same booksellers stocked their works, the same critics reviewed them. Le Prince de Beaumont wrote *La nouvelle Clarice* in reaction to Richardson's *Clarissa,* while Riccoboni translated Fielding's *Amelia* and was influenced by Rousseau (just as he was influenced by her); all were popular with the same audiences. I have no intention of claiming that women writers of the period were uniformly interesting or distinguished, and I recognize that there are different reasons for studying different writers.

But late eighteenth-century novelists like Riccoboni, Charrière, and Souza deserve a distinguished reputation. If novels by them and other women were not included in the canon that was formed in the next century, the explanation is not to be found in the early status or stature of these works. The reasons that they were forgotten have more to do with content: unlike certain canonical novels, these intense representations of the domestic were not on the whole vehicles for meditation on war, dueling, or even gardening. The questions they raise—the passionate nature of women, the economic necessity and indeed the very possibility of marrying and remarrying, the livability of contemporary marriage, the significance of mothering and domesticity—as much as the way in which they raise them, didn't appear sufficiently important to the literary establishment.

My analyses aim to show that these are in fact works whose subtle subversions undermine social systems and power bases, womanly works that scratch away at a monolithic vision of the sensibilities and prescribed behavior of "the fair sex" (a vision that, of course, had been largely created or at least accepted by women). The very writing of such works, their contemporary and posthumous reception, and their exclusion from the canon are eloquent events in the history of literature and society.

The organization of this book into a series of somewhat discrete chapters represents a decision made not despite but because of persistent neglect or critical misreadings and the relative obscurity of certain of the novels in question. This body of work does not lend itself to easy categorization, but demands sustained analysis, a willingness to look closely at the play of moral and social language, metaphors and ironies. Texture and sense are better understood by examining specific novels at length than by reciting "feminine themes" and "types" or by according consistent preeminence to biographical material.

Such an organization allows me to explore the psychological continuities of women's narratives, while also underscoring their heterogeneity. Various gestures of defiance and compliance on the part of heroines disclose an abiding preoccupation with marriage, while they also reveal a lively interest in related concerns as diverse as slippery streets and illicit pregnancies in Charrière's novels, widowhood in Riccoboni's, ugliness in Montolieu's, and mothering in Le Prince de Beaumont's.

I emphasize such variations in part as a counterweight to the leveling agenda of critics who have insistently read women novelists as "eternally themselves" and their novels as examples of myopic tendencies, as the creations of an "unfaithful" womanly memory which stores "une foule de pseudo-faits bien menus, qui prennent une importance considérable dans leur esprit et dans leur imagination" ["a host of very tiny pseudo-facts, which take on a considerable importance in their minds and imaginations"] (Mooij 9).

Allegations of "myopia," "unfaithful memories," and "pseudo-facts" doubly disparage women's supposed autobiographical inclination: although women write solely about what happened to them, their little heads can't even get *that* right.[21] This notion of women's imaginative seduction by "very tiny pseudo-facts" makes an interesting contrast with a critic's praise of Denis Diderot's brilliant use in fiction of the "little facts" *he* files away: "C'est avec de petits faits vrais, pris de droite et de gauche, que se contruisent toutes les oeuvres proprement géniales" ["It is with true little facts, taken from left and right, that all the works of real genius are constructed"].[22] I propose to explore those gender-weighted "facts" and "pseudo-facts" in women's writing.

In narratives whose springboard may be personal experience, but whose heroes and heroines are artistically blended from social and literary convention and moral allegory, we can see, in George Eliot's phrase, woman's mind passing "like an electric current." A close reading of these novels reveals distinctly female voices speaking, in the language of eighteenth-century convention, about issues of power and gender which, after being resolutely driven underground, have finally reached the surface of our social consciousness.

CHAPTER 2

SPEECH AND SAINTLINESS

Jeanne Le Prince de Beaumont

The year 1748 saw the appearance of a quarto brochure (or "feuille volan-te") by the Abbé Gabriel François Coyer: *L'année merveilleuse, ou les hommes-femmes* [The wonderful year, or the men-women]. This was a spirited attack on society, and especially on women, in the guise of an astrological prediction: the first of August 1748 would witness the con-junction of five planets that had been drawing together since the begin-ning of time. This event would in turn produce "the wonder of wonders": men would be changed into women and women into men. Inevitably, such a transformation would be to the detriment of the male.

A number of rejoinders appeared almost immediately, and among those who rose to the defense of women was Jeanne Marie Le Prince de Beaumont (1711–80). Her response is a powerful example of early modern feminist reaction to a narrow, misogynistic view of woman. The interest of this polemic for a study of women novelists lies in its articula-tion of the very conditions of possibility for feminist writing in the eighteenth century. By that I mean the ability of a writer like Le Prince de Beaumont to challenge firmly entrenched hierarchies and to "decon-struct" male discourse, of which Coyer's may be seen as a paradigmatic example. Such polemic may provide a conceptual framework for the cultural and narrative manifestations of the subjects of authority, lan-guage, sex, and society that concern us here.

A sister of the painter Jean Le Prince, Jeanne Marie Le Prince de

Beaumont was born in Rouen. She was thirty-seven years old in 1748, the author of a novel, *Le triomphe de la vérité ou mémoires de M. de la Villette* [The triumph of truth or memoirs of M. de la Villette] (1748), and the mother of a little girl; she had had her marriage to the child's father annulled a few years earlier. Faced with the necessity of earning her living, she was on the point of establishing herself in England, where she would remain for fourteen years as governess to aristocratic families. She returned from England in 1762 to settle near Annecy, where she helped raise her grandchildren (one of whom would become the mother of Prosper Mérimée). Le Prince de Beaumont lived to be nearly seventy and became one of the era's most prolific writers.

She published about seventy volumes; these include the novels that I shall discuss shortly as well as treatises on education (for example, *Education complète*), works of Christian inspiration (*Les Américaines ou la preuve de la religion chrétienne par les lumières naturelles* [American women or proof of the Christian religion by natural lights], *La dévotion éclairée* [Enlightened devotion]), and anthologies intended for children, adolescents, and young women (*Magasin des enfants, Magasin des adolescentes, Magasin des jeunes dames*).

Not only did she establish the genre of children's literature in France, but as the first woman to found and edit a magazine she also played an important role in the development of journalism. Her *Nouveau magasin français,* written in French and published in London in the 1750s, addressed women's issues through stories, poems, letters, and editorials.[1] According to a 1769 publication, the *Dictionnaire historique portatif des femmes célèbres,* her writings were "entre les mains de tout le monde" ["in everyone's hands"] (1: 309). They were also reedited throughout the next century and widely translated.

Any currency that her name retains, however, is chiefly owing to its appearance on the cover of editions of *La Belle et la Bête* (Beauty and the Beast). The fairy tale was first published in 1740 by Gabrielle de Villeneuve, but Le Prince de Beaumont condensed the story from nearly two hundred pages to twenty-two and included the now-classic version in her *Magasin des enfants* (1758).[2] *La Belle et la Bête,* to which I shall return in chapter 7, is today without doubt the best-known work of fiction published by any woman in the eighteenth century.

Her adversary in the *Année merveilleuse* exchange, the Abbé Gabriel François Coyer, was four years her senior and likewise at the beginning of his literary career. He would become a noted satirist and popularizer, whose writings, while often glosses on the works of such authors as Swift and Voltaire, were important to the propagation of ideas. His *Développement et défense du système de la noblesse commerçante* (1756) expressed his rejection of traditional ideas about the role of the nobility in contemporary society, while his *Plan d'éducation publique* (1770) has been said to contain "some of the most revolutionary proposals of any contemporary work on that subject."[3] In a tale called *Chinki* (1768), Coyer satirizes fiscal legislation and assails the land tax.

Publications such as these had a considerable effect on the dissemination of abstract ideas. But Coyer's earliest publications date to the middle of the century, when he launched four satirical, semifrivolous broadsides: *La découverte de la pierre philosophale* [The discovery of the philosopher's stone], *La magie démontrée* [The proof of magic], *Plaisir pour le peuple* [Pleasure for the people], and what was to become his most popular work, *L'année merveilleuse*. Collected and reissued in 1754, along with other occasional pieces, in a compendium titled *Bagatelles morales*, they reflect the period's anglomania in their heavy borrowings from English writers.

The title and principal conceit of *L'année merveilleuse*—the transformation of the sexes—were taken from a pamphlet emanating from the famous Scriblerus Club and considered to be the work of Alexander Pope and Dr. John Arbuthnot: *Annus Mirabilis or the Wonderful Effects of the Approaching Conjunction of the Planets Jupiter, Mars and Saturn*. The Pope-Arbuthnot piece is bawdy and heavy-handed, most of its humor relating to the consequences for virginity, seduction, and rape of the universal sex change that would accompany the celestial phenomenon: "The cruelty of scornful mistresses shall be returned; the slighted maid shall grow into an imperious gallant, and reward her undoer with a big belly, and a bastard."[4]

Coyer's social satire, on the other hand, is more mordantly antifemi-
nist, though hardly ribald. His principal theme is the silliness of women.
By depicting the ludicrousness of men behaving in the mindless way he
attributes to women, he sarcastically attacks the manners and morals of
the upper classes, especially female. "Les hommes se flattent-ils d'être
hommes encore longtemps?" ["Do men feel sure that they will continue
much longer to be men?"], he asks. Obsessed with trivia, ruled by vanity
and caprice, they have already begun to fuss and simper. There have even
been cases of men developing that quintessentially female affliction, the
vapors: "Je tirai dernièrement mon flacon pour un seigneur à qui son
intendant rendait des comptes" ["I took out my smelling salts not long
ago for a nobleman whose steward was detailing his finances"]. Coyer
predicts that it will get worse:

> Que désormais notre surprise cesse donc en voyant des individus
> mâles en boucles d'oreilles faire de la tapisserie, donner audience
> dans leur lit à midi, interrompre un discours sérieux pour converser
> avec un chien, parler à leur propre figure dans une glace, caresser
> leurs dentelles, être furieux pour un magot brisé, tomber en syncope
> sur un perroquet malade, dérober enfin à l'autre sexe toutes ses
> grâces. (32)

> [We should therefore no longer be surprised to see males in ear-
> rings making tapestries, receiving guests from their beds at noon,
> interrupting a serious conversation to have a word with their dogs,
> speaking to themselves in a mirror, stroking their lace, becoming
> furious over a broken porcelain, fainting over a sick parrot—in other
> words taking over all the graces of the other sex.]

Of the sundry instances of female silliness, the ultimate is their speech:
women talk too much. Too many flights of fancy, too much small talk and
exaggeration. This serves as a prelude to Coyer's most suggestive point:
the changes that he chiefly deplores relate to three male characteristics
which, he maintains, traditionally distinguish men from women: "parler
peu, penser beaucoup, et dominer" ["speak little, think a lot, and rule"]
(34). Coyer sketches the relation between man's crafty and well-crafted

laconism, on the one hand, and his capacity for governing and for writing and interpreting history, philosophy, and theology, on the other. Their economy of expression would seem to suit men for critical analysis and serious writing, on the grounds, apparently, that the less said the better. In contrast, female excess of expression disqualifies women for anything but social conversation and the composition of light verse and novels— activities and genres to which Coyer, like most of his contemporaries, would refuse high literary station.

L'année merveilleuse captivated the public. Fréron's review of 10 July 1749 notes: "Jamais brochure n'a été lue avec tant d'avidité. Les grands et les petits, les gens d'esprit et les sots, Paris et les provinces lui ont fait le même accueil" ["Never was a brochure read more eagerly. The great and the small, the witty and the foolish, Paris and the provinces, all have given it the same welcome"].[5] Jules Gay reports that there were so many copies in circulation that the postal service made unusually high profits (1: 227). In fact, however, if the satire is uncommonly lively, both its thematics and its object are conventional. The period often elucidated social or moral foibles with stories of men and women, masters and slaves, rich and poor exchanging places. That women babble was alleged with regularity, and the conviction that the most fashionable among them dissipated time and energy on trivia was likewise widespread. The feminization of males and of French society itself was also a frequent theme, underscored by Jean-Jacques Rousseau, among others.[6]

At heart, of course, *L'année merveilleuse* attacks not just women, but society. Coyer censures social vices by caricature and implicitly posits a series of binary oppositions. Masculine and feminine being the fundamental allegory of difference, whatever approaches perfection is in Coyer's scheme charged with a masculine value, while society's deviation from perfection is qualified as feminine.

Less witty and polished, but actually more original, is Le Prince de Beaumont's *Lettre en réponse à L'année merveilleuse* [Letter in response to The wonderful year], which appeared in quarto the same year, ostensibly in Nancy.[7] The *Lettre en réponse* fills only seven pages, half the length of Coyer's piece. Formally, it is not a rejoinder: although she addresses many of her remarks to men, the principal addressee of the piece is an unidentified "Madame" who has asked for her reaction to *L'année merveilleuse*. This strategy is essential. When Coyer valorizes the intentionality of masculine thought, he betrays how deeply rooted his discourse is in a patriarchal society where man's firm control makes speech itself all but superfluous: relegated to woman, words ultimately become the sign of her triviality.

In resorting to the female writing that Coyer disdains, Le Prince de Beaumont addresses herself in the first instance not to Coyer, but elsewhere—to the other, to woman—and thus privileges dialogue with someone of her own sex over debate with the male adversary. In this early piece, the bias that will characterize her writing is already evident: for three decades more, she will write not just *about* women, but *for* women, dedicating her life to their education, steadfastly maintaining that science is open to the female mind and that a whole range of expression is accessible to the female pen. Her mission is not to change society, but to elevate the female sex, an agenda that is already laid out in the *Lettre en réponse*.

Differentiating between Coyer's meretricious critique of feminine pastimes and his account of the attributes distinguishing the sexes, she chooses to gloss the latter:

> *Les hommes*, dit-il, *naturellement parlent peu, pensent beaucoup, aiment à dominer*. Je conviens de ce qu'il avance; mais je le prie d'examiner si ces caractères distinguent aussi avantageusement son sexe d'avec le nôtre, qu'il l'insinue. (2)

> [Men, he says, naturally speak little, think a lot, and like to rule. I admit what he says; but I beg him to examine whether these characteristics give his sex as much of an advantage over ours as he insinuates.]

Her initial agreement conceals a different reading strategy. She does not dispute Coyer's characterization of traditional male (and, by opposition, female) attributes, but she regards them as symptomatic rather than analytical and identifies deep causes redounding either to woman's credit or man's discredit. That is to say, she distinguishes between Coyer's categories and his interpretation. The discrimination she makes not only sorts out intrinsic physical and metaphysical differences between man and woman but also challenges the basis of his hierarchy.

Pushing his pretentions of male concision to their logical extreme, she associates men with silence and women with speech. "Pour que le silence fût préférable à la parole," she reasons, however, "il faudrait que le néant fût au-dessus de l'existence" ["For silence to be preferable to speech, nothingness would have to be higher than existence"] (2). This is contrary to the natural order, where action is necessary for the construction and conservation of all beings.

Action is therefore a perfection, idleness a defect, and a being is all the more perfect for the ability to act—or to speak—at length. Women, moreover, speak not just more but better than men, and as proof Le Prince de Beaumont marshals anthropological evidence and social observation. Peasant girls think and speak better at fifteen than boys at twenty-five; and in polite society women provide most of the topics of conversation. The proof that men find such conversation to their liking is that they spend long hours in female company, "aux dépens de [leurs] occupations les plus graves" ["at the expense of (their) most serious business"] (4).

But her response has an ontological basis as well. The silence that Coyer implicitly extols seems to flow from an unspeakable primeval mystery, and from it somehow radiates male power. In trivializing speech, Coyer appears to suggest something antecedent to language, an eternal reality that needs no expression in time or words. For this ultimate presence acknowledged by silence, Le Prince de Beaumont substitutes a void: for silence to be preferable to speech, nothingness would have to be above existence. She demystifies silence: in speech reside vitality, continuity, responsibility, truth.

Regarding Coyer's second point, that men think more than women, Le Prince de Beaumont explains that they must work hard to articulate even ordinary thoughts whereas, in contrast, women's facile style testifies to how little effort writing requires of them and helps to explain why they make the most important contributions to the Republic of Letters.[8] Nor does Le Prince de Beaumont dispute Coyer's final point regarding male rule, although she does maliciously alter his formula. Where he alleged that men rule, she credits him with saying that they like to rule and declares that their perennial subjugation of women gives ample proof. In other words, what Coyer sees as propensity to deep thought, Le Prince de Beaumont reads as slowness and dullness of intellect; what he describes as natural fitness for governing, she claims is perverse pleasure in mastery and manipulation.

For Le Prince de Beaumont, as for European feminists as far back as Christine de Pisan, no biological justification for the subjection of women exists: it is culturally determined (Kelly, *passim*). Masculine domination, far from signaling superiority, bears witness to men's flaws. This part of her argument flows into an explicit affirmation of female superiority: women are by nature upright and faithful; men, duplicitous and inconstant. Knowing themselves incapable of virtue, men establish a double standard; while making laws to dispense themselves from the practice of morality, they institutionalize an insidious education for women that is designed to inculcate frivolity. The message of the *Lettre en réponse* is that woman's natural qualities are compromised by her wretched education—a conviction that echoes through the writings of other French women authors of the period (for example, Françoise de Graffigny, Anne Louise Elie de Beaumont, and Marie Jeanne Riccoboni). An extended metaphor in the *Lettre en réponse* compares women to loam in which thorns are sown and from which fruits and flowers are unseasonably pulled: the miracle is that any plants at all survive. Thus does Le Prince de Beaumont argue against both the theory of female faults and the kind of social and educational conditioning that could make it self-fulfilling.

The skirmish between Coyer and Le Prince de Beaumont may be seen as part of a vast centuries-old debate about female inferiority, whose extreme version poses the question of whether women have souls. Such controversy is related to a tradition that considered the seduction of Eve and Adam as the result of unwise speaking and listening and that, by implication, valorized taciturnity. We are, indeed, reminded of Eve's original subversive speeches when Coyer deplores the adeptness of young women at seducing mature men. Coyer evokes it in terms of female discourse and male action:

Une fille de seize ans dit à un homme de quarante, au lieu d'examiner dans votre cabinet, si ce malheureux conservera sa fortune ou la perdra, regardez-moi tous les jours pendant plusieurs heures, il la regarde; aimez-moi plus que votre femme, il y consent; ruinez-vous pour moi, il se ruine. (36)

[A girl of sixteen says to a man of forty, instead of going to your study and looking into the question of whether that poor man will retain his savings or lose them, look at me every day for several hours: he looks at her; love me more than your wife: he agrees to it; ruin yourself for me: he ruins himself.]

Le Prince de Beaumont responds, as we have seen, by positing the social utility of woman's speech. Her related defense of the female heart and mind as virtuous is not unexpected: contemporary authors of both sexes were maintaining the same thing. A little over a decade earlier, for example, Madame Galien in her history of famous women called *Apologie des femmes appuyée sur l'histoire* (1737) argued from the Bible that woman, made from Adam's rib, formed from the clay of the earth, is more noble than man; her original sin is less serious than man's, her body more beautiful than his, her soul "infinitely more elevated" (10–11). Galien likewise congratulated women on their "pleasing volubility" (19)—doubtless the gift of a grateful creator. Le Prince de Beaumont also locates her discussion in a theological context by means of a biblical point of reference, going beyond the defense of the soul and making a claim for the female body as more perfect in origin than that of the male.

Her argument, like Galien's, is a persiflage of the standard notion of masculine primacy and perfection. She remarks that God fashioned Adam from the vilest dust, but only after working over this first creation did He judge it worthy to serve in the formation of woman. A metaphor from painting helps make the point: the last strokes of the brush produce the masterpiece. Woman is God's masterpiece, on which He lavished His final brushstrokes: "Il forme la femme; tout est accompli" ["He creates woman; everything is done"] (5). And He creates no more. The heretical implications of her rationalization are of a piece with the argument for the superiority of speech over silence. Man's claims to precedence issue from his participation in some primary essence: primordial silence, primal dust; but for Le Prince de Beaumont the derivative is in each case the chef d'oeuvre. Thus does she parody man's pretentions to divine essence.

In the final analysis, Le Prince de Beaumont's recognition of the function of words in both writing and speaking contrasts with Coyer's perception of words as a transparent means of conveying extraverbal truth. Even more compellingly, the polemic is an example of a subordinated group using the marks of its subordination as images of power. While misogynist literature frequently accused women of volubility, Le Prince de Beaumont eschews the obvious response: refutation of the accusations. Instead, she uses Coyer's own arguments against him, not to assert the equality he denies women, but to claim a paradoxical female preeminence, basing it on the very characteristics he views as flaws.

In other words, she incorporates the notions that nourish male bias in her creation of a vigorous image of woman as physically dignified, morally estimable, and intellectually redoubtable. She makes explicit her idea of the extent of female superiority in her concluding summary: everything that, by man's own account, differentiates him, is in fact to woman's advantage. Consequently, in spite of men's far-reaching prerogatives, women would be ill-advised to wish for any such transformation as *L'année merveilleuse* describes. A mock legal appeal is appended, requesting, "au nom de tout le sexe" ["in the name of all the fair sex"] that Nature permit no metamorphosis.

Later that year she published another quarto brochure which forms a sequel, titled *Arrêt solemnel de la nature, par lequel le grand événement de l'année 1748 est sursis jusqu'au premier août 1749* [Solemn decree of nature, whereby the great event of the year 1748 is postponed until 1 August 1749].[9] This, like the preceding pamphlet, takes the form of a letter addressed to "Madame." It describes a vision. Seated at the foot of a tree in the area outside of Paris already known as the Champs Elysées, at eleven o'clock on the night of 31 July—the night before the transformation of the sexes is to occur—the author is rereading her petition when the glorious apparition of the goddess Nature occurs.

33

Demonstrating that nature is preferable to art, she appears in two successive guises: first in the simplicity of a divinity; then as a fashionable lady, ornately dressed, rouged, and powdered. Nature grants a year's reprieve: if women use that time to advantage, no metamorphosis will occur. She condescends to leave behind a code intended to "remettre le beau sexe dans son état primitif" ["restore the fair sex to its original state"] (6), whose fifteen rules make clear that Le Prince de Beaumont's ideas of reformation and restoration affect two principal areas: attire and chastity.

The code discourages excessive adornment, elaborate dress, and perfumes. No woman may spend more than half an hour dressing, discuss her attire for more than three minutes, conceal her age, or encourage more than one suitor at a time. Women whose husbands philander may use only sweetness to woo them back, under pain of seeing them become incorrigible. No rules are given for unfaithful wives, because they are sufficiently punished by their own remorse and their lovers' scorn; or for coquettes, whom Nature finds unworthy of her concern.[10]

The defense of woman's language in the *Lettre en réponse* is implicitly joined in the *Arrêt solemnel* to an identification of female nature with Nature and to an effort to extend and embellish that identification. Considered in tandem, the two works appear to imply that Nature, spontaneous and sincere, disdains not only the manipulation of adornment and cosmetics, but also the political manipulation to which men are led by their love of power and finally, the rhetorical manipulation exercised by male language, which is highly reflective, overdetermined, and sophistic. Artistry in dress and behavior rivals sophistry and is likewise despicable.

Le Prince de Beaumont's argument for woman is an argument against the male mystique. While Coyer insinuates the existence of some mysterious, original perfection that man imitates, Le Prince de Beaumont rejects the strategy of imitation by denying masculine claims to the excellence of silence, refusing to emulate men, and preferring dialogue with women. In counterpoint, she subversively rewrites Coyer's allegations of female inferiority as an account of female difference and argues in effect for the superiority of the derivative over the primordial. Whereas Coyer

34

implicitly conceives thought as preverbal, and words as eccentric, she outlines an opposing position that defends woman's language as differentiated and energetically dispersed.

Le Prince de Beaumont's notions of right conduct may strike us today as quaint, unless we are willing to view her idea of chastity, in the tradition of Aristophanes' *Lysistrata*, less as a constraint than as a positive, emancipatory value. It helps her to define woman against man and to put a high value on female self-sufficiency. I shall argue for a similar reading of her novels, in which the inviolate chastity of dutiful heroines sets them apart from a phallocentric culture. Those novels have not been printed for two hundred years. Needless to say, they have received little or no critical attention.

There are exotic didactic works like *Civan, roi de Bungo, histoire japonaise* (1754),[11] but her four major novels—*Lettres de Madame du Montier* (1756), *Lettres d'Emérance à Lucie* (1765), *Mémoires de Madame la baronne de Batteville* (1766), and *La nouvelle Clarisse* (1767)—all take the epistolary form. They run to hundreds of pages each and implicitly advance some of the same fundamental notions as the *Lettre en réponse* and the *Arrêt solemnel,* including the inferiority of artifice to nature, the moral and social value of women's speech and activity, the importance of education and self-reliance for women, and their natural superiority.

All the novels exhibit numerous peripeteia of convention, while they give play to the tribulations of a virtuous young woman who models herself on a saintly older one. They specifically raise concerns about the necessity of getting married and about the possibility of happiness in marriage: "Je conseille à celle qui veut jouir de la vie, comme on parle dans le monde, je lui conseille, dis-je, de se vouer au célibat, c'est le seul état qui lui convienne" ["I advise any woman who wants to enjoy life, as they say in society, I advise her, I say, to make a vow of celibacy, it's the only condition that will suit her"], proclaims the author's mouthpiece in *Lettres d'Emérance à Lucie* (1: 16). Although on the surface, they appear to subscribe to that era's version of the double standard, the novels, like the *Lettre en réponse* and the *Arrêt solemnel,* can be read as a credo of female dignity and perfectibility.

LETTRES

.DE MADAME

DU MONTIER

.Recueillies par Madame LE PRINCE
DE BEAUMONT.

TOME PREMIER.

A LYON

Chez PIERRE BRUYSET PONTHUS ;
rue Saint Dominique, près du cloître
des RR. PP. Jacobins.

M. DCC. LXVII.
AVEC APPROBATION ET PRIVILEGE DU ROI.

Title page, Jeanne Le Prince de Beaumont, *Lettres
de Madame du Montier,* vol.I (Lyon: Bruyset Ponthus,
1767). Collection of Robert L. Dawson.

The last of the novels, *La nouvelle Clarice,* is both the most self-conscious and the most optimistic; in the way it examines questions of parental authority and domestic arrangements, it owes a good deal to Richardson and Rousseau. From the former it takes its title and principal concern: the legitimacy of a young woman's accepting a man's help in fleeing an unreasonable father. In circumstances not unlike those that beset Richardson's Clarissa, Clarice redeems herself by marrying her accomplice, who luckily is an upstanding young man. This gives her confidante occasion to expand on the plot of Richardson's novel and to censure its "dangerous details" and "dirty ideas" (2: 31).

Clarice's story, we are given to understand, is far more moral. From Rousseau the novel takes the inspiration for its second volume, an account of Clarice's married life on her husband's estate, where she distributes money and advice, plants vegetables instead of flowers (subordinating, like Rousseau's Wolmar, "l'agréable" to "l'utile"), teaches the peasants cleanliness, and feeds abandoned babies with a concoction of milk and barley water. This domestic ideology is grounded in Christian morality and forbearance.

Excesses of plot and language characteristic of many eighteenth-century novels of adventure and sentiment—"retire-toi, monstre que l'enfer a vomi pour ma perte" ["away with you, monster vomited up by hell for my perdition"] (2: 154), screams Clarice to a half-brother whom her corrupt father wants her to wed—are offset by whimsical details: the man Clarice actually marries earns his keep as assistant to a wigmaker, a former mistress having taught him to roll her curls. Like her other novels, this one hones the themes of *La Belle et la Bête* and *Arrêt solemnel:* physical beauty does not signify; worldly values entail difficulties; goodness is its own reward.

In view of the complexity of her plots, which may follow a large cast of characters across generations and through multiple adventures in Europe and America, I have chosen for purposes of clarity to focus my discussion on two of the novels: *Lettres de Madame du Montier* (hereafter *Madame du Montier*) and *Mémoires de Madame la baronne de Batteville* (hereafter *La baronne de Batteville*). Both enjoyed considerable popularity.[12] The

Abbé Sabatier de Castres, author of a dictionary of French literature, *Les trois siècles de la littérature française,* first published in 1772, mentions these two novels alone among works by Le Prince de Beaumont particularly worthy of note (3: 560–61). Their illustration of Le Prince de Beaumont's convictions about women's education and the bases of conjugal harmony and their explicit moralizing set them off even from that period's highly moralistic fiction.

But while her anthologies and occasional writings like the *Lettre en réponse,* either in form, content, or both, teach the urgency for women of access to reason, what intrigues me about these novels is that they obliquely call into question the usefulness of reason in its accepted sense. I do not wish to make an exaggerated claim for works that can strain the modern reader's tolerance for didacticism and implausibility. But despite the conventionality of certain plot elements and the conservatism of her rhetoric, these novels strategically explore the implications for women of the Enlightenment's linking of reason and virtue while they suggest, ultimately, that the mind's emancipation is the freedom most to be cherished.

Her heroines, moreover, are strangely engrossing and secretly subversive, both in their unusually strong sense of social responsibility and in their tacit resolve not to be victimized by men's passion. In *Madame du Montier,* eighteen-year-old Mademoiselle du Montier is the eldest child of an ancient but penniless family and seems destined for a life of provincial obscurity when Providence throws an old friend of her father, the wealthy marquis de ***, across her path. Dazzled by her qualities of mind and soul, he obtains her hand and whisks her away to the court at Turin, where he is in the service of the king of Sardinia. For the rest of her wedded life, she exchanges letters with the mother whose counsel she scrupulously follows. Only once does she experience passion, for a courtier named Mastrilli, and she hardly understands what is happening to her. When an insightful Madame du Montier reveals to her naïve daughter that her interest in Mastrilli is love, the young marquise resolutely dismisses him; but the episode has helped her to understand that whatever she and her *husband* feel for each other, it is not passion. Various other

38

trials—her husband's philandering, her children's death, her sister's calumnies, social ostracism—allow her to polish her already shining virtue.

While other heroines of the period moan and groan about their troubles, this one displays an inner strength that enables her to follow the advice of her mother: "surtout point d'abattement" ["most of all, no despondency"] (1: 168, 180). When at thirty she is widowed and free to marry Mastrilli, she prefers, like the widowed princesse de Clèves, to dismiss the man she loves; she arranges his union with a younger sister and adopts a life of charitable works. Hagiography has already begun: her mother is transcribing and circulating their letters.

Although the book incorporates several voices in addition to the predominant ones of the marquise and her mother, it is arranged in a straightforward manner: a letter is sent, the response appears in the next letter. Little sense is conveyed of the passage of time, although a simple calculation reveals that the novel covers about twelve years, since we know the heroine is eighteen at the time of her marriage and thirty when she is widowed at the end. Despite its length, the plot has a relatively sharp focus, with few of the digressions so frequent in multivolume novels of the period. Le Prince de Beaumont does not lose sight of the fact that this is the story of a marriage: it begins when the bride goes from France to Savoy with her husband and ends when, newly widowed, she returns to her mother.

Two years after the publication of *Madame du Montier,* an English translation appeared as *History of a Young Lady of Distinction, in a Series of letters that passed between Madame du Montier, and the Marchioness de ****. The title page contains this description of the contents:

> Wherein are laid down the Instructions and Councils of a discreet and affectionate Parent, for her Daughter's Conduct upon the Stage of the great World, and in the more amiable and humble Station of a Wife and Mother; as well in her Condition of Prosperity and Happiness, as under the severest and most affecting Trials. Also, such Sentiments of Gratitude, Duty and Respect, as exhibit a Heart overflowing with the most exalted Love and filial Piety towards an unfaithful Husband and a fond and endearing Parent. The whole

forming an instructive and agreeable Companion to the Ladies in every Condition of Life.[13]

The passage aptly characterizes the novel's didactic nature, and the translator has insured that no reader opening the book can have any doubt about what she will find in it.

If the French editions, unlike the English, bear no title-page description of contents, the morality of the work is nonetheless prescribed by three preliminary pieces: dedication, foreword, and preface. The book is dedicated to a certain marquise de Rosan who, according to the author, resembles the title character in her infallible sense of what constitutes a proper female education. Then a four-page foreword echoes the themes of the dedication pages: maternal wisdom and filial docility. Finally, a slightly lengthier "editor's preface" addresses the question that must occur to the reader who has come this far, that of the book's readability:

> Mon Dieu! que votre Madame du Montier est dévote, me disait une personne qui avait jeté les yeux sur les lettres qui venaient de m'être remises, et que je n'ai fait que copier. Ne pourriez-vous pas retrancher quelque chose des sermons qu'elle fait à toute sa famille? A coup sûr cela ennuyera. (1: xi)

> [Goodness! How pious your Madame du Montier is, said someone who had seen the letters that had just been given to me, and that I have done no more than copy. Couldn't you eliminate some of the sermons to her family? People will surely be bored.]

The "editor"—Le Prince de Beaumont herself, according to the title page—defends the work on three counts. In the first place, the severe morality of these letters is suited to an era so corrupt that readers are becoming bored with libertinism and interested in "facts."[14] In the second place, if these are indeed true letters (and who, she asks, can prove that they are not?), then the editor must respect her text. And, finally, verisimilitude itself forces her to refuse to attenuate the tone. She explains this last scruple with the following reasoning:

40

On aurait raison de regarder ces lettres comme une fiction mal digé-
rée, si la marquise et sa mère avaient conservé leur raison et leur vie
au milieu de tant de coups si terribles et si redoublés, sans le secours
tout-puissant d'une foi très vive. (xiv–xv)

[People would be right to consider these letters a half-baked fiction,
if the marquise and her mother had held onto reason and life among
so many terrible afflictions, without the all powerful help of a living
faith.]

In an epoch that valued authenticity over imagination and history above
fiction, Le Prince de Beaumont interweaves questions of truth, verisimilitude, reason, utility, and morality into a suggestion that these letters can
combat the depravity of the times because they are factual rather than
fictional. In addition, they are credible, she maintains, in that saintliness is
a natural outcome of suffering. And why should not the love of God
produce the same miracles of behavior as profane passion? This concern
with the *vrai* and the *vraisemblable* runs through most novels of the early
and the middle century, including others by Le Prince de Beaumont.[15]
She adduces the very aspects of her work that may seem most far-
fetched—the uncommon benevolence of her heroines, their uncomplain-
ing submissiveness to Providence, their readiness to forgive the worst
offenses—as paradoxical evidence of "the facts."

Starting with her preface, then, in considering women's plights, she
begins rewriting what is commonly understood as the plausible, the reasonable, and the factual. Near its end, she makes explicit her intention to
"prouver la possibilité du bonheur dans les états les plus pénibles"
["prove the possibility of happiness in the most painful circumstances"]
(xvi). Novels, of course, are generally concerned with the possibility of
happiness, and endings are conventionally labeled happy or unhappy. In
the eighteenth-century novel, outcomes tend to be highly stylized: either
a happy marriage or retirement, typically to a convent. Instead, Le Prince
de Beaumont's heroines emerge from highly problematic marriages to
end up alone, enjoying a transcendent solitude.

Their beatification is closely associated with their perspective on wealth and with the refusal of the artificial and the meretricious that Le Prince de Beaumont preached in the *Arrêt solemnel*. Virtually every heroine of Le Prince de Beaumont discovers that money is an obstacle to perfection; the young marquise in *Madame du Montier* has the greatest success in divesting herself of fortune and income. The heroine of *La nouvelle Clarice* is just as highly motivated but less successful, although the theme itself is even more predominant in this novel. Despite Clarice's indefatigable efforts to disburden herself of portable and real property in order to live a saintly life, she is still rich in the end, thanks to the well-meaning intervention of friends less advanced in saintliness. But her riches are the subject of continual discussion and negotiation: page after page supplies details of the exact sums left her by her aunt, required for her maintenance, usurped by her father; of the precise value of clothes and jewelry and the sums for which they are sold or pawned.

The novel goes to paradoxical lengths to prove that wealth is a useless burden, even a misfortune. Economic concerns relating to the possibility of women's happiness run all through the works I discuss in this study, where countless heroines like Mademoiselle du Montier must marry to survive. But in the novels of Le Prince de Beaumont, once survival is insured, women may try to reject membership in a consumer economy as one aspect of their private revolt.

In 1766, ten years after the publication in book form of *Madame du Montier, La baronne de Batteville* appeared, with a plot more romantic and larger in scale. Its subtitle, "la veuve parfaite" ["the perfect widow"], announces, like the prefatory material in the earlier work, an upbeat moral tone. Here Julie, baroness of Batteville, writes a series of letters to a friend, interpolating her life's story. As a girl, she is affianced to des Essarts, whom she loves. The plague in Marseille in the 1720s separates them, and des Essarts behaves heroically through a series of prodigious adventures. With the help of a razor, he delivers the baby of a dying plague victim and contracts the disease. Robbed, beaten, and interred alive, he is eventually born again, rising from a ditch of corpses to travel to America and become a still more devout Christian.

Julie, meanwhile, presuming him dead, is cajoled by her mother into marriage with a doting older man, the wealthy baron of Batteville. When their child, also named Julie, is about twelve, des Essarts reappears on the scene and saves the lives of mother and daughter in a fire. The baron shortly dies, and his widow, thirty-two years old, is now free to marry des Essarts, who still adores her. Instead, in a gesture that recalls (and goes beyond) both the widowed princesse de Clèves refusing the hand of the duc de Nemours and Rousseau's Julie attempting to marry St. Preux to her cousin Claire, Le Prince de Beaumont's heroine persuades her former suitor to marry her daughter.[16] The couple live happily ever after, the baroness emerging from her convent retreat only to attend the births of her twelve grandchildren, all of whom become, like their progenitors, prodigies of virtue.

The continuity of female concerns and temptations and the exemplary value of the sublime and sublimated virtue of the baroness are suggested by the repetition of her life patterns in the experience of her daughter. These include love at first sight, not just for a man, but for *the very man* her mother loves; the precipitate decision to enter a convent, from which she must be doggedly dissuaded by the menaces of family members, priests, and nuns; a stubborn determination to sacrifice her own happiness to her mother's well-being; and the ultimate acceptance of a marriage arranged by the mother. The daughter in question bears not only an uncanny physical resemblance to her mother, but also her name.

Most of Le Prince de Beaumont's heroines are neither humorous nor volatile, nor, except for fleeting instances, impassioned. The young heroine of *Lettres d'Emérance à Lucie* explains that she is satisfied to feel only friendship for her older husband and that remaining virtuous "tires her" not at all (2: 48). Like Lucie, the others are not so much psychologically resilient as Christianly docile. In an era whose literature enshrined the ideals of sensibility, including the conviction that legitimate passion ennobles both subject and object, these novels contend that virtue lies squarely in the refusal not just of adulterous love, but ultimately of all passion.

It is clear to every character in *La baronne de Batteville* that God opposes the marriage of Julie and des Essarts, whose character, fortunes, and family connections would appear to suit them ideally to one another. Divine opposition is apparently based on the principle that one must *not* marry for love, no matter how legitimate such a union might seem, and subsidiary plots in *La baronne de Batteville* reinforce the point.

Unlike many of her contemporaries, Le Prince de Beaumont does not glorify the discovery of love; instead she systematically discredits passion. Her letter-writers spin aphorisms such as: "Il arrive rarement que l'amour d'un homme survive à l'estime, et il est encore plus rare que cette estime se conserve après qu'on s'en est rendue indigne par une faiblesse" ["It is rare that a man's love outlives respect, and even rarer that his respect is sustained after a woman has made herself unworthy of it by yielding to him"] (*Montier* 1: 294). When the heroine of *La baronne de Batteville*, still single, is led to believe that her beloved is dead, she reacts with palpable relief: "La mort de M. des Essarts me parut un coup de miséricorde qui avait daigné m'arracher à une passion dont l'excès me rendait criminelle" ["The death of Monsieur des Essarts seemed a stroke of mercy which unshackled me from passion whose very excess was criminal"] (70).

Years afterward, even though they are again free to marry, she and des Essarts persist in referring to their love through an age-old vocabulary of illness and cure: "Je pensai alors au seul remède qui pouvait me guérir radicalement, c'était le mariage de ma fille avec des Essarts" ["Then I thought of the only remedy that could radically cure me: the marriage of my daughter and des Essarts"] (178). Still later, when a correspondent laments the infidelity of her husband, the baroness replies complacently: "Votre histoire est celle de toutes les filles qui se marient par inclination; je m'attendais à ce qui vous arrive" ["Yours is the story of all girls who marry for love: I expected this to happen"] (215).

The question of the nature of happiness earlier raised in *Madame du Montier* is raised again when the heroine of *La baronne de Batteville* writes: "Je suis heureuse; mais il s'en faut beaucoup que vous ayez la moindre idée de la nature du bonheur dont je jouis; et sans de certaines circonstances, il ne tiendrait qu'à moi de le regarder comme une infortune" ["I'm happy; but you are far from understanding the least thing about the happiness that I enjoy; and it is only because of certain circumstances that I myself don't consider it a misfortune"] (1–2). She alludes to the disappointments that underlie her apparently comfortable life and explains that God has given her a felicity independent of all that surrounds her.

"Independent" is a key word, suggesting a happiness that is wholly subjective, yet also free of illusions. It contrasts with the posture of the romantic heroes: in Chateaubriand's *René* (1802), for example, the heroine's "renunciation" is fraught with illusion and a death urge, a kind of emptying out of self. But well into Le Prince de Beaumont's novel, the baroness notes, "Je suis heureuse parce que je suis sans remords, je renouvelle mon sacrifice à tous les instants" ["I'm happy because I have no remorse, I renew my sacrifice every instant"] (177). In much eighteenth-century fiction, the word "bonheur" carries a sexual charge: a woman who agrees to "faire le bonheur" of her lover, goes to bed with him. But as it appears in Le Prince de Beaumont's novels—as a result of sacrifice and practically synonymous with renunciation—"bonheur" suggests a spiritual configuration of themes.

The wedding of Julie and the baron of Batteville is one of Le Prince de Beaumont's most hallucinatory scenes, the altar serving as locus both of the family's sacrifice of Julie and of Julie's sacrifice of passion. She has repeatedly explained to her mother, to the abbess of the convent where they live, to her confessor, and to the baron himself that she prefers the veil to marriage. But each of her interlocutors misconstrues her words and chooses to view as provisional consent what she intends as categorical refusal. She is propelled to the altar by feelings of gratitude (toward the old baron), responsibility (toward her penniless mother), and guilt (her confessor having pointed out the "indecency" of love for the putatively dead des Essarts). In a convent, with few witnesses, more or less against her will, the young woman is given over into the hands of an older man, and her aversion for the business is suggested in a brief notation: "L'étendue des devoirs que j'allais m'imposer m'effraya" ["The breadth of the obligations I was about to take on frightened me"] (99).

The forced marriage is a staple of fiction from one end of the century to the other, and this scene echoes countless others. The heroine of Catherine Durand Bédacier's first novel, the exaggeratedly romantic *La comtesse de Mortane* (1699), is conducted to the altar one night, "more dead than alive," by her authoritarian mother (1: 34). Almost a century later, Adelle, the teenage protagonist of Mérard de Saint-Just's *Mon journal d'un an*, is likewise lured by her stepmother to an abandoned chapel at midnight, tricked into signing a marriage contract, and forcibly united to a loathsome specimen of mankind. Like Madame de Mortane, she describes herself as a victim. Whereas Madame de Mortane's mother is arrogant and ambitious, however, and Adelle's stepmother is dissolute and cruel, all the bride's tormentors in Le Prince de Beaumont's novel are in the service of Providence, and the groom is good at heart.

Le Prince de Beaumont's ideal woman recognizes marriage as a social and economic necessity and endures a few years of life with a man whom she cannot love in sensibility's sense. Madame du Montier's reflection on marriage in a letter of consolation to a young woman who has been forced into a convent—"Si le mariage avait un noviciat, on n'y verrait guère de professes" ["If there were a novitiate for marriage, very few would enter the order"] (2: 329–30)[17]—could function as epigram to Le Prince de Beaumont's novels and, indeed, to a large body of fiction by eighteenth-century women writers. Following the tradition of *La princesse de Clèves,* many heroines, especially in novels by women, choose seclusion and good deeds over amorous involvement or marriage, and such a theme was handled in ways running the gamut from the somber to the humorous.

Marie-Anne Robert's *Nicole de Beauvais ou l'amour vaincu par la reconnaissance* [Nicole de Beauvais or love vanquished by gratitude] (1767) is a lighthearted story about a peasant whose naïveté leads to endless sexual misunderstandings, and who, like the heroines of Le Prince de Beaumont, finally opts for a celibate life of friendship and charity. What distinguishes Le Prince de Beaumont's novels from Robert's and those of others is their moral intransigence: a continual peeling away of worldly values and goods parallels the gradual rejection of passion and remarriage.

It seems to me that there is a feminist dimension to the rigorous chastity of Le Prince de Beaumont's heroines, suggested both by the configurations of her fictions and the broader context of her feminist preoccupations (preoccupations that are made insistently clear in the *Lettre en réponse*). It is plausible to read her mature heroines' refusal of their sexuality as a victory over patriarchal culture. That culture included, of course, a set of legal structures guaranteeing the subordination of women, who "lived in a sort of permanent minority" (Traer 139) both as daughters and as wives. The widow, on the other hand, enjoyed a significant degree of freedom—a fact with implications that I shall consider in chapter 4.

But it is also important to note that in the eighteenth century, female sexuality was normally associated with the years known today as adolescence. The period's fiction amply demonstrates that in her twenties a woman was considered mature, sometimes even overripe, and at thirty often beyond desire. (When Marie Armande Gacon-Dufour specifies in a polemical text entitled *Mémoire pour le sexe féminin, contre le sexe masculin* [1787] that by the age of forty-five, female passion is extinguished, the relatively advanced age she suggests gives evidence of liberal views [43–44].) Libertine novels especially center female worth on sexuality, and the heroine's power in such novels derives directly from her ability to arouse sexual feelings and to manipulate them for her own ends.

Le Prince de Beaumont's thirtyish heroines, on the other hand, are regarded as sexually viable when they willfully disengage themselves from love and reject the uterine economy, and their final liberation occurs in and through single life. Her originality resides partly in the perception that an exceptional virtue may enable woman to define herself against and without man. ("Virtuous" was not on the whole a useful epithet for a man.) So her heroines start afresh in widowhood, dismissing sexual involvement and emphasizing instead mother-child bonding: love for her daughter, writes the baroness, "acheva de remplir le vide qui était resté dans mon coeur depuis que j'en avais banni des Essarts" ["finally filled the void that had been in my heart ever since I had given up des Essarts"] (102). Indeed, the mother-daughter relation is consistently privileged in Le Prince de Beaumont's novels, usurping the customary position of relations between men and women.

47

While other characters in the novel try to talk "reason," encouraging the widowed marquise to accept the hand of Mastrilli or the widowed baroness to marry des Essarts who has remained faithful for sixteen long years, the author endorses the eccentric choice of celibacy, locating the culmination of their heroism in their refusal of remarriage. Le Prince de Beaumont's novels are striking for their enlistment of self-abnegation in an alliance with godliness against patriarchal norms. In the last analysis, her Christian morality, like the valorization of speech over silence, may be a specifically female strategy. If not militant, it appears at least separatist: the pietism of her heroines represents a sort of internal revolt against Enlightenment.

It is undeniably convenient for patriarchy when the form of protest used by women is withdrawal or refusal to participate rather than active revolt. From a twentieth-century point of view, there is more than a little poignancy in these equivocal gestures of renunciation, in the stance of female characters whose need for autonomy seems to require them to give up their sexuality. The feminism of eighteenth-century authors is not necessarily congruent with our own. As I suggested in my last chapter, the interest of these fictions lies not in outright demonstrations of revolt, but in a subtle questioning of social institutions, in a sometimes almost imperceptible slippage in terms, or in the covert revision of conventional plot elements. In these allegories about personal fulfilment, displays of rebellion may take shapes that suggest ambiguous relations to social and literary convention.

In his chapter on "The Faux Dévot," Erich Auerbach discerns a tight mesh in the French seventeenth century between notions of virtue, reason, and verisimilitude. Reason and common sense seemed perfectly compatible with "la bienséance" and extreme manifestations of adherence to duty and concern with dignity or "gloire."[18] A century later, Le Prince de Beaumont suggests a configuration at once similar and different. The preface to *Madame du Montier*, as we have seen, problematizes the mostly unquestioned alliance between nature and reason, defending her characters' apparently abnormal psychology on the unusual grounds of its verisimilitude, its "natural" logic. This justification may seem paradoxical to us, but it coincides with Auerbach's reading of the perspective of the preceding century: to contemporaries and to generations following, the psychology and exaggerated behavior of Racine's characters seemed perfectly real, valid, and even exemplary.

Yet while Le Prince de Beaumont stresses the validity and exemplary nature of her characters' obsessional purity, in another way she diverges radically from the earlier ethic, for in their implicitly hostile compliance with the demands of patriarchy her plots seem to oppose the notion of virtue to that of reason. In the very heart of the age of reason, and while her own manuals and journalistic writing stress the importance of reasoning for women, her novels subversively question its usefulness. Hers are not the unpleasant versions of a later century—the Victorians' denigration of reason—but a gradual and complicated (and, for our own era, in some ways rather beguiling) novelistic disengagement of reason and virtue. She might be protesting that "reason" only meant, as Louise d'Epinay put it, "suivre les avis qu'on vous donne" ["following the advice you're given"].[19] In spite of the conservatism that leads her in all her writings to an overt endorsement of the proprieties, we find in these novels tacit suggestions of the recognition that some of these very proprieties were arbitrary inventions, systems of closure, and obstacles to female self-knowledge. While her didactic and journalistic writing preaches "reason" and the fulfillment of one's obligation to society through marriage and reproduction, the novels may be read as suggesting a quiet but self-assured renunciation of this sort of traditionally "reasonable" behavior. Heroines withdraw from society's established frameworks and refuse its pressures for marital sex, subservience, and endurance of the double standard. As individuals, her mature, carefully educated, and richly experienced heroines end up choosing an exalted, autonomous, and unreasonable course of virtue, allying themselves with God and embracing chastity as a path to integrity and a means of control.

CHAPTER 3

DOXAL VIRTUE

Anne Louise Elie de Beaumont

If marriage is a major structuring principle in the eighteenth-century novel, functioning as the crucial event whose occurrence (or absence) concludes numerous stories, then the question of marriageability, of whether or not a given woman is "right" for an exalted marriage, is a compelling aspect of plot. This question may be explored through the interplay of two kinds of phenomena: the performing skills of sexually experienced women, and men's received ideas about female virtue and male honor.

The Madame de la Pommeraye episode in Diderot's *Jacques le fataliste et son maître*[1] is one of the best known of eighteenth-century tales and has been seen as a kind of paradigm for gender relations in the novel and in society. It is a story of marriageability and marriage, and the relation between the marquis des Arcis and the young whore who becomes his wife illuminates the role played in fiction by rather dubious doxies, in both homonymic senses of that term: on the one hand, problematic women—sweethearts and prostitutes—and on the other, doctrines and myths about womanizing and wiving which may be more problematic still. In particular, it poses questions of social consciousness and sexual morality that provide a useful perspective on plots typically turning on courtship and matrimony.

The marriage of Diderot's marquis, the event with which the la Pommeraye story virtually ends, is prepared by the early account of the affair between him and Madame de la Pommeraye and the reasons for their breach. Critics are wont to call it a case of "infidelity" on the part of des Arcis. Yet infidelity in love and marriage is normally constituted by an instance of deviance. By all appearances, the lover of Madame de la Pommeraye, despite a history of philandering, has of late committed no such act. There is not a single suggestion that he has so much as experienced a specific attraction for another woman. What, then, has he done?

Peu à peu, il passa un jour, deux jours sans la voir; peu à peu il manqua au dîner-souper qu'il avait arrangé; peu à peu il abrégea ses visites; il eut des affaires qui l'appelaient: lorsqu'il arrivait, il disait un mot, s'étalait dans un fauteuil, prenait une brochure, la jetait, parlait à son chien ou s'endormait. Le soir, sa santé, qui devenait misérable, voulait qu'il se retirât de bonne heure: c'était l'avis de Tronchin. "C'est un grand homme que Tronchin! Ma foi! je ne doute pas qu'il ne tire d'affaire notre amie dont les autres désespéraient." Et tout en parlant ainsi, il prenait sa canne et son chapeau et s'en allait, oubliant quelquefois de l'embrasser. (145–46)

[Little by little, he spent a day, two days, without seeing her; little by little, he missed the suppers that he had arranged; little by little, he shortened his visits; he was called away by business: when he arrived, he said a word or two, stretched out in an easy chair, picked up something to read, tossed it aside, spoke to his dog or fell asleep. In the evenings, his health, which was becoming very poor, obliged him to withdraw early: that was Tronchin's advice. "He's a great man, Tronchin! My word, I wouldn't be surprised if he cures that friend of ours whom the other doctors have given up on." And so saying, he picked up his cane and his hat and left, sometimes forgetting to kiss her.]

What has he done? Forgotten dates, fallen asleep in the evening, attended more to his dog than to his mistress, neglected to kiss her goodnight. In short, neither more nor less than to behave like a husband rather than a lover. Madame de la Pommeraye winds up despite herself with a weary companion whose health and digestion motivate him to go to bed early and alone.

With this caricature of marriage the episode begins; to this experience of a love affair turned conjugal, Madame de la Pommeraye reacts with resentment. Rejecting the pseudo-marriage, just as she earlier declined his proposal, she determines to humiliate the very institution of marriage; but in so doing she succeeds in opening up the whole range of questions about male and female identity, about the meaning of legitimacy and the function of performance in human relations. In an example of supreme but ironically miscalculated revenge, she marries off the marquis to the most unmarriageable of women. The bride, called Mademoiselle d'Aisnon, has a practical-minded mother, the face of an angel, and a talent for mimicking virtue.

But the marquis des Arcis, after the initial nasty shock of discovering his wife's vile past, nonetheless resolves to live happily ever after. He seems to take to heart the sensible dictum enunciated by Boudier de Villemert in a 1758 treatise titled *L'ami des femmes* [Women's friend]: "La première loi que doivent s'imposer des époux, est de s'interdire tout examen et tout regret après le mariage conclu" ["The first law for a husband and wife to adopt is to banish all scrutiny and all regret once the marriage has been contracted"] (176).

Diderot's hero has traits and experiences in common with another fictional marquis of the period: the young protagonist of *Lettres du marquis de Roselle* (1764) by Anne Louise Morin Dumesnil Elie de Beaumont (1729–83). The standard biographical sources give little information about the author apart from her birth in Caen and her death in Paris. The wife of a well-known lawyer, she collaborated on her husband's work and signed her own name to few publications. She was commissioned to complete an unfinished and complicated historical novel by Claudine de Tencin, *Anecdotes de la cour et du règne d'Edouard II, roi d'Angleterre*, for its 1776 publication.

Joachim Merlant recounts with admiration an anecdote that he calls the "story of her marriage": as a poor young woman, she became engaged, but when her father's death made her rich, her family urged a more brilliant alliance on her; she persisted, however, in her original plan to marry Jean-Baptiste Elie de Beaumont. "Elle fut heureuse" ["She was happy"], Merlant states categorically (16).

Lettres du marquis de Roselle is itself a reflection on the social problems involved in marrying and a woman's chances for happiness in marriage. Like the Madame de la Pommeraye episode, moreover, it investigates the moral choices associated with eroticism and myths of womanhood and honor. It inquires above all into the meaning of womanly virtue. At the heart of both these stories are questions about the extent to which men and women can really understand each other; both comment on male anxiety about what one possesses in a wife and female anxiety about being or appearing to be what a husband thinks he possesses. By plotting the intersections between them, I hope not only to show the similarities and differences between two provocative versions of beguiling women and gullible men, but also to illuminate the way one woman's work opens up familiar words to new meanings.

Elie de Beaumont's hero—twenty years old, orphaned, and an authentic *belle âme*—is introduced by his corrupt companion, Valville, to an actress named Léonor, who senses in him the possibility of more than just passing material gain. By means of schemes and play acting no less complicated than what Madame de la Pommeraye directs in the Diderot tale, Léonor, like Mademoiselle d'Aisnon, makes an elaborate display of devotion and chastity, withholding from the marquis favors that have been liberally bestowed on his predecessors. The story, much longer than Diderot's, is told from shifting points of view in the form of 143 letters written by all of the main characters and spanning a period of twelve months, from November of one year to November of the next.

Elisabeth de Fontenay points out that in the eighteenth century the institution of religion was frequently in the service of men, permitting them the enjoyment of women and the satiation of "perverse desires," which the civil and moral code would not otherwise have tolerated (43). In the two stories at hand, however, it is not the noblemen but the harlot and the comedienne—the *fille de joie* and the *fille d'opéra*—who appropriate the discourse and gestures of religion as major elements in their strategies of engrossment and entrapment. Here religion masks the ferocity of *female* ambition and desire. Like des Arcis, Roselle is taken in by the lure of the demon-angel, his obsession ever intensified by her refusals.

LETTRES

DU MARQUIS

DE ROSELLE.

Par Madame * **.

PREMIERE PARTIE.

A LONDRES.

Et se trouve

A PARIS,

Chez Louis Cellot, Imprimeur-
Libraire, grand'Salle du Palais,
& rue Dauphine.

M. DCC. LXIV.

Title page, Anne Louise Elie de Beaumont,
Lettres du marquis de Roselle, vol. 1 (London
and Paris: Cellot, 1764).

LETTRES

DU MARQUIS

DE ROSELLE.

Par Madame E. D. B.

NOUVELLE ÉDITION.

À LONDRES,

Et se trouve

A PARIS,

Chez L. CELLOT, Imprimeur-Libraire,
rue Dauphine.

M. DCC. LXX.

Title page, Anne Louise Elie de Beaumont, *Lettres
du marquis de Roselle* (London and Paris: Cellot, 1770).
Collection of Robert L. Dawson.

In Diderot, appearances eventually become reality: Mademoiselle d'Aisnon unexpectedly makes des Arcis a fine wife; but in Elie de Beaumont, the appropriation of the motifs of religion in no way disturbs the fixities of identity imposed by a patriarchal universe: women's performing skills, their ability to orchestrate the feigned extremes of devotion and passion, only confirm their social limitations. Despite their capacity for change, an emotional stage, a play of surfaces, remains all that is available to them.

The marquis de Roselle, then, resists the reasoning of those who try to enlighten him, including his sister and brother-in-law, his good friend Ferval, and a family friend named Madame de Narton. Much of what they and others have to say turns on the question of what "virtue" really is. Even his libertine crony Valville sermonizes him:

Tu te laisses prendre par un faux air de vertu; quelle extravagance! Quand cette vertu serait vraie, il faudrait être bien dupe pour s'attacher à une femme qui l'afficherait. A quoi cela mène-t-il? (65)

[You're letting yourself be taken in by a false appearance of virtue; what absurdity! Even if this virtue were real, you'd have to be a fool to get involved with a woman who made a show of it. Where does it lead?]

It leads, of course, to marriage. The marquis, refusing to believe in Léonor's duplicity, offers jewels and carriages, which Léonor, like Mademoiselle d'Aisnon, astutely declines. And when he proposes a secret marriage with the contractual gift of half his fortune, she declines even this, determined to acquire, as she says, "le nom et le rang de la marquise de Roselle" ["the name and rank of the marquise de Roselle"] (165).

And so Roselle, just like des Arcis, ultimately proposes a formal marriage, with due decorum and ceremony. But here the texts diverge. For while des Arcis does indeed wed the beautiful harlot, Roselle is saved *in extremis*. Just as the wedding begins, Ferval bounds into the room with proof of Léonor's duplicity: he has bought the letters she wrote to a confidante detailing her machinations and ambitions. Léonor is sacrificed so that the tension between the personal and social needs of nobility may be resolved, and Roselle is spared the mortifying acquisition in wedlock of damaged goods. The daring redefinition of marriageability has apparently failed and the female stage has collapsed, leaving intact the truisms of patriarchal identity.

The second half of the novel—another 200 pages—details the events of the succeeding months: a wiser Roselle, restored to the bosom of his family, is introduced to another young woman, Ferval's beautiful sister, as noble and good-hearted as she is penniless. She makes Roselle the perfect wife. Léonor, meanwhile (not unlike Madame de Merteuil in *Les liaisons dangereuses*) is punished for her sins by the loss of health and beauty. In the end, however, at the urging of his wife, Roselle provides the dowry needed for Léonor to enter a convent. The last letter is addressed to Roselle by a repentant Léonor, flagellating herself and promising to devote what remains of her miserable life to prayer. The Elie de Beaumont novel, then, serves us up a conventional ending. But if it gives the victory to "virtue," that victory involves an interesting extension of the female performance: throughout the novel, the necessary mobility and fluidity of women's social identity put into question the psychological clichés to which the ritualized quality of their various roles would seem to confine them.

In July 1764, the *Correspondance littéraire* exercised its usual acerbic wit on the novel:

> Il fallait un prodigieux génie pour rendre cette situation susceptible d'intérêt, et madame de Beaumont n'en a pas l'ombre. Son roman a pourtant eu une sorte de succès; c'est qu'il est rempli de sentiments honnêtes et d'une sorte de morale à la portée de tout le monde; on y trouve même quelques sermons assez chauds. On ne peut refuser de l'estime à une femme qui a écrit les *Lettres du marquis de Roselle;* mais on l'estimerait encore davantage si, après les avoir écrites, elle les eût jetées au feu, parce qu'elle en aurait senti la médiocrité. (Part 1, 4: 156–57)

> [It would have taken an exceptional genius to make this situation engaging, and Madame de Beaumont has not the shadow of such

genius. Her novel has nonetheless had a modest success; it is filled with honest feelings and a kind of morality within everyone's reach; there are even some rather heated sermons. We cannot refuse to respect a woman who wrote *Lettres du marquis de Roselle*, but we would respect her even more if, after having written it, she had thrown it into the fire because she realized how mediocre it was.]

But a few months later the same reviewer grudgingly acknowledged that the novel had had "un succès presque universel" ["almost unanimous success"] (Part 1, 4: 365). In the preface to *Agathe et Isidore* (1768), Benoist writes that it has long been the case that the most successful novels are in letter form and as evidence cites half a dozen titles, including *Lettres du marquis de Roselle*.[2] Sabatier de Castres expressed a still more general approbation when he wrote of his compendious *Les trois siècles de la littérature française:*

Un mélange heureux de morale et d'intérêt, d'instruction et de senti-ment, de chaleur et de simplicité, rend cet ouvrage très propre à faire sentir les égarements d'une jeunesse trop passionnée, et à la rappeler aux lois de la sagesse et de la raison. Il est d'ailleurs écrit d'un style pur et souvent élégant; on désirerait seulement qu'il fût un peu plus varié. (2: 237)

[A judicious mixture of morality and interest, of instruction and sentiment, of warmth and simplicity, makes this work very suitable for impressing on overly impassioned youth the error of their ways, and for bringing them back to the laws of wisdom and reason. It is written, moreover, in a pure and often elegant style; one could only wish that it were a little more varied.]

Sabatier's assessment resonates with that of most critics from contempo-raries through the early twentieth century: the work is admirable, moral, and educational, one of those few, as La Harpe remarked, which one could with impunity put in the hands of young women (*Oeuvres* 14: 27). There were no fewer than thirteen reeditions in the fifteen years after its original 1764 publication.

It was a popular novel, then, but—like most novels by women—it fell from sight during the nineteenth century and has been little alluded to since. The la Pommeraye episode, on the contrary, as part of a "canonical" text, has been amply studied. Critics tend, for the most part, to discuss it in terms of several broad movements: seduction, betrayal, jealousy, and vengeance. But reducing Diderot's tale to such a schema neglects the specific nature of the relation between des Arcis and Mademoiselle d'Aisnon, a connection structured by the givens of the condition and civil status of eighteenth-century woman, as well as the tension between human values and social equilibrium.

The *Lettres du marquis de Roselle,* where Roselle avoids Léonor's trap and the good Mademoiselle de Ferval wins the hero's hand, quite evidently differs in tone from Diderot's humorously cruel story, where events conspire to throw des Arcis in the nuptial bed of Mademoiselle d'Aisnon. A comparison of the two stories nonetheless allows a displacement of critical emphasis from considerations of jealousy and revenge to questions of liberty, justice, and passion in different guises.

Stories whose impetus was the powerful sexual impulse of undiscriminating noblemen seem to have been particularly attractive to the female imagination. Such plots could put starkly into play the inequalities of social reality, the importance of marriage for a woman's survival, and the ways in which marriageability was differently defined for men and women. An interpolated story in *Les noeuds enchantés* [The enchanted knots] (1789), an oriental tale of "aventures galantes" by Fanny de Beauharnais, incorporates several essential elements of the stories by Diderot and Elie de Beaumont. The mother of Mlle *** explains to her daughter, who possesses little more than her beauty and musical talents, that the world is a vast theater where everyone must play a role and sometimes even change parts several times a day.

When the libertine count de *** falls in love and tries to seduce the daughter, the mother mounts an elaborate play; the daughter (whose morals are, at best, "equivocal") is told to feign deep feeling and to "parler vertu, devoir, honneur" ["talk virtue, duty, honor"] (2: 34). So doing, they shrewdly turn the count's seduction plan into a marriage proposal. Once she has acquired the essential noble name, the new countess unscrupulously sets about acquiring a fortune to match it. In the blink of an eye, thanks to her money and her name, she is "metamorphosed" into a "lady of quality" and "a virtuous woman" (2: 46).

Gabrielle de Villeneuve's popular novel, *La jardinière de Vincennes* (1753), is a more developed and rather more uplifting example of the Cinderella version of this plot. In five tomes and over 500 pages, it tells the story of the twenty-year-old marquis d'Astrel, who falls in love with a golden-haired milkmaid and offers her money, then more money, and finally a secret marriage in return for her favors—all of which her mother declines on her behalf. The refusals intensify the marquis's desire to the point where he becomes violently ill. Up to here, the story line is similar to that of *Lettres du marquis de Roselle*. But the marquis d'Astrel's mother, in order to save her son's life, agrees reluctantly to a public marriage, and the beautiful blonde is then revealed to be the impoverished scion of an aristocratic family and therefore an appropriate wife for the marquis.

Villeneuve is known to posterity principally for her fairy tales, and the fairy-tale resolution of her major novel is conventional and predictable; none of the characters learns, grows, or changes much. She registers a hard-won victory against social prejudice (the marquis marries the milkmaid) only to undermine it (the milkmaid was not just a milkmaid after all).[3] Diderot's tale and Elie de Beaumont's novel offer considerably richer allegories.

If they both contrast male credulity with female guile, Diderot's subtext is evoked in his essay *Sur les femmes,* when he situates a highly rhetorical version of "female psychology" within the reality of male "despotism," as he calls it: of women he writes:

> Impénétrables dans la dissimulation, cruelles dans la vengeance, constantes dans leurs projets, sans scrupules sur les moyens de réussir, animées d'une haine profonde et secrète contre le despotisme de l'homme, il semble qu'il y ait entre elles un complot facile de domination, une sorte de ligue, telle que celle qui subsiste entre les prêtres de toutes les nations. Elles en connaissent les articles sans se les être communiqués. (253)

[Inscrutable in their dissimulation, cruel in vengeance, determined in their plans, unscrupulous in their manner of succeeding, prompted by a deep and secret hatred for man's despotism, they seem to be involved in a plot to rule, a sort of league, such as the one linking priests of all nations. They know its articles without being in communication with each other.]

In the story from *Jacques le fataliste,* what appears to be indeed just such a "plot" when viewed from the perspective of Madame de la Pommeraye looks different from the point of view of Mademoiselle d'Aisnon. As prisoner of a social and sexual economy, her only chance for survival is the so-called cruel and unscrupulous "dissimulation" that Diderot attributes to women.

But in the context of the Elie de Beaumont novel, Diderot's clandestine "plot" becomes an instance of solidarity, the instinct for which explains why the good Mademoiselle de Ferval sees that women like Léonor—the very ones who lead men to perdition—are in fact the victims of the men they seduce, and in the end extends a helping hand to her husband's ex-lover (Merlant 24). Of course, from a feminist point of view, both these texts may be read as stories not so much about "plots" as about working women. They portray women trapped by economic and affective systems in which pretense and opportunism are their only tactical weapons. Léonor, Mademoiselle d'Aisnon, and her mother use their talents and intelligence to exploit the ambiguities of language and religion, and attempt to transform precarious situations of dependence into comfortable survival.

The question of marriageability is the vehicle by which is instigated a critique of so-called female psychology, which is revealed as a caricature of surfaces produced by the dire, incessant necessity of performance. If male freedom generates a certain psychological uniformity, female enclosure paradoxically results in a surprising variety of performance. Indeed, the texts at hand are by their nature dramatic: the epistolary novel is, of course, an analogue of drama, and Diderot's fiction also typically takes on a quasi-dramatic structure. In the Diderot story, cast in the form of a dialogue among Jacques, his master, and their hostess, Madame de la

Pommeraye is the writer-director whose scenario unfurls before the audience, although in the end the lead actress escapes her control.

In the *Lettres du marquis de Roselle*, Léonor's very profession as opera performer symbolizes both the inadequacy of appearances and the seductions of an ignoble world. But her play finally collapses. More than Diderot, Elie de Beaumont poses the question of virtue itself in theatrical terms—in terms of dramatic speeches, audiences, spectacles, successes, failures, and the inability to distinguish between reality and appearance.

Both texts conclude with what Henri Coulet calls the spectacle of the repentant Madeleine. Madame la Marquise des Arcis literally throws herself at her husband's feet, declaring, "Quel que soit le sort que vous me préparez, je m'y soumets" ["Whatever the fate you have in store for me, I submit to it"] (194–95).[4] An ailing Léonor metaphorically strikes the same pose as she writes from her sickbed to Roselle's new wife: "Je me jette à vos pieds, je remets ma destinée entre vos mains" ["I throw myself at your feet, I put my fate in your hands"] (355). This final "fall" of the "fallen woman" is in each case her finest performance.

Elie de Beaumont's novel caught the public's interest sufficiently to inspire a sequel that appeared one year after its publication: *Lettres de Sophie et du chevalier de* ***, *pour servir de supplément aux Lettres du marquis de Roselle* [Letters of Sophie and the chevalier de ***, to serve as a sequel to the Letters of the marquis de Roselle], by François Georges Fouques Deshayes, known as Desfontaines. Early on, Sophie, an honest young actress, receives from an aging go-between some unsolicited advice which makes explicit the ambiguous relation between doxal virtue and the doxy's performance—a relation that we have deduced from Elie de Beaumont's story:

> Vous avez sur la vertu de fort mauvaises idées, et vous prenez à gauche: la vertu et l'honneur consistent à faire son chemin. . . . Le temps de la jeunesse est précieux, et vous devez vous employer avec fruit .
>
> Premièrement, faites politesse à tous les hommes, surtout à ceux qui sont riches.

Secondement, agacez-les toutes les fois que vous en trouverez l'occasion: il y a beaucoup d'hommes qui aiment à être agacés.

Troisièmement, quand vous avez affaire à des gens d'un certain âge, faites-leur entendre que vous ne pouvez souffrir les jeunes gens: il n'y en a pas un qui n'en soit la dupe et qui ne vous donne jusqu'au dernier sou. Vis-à-vis des jeunes gens, au contraire, soyez folle, dissipée et très coquette: il n'y en a pas un qui, pour vous conserver et vous enlever à un rival pour lequel il croira que vous avez de l'inclination, ne se ruine de fond en comble. Ils mangeront leur bien par amour-propre et vous en aurez le profit.

Quatrièmement, ne vous laissez jamais séduire par les promesses, mais par la bourse. N'accordez rien qu'argent comptant. (1: 30–32)

[You have some very mistaken ideas about virtue, and you're going about it wrong. Virtue and honor consist in making one's way. . . . The time of youth is precious, and you should make good use of it.

First of all, be very polite to all men, especially the rich ones.

Secondly, lead them on whenever you can. There are a lot of men who like to be led on.

Thirdly, when you're dealing with middle-aged men, give them to understand that you can't abide young men. There's not a one who won't be duped and give you his last sou. With young men, on the contrary, act extravagant, dissipated, and very coquettish: there's not a one who, to keep you and take you away from a rival he thinks you like, won't totally ruin himself. They'll squander their wealth out of vanity and you'll be the richer for it.

Fourthly, never let yourself be seduced by promises, only by money. Concede nothing except for cash.]

Sophie, who is despite her profession a paragon of continence and constancy, rejects this counsel. When she decides, for the sake of her reputation, to leave the theater and do "hand work," she shapes her definitive role. The chevalier whom she loves—recently become a marquis—at last proposes marriage, with his father's blessing. Sophie's marriageability is thus a dialectical process, a theatrical transcending of the "lower," literal theatrical mode.

Women's power seems to reside in no original attribute, but rather in the quality of their performance, whereas in the case of our various marquis, the title itself generates strength. An unequivocal identity is their birthright. Women, disenfranchised, have neither birthright nor status; without autonomous roles, they must create an identity that will ensure survival. *Lettres du marquis de Roselle* suggests that their "virtue," like all else, results from the inescapable necessity of staging their lives in reference to a script written according to alien precepts for an audience that owns the theater. The quintessential role at which they must succeed, of course, is that of pleasing men—"la femme est faite spécialement pour plaire à l'homme" ["woman is specially made to please man"], writes Rousseau in *Emile* (4: 693)—while the men they have to please are poor readers and naive spectators. These stories ask implicitly to what extent the assigned female role can be modified without social upheaval or personal disaster.

Whereas the marquis of all three novels assume that identity and status are absolute and original, the women are subversive precisely because they understand that virtue is no less a performance than sexual satisfaction. If, when all is said and done, Diderot's protagonist, Mademoiselle d'Aisnon, puts on a more convincing show than Elie de Beaumont's Léonor, let us recall that, in contrast, her sexual performances were apparently wanting; as her mother complained to Madame de la Pommeraye, the daughter has no "esprit de libertinage, rien de ces talents propres à réveiller la langueur d'hommes blasés" ["notion of libertine pleasures, none of the talents needed to awaken blasé men from their torpor"] (162). With her mother and Madame de la Pommeraye to direct her, she manages to compensate for the weakness of those early efforts by the professionalism of the final representation. Conversely, Léonor's performances are instinctive and outstanding, and she writes and directs her own subsequent exhibition of virtue. High society, however, does not allow itself to be entered by the likes of her, so her climactic final act, the wedding, miscarries, and Léonor winds up in a convent cell—reversal and parody of the boudoir—embracing the religious faith she once pretended to have.

But Elie de Beaumont's hero, the marquis de Roselle, acquires a wife after all, although the resolution of the plot is different from what happens in Diderot: Roselle marries Mademoiselle de Ferval, the sister of his true friend. The ending, then, is more conventional than Diderot's, although in some ways more disturbing. If the worthy provincial beauty wins the hero, it is not only because by her goodness she deserves him, but also because, in the final analysis, she gives a good performance. Mademoiselle de Ferval has been taught to act as men want her to (or, at least, as women think men want them to), an especially important skill given her noble family's lack of fortune. On her wedding day, her mother recapitulates the entire sense of the daughter's education, imparting an extended lesson on behavior requisite in a wife, on the quality of performance necessary to hold a husband. I quote only a portion of the long passage in question:

> Notre partage, surtout dans le mariage, c'est la douceur, la complaisance, les attentions tendres, et tout ce qui peut attirer la confiance et l'attachement. . . . Une femme tendre, vertueuse, et raisonnable, qui malgré tous ses efforts se voit en butte à la mauvaise humeur d'un époux; qui n'a jamais la douceur de s'entendre applaudir sur les meilleures actions; qui même est obligée de les cacher, et de paraître avoir des torts pour se faire supporter; qui dérobe son malheur à tous les yeux; . . . qui tâche au moins de sauver les dehors, et de faire paraître son mari vertueux et raisonnable; qu'une telle femme est grande! qu'elle est estimable! mais qu'elle est malheureuse! (343–44)

> [Our lot, especially in marriage, is gentleness, obedience, tender attention, and everything that can attract confidence and affection. . . . A loving, virtuous and reasonable woman, who despite her best efforts sees herself exposed to a husband's ill humor; who never has the pleasure of being commended for her best deeds; who is even forced to hide them and to appear to have shortcomings in order to

be tolerated; who conceals her misery from all; . . . who tries at least to save appearances, and to make her husband look virtuous and reasonable; how great is such a woman! how worthy of respect! but how miserable!]

And again, a few pages further on: "Obéissons pour régner; assujettissons-nous aux petites choses, pour jouir des grandes. . . . Le soin de plaire . . . doit être notre premier objet" ["Let us obey in order to rule; let us be governed in the little things, in order to enjoy the more important ones. . . . Trying to please . . . should be our first objective"] (348–49). The discourse of masculine desire ignores female selfhood; it is characterized by expansion, by the assumption that absolutes exist, and by physical impulsions. Female discourse, on the other hand, is shaped by compression and restraint, and female pragmatics demands a display of sincerity, a ready mask and a persuasive voice.

The advice from the mother of the bride echoes the recommendations from the eponymous letter-writer in Le Prince de Beaumont's *Lettres de Madame du Montier* to her newly wedded (and also undowered) daughter: treat your husband tenderly, act as if he had no faults, and never embarrass him. Always try to please. If he is unfaithful, let there be no acrimony. Above all, do not expect much happiness in marriage, even from the best of husbands. Orthodox marriage, for Le Prince de Beaumont as for Elie de Beaumont, demands not simply that a woman maintain the appearance of goodness and virtue, but also that she make even a foolish and philandering husband look righteous and decent. Marriageability is the ultimate manipulation of appearances. Although she is genuinely benevolent and sensitive, then, Mademoiselle de Ferval's success in marriage nonetheless depends on her capacity to perform adequately, to appear to obey in order to gain some control of her circumstances.

Her education, like that of the genteel but impoverished young heroines of Le Prince de Beaumont, has taught her to gauge her audience and to respond modestly and appropriately to it. Here is the testimony of Roselle's sister when his bride makes her entrance into Parisian society:

Elle me semble réunir toutes les sortes d'esprits. Chacun peut croire qu'elle a le sien, tant elle sait se mettre à l'unisson. . . . Elle a toujours pris le ton qu'il faut avec toutes les personnes qu'elle a vues. (359)

[She seems to me to incorporate all ways of thinking. Everyone believes she thinks like them, because she is so good at agreeing with everyone. . . . She has always struck the tone that was right for the company she was in.]

Léonor, too, realized the urgency of appropriate speech and behavior, announcing confidently that if she ever became a marquise, she would adopt the proper "tone" (164); but Léonor was obliged to make an inauspicious exit before the final curtain.

If the stories are similar, then, the fates of the heroines differ dramatically. Both, it is true, are redeemed in the grand finale. In Diderot's text, social redemption is possible: Mademoiselle d'Aisnon marries and acquires a noble name. But for Léonor, redemption is moral and marginal: she repents and is saved, but far away from high society and the marquis. She is sacrificed so that someone else may be happy and aristocratic ethics may be preserved. Woman's radical alienation is clearer in Elie de Beaumont; and yet with that alienation comes autonomy. While Mademoiselle d'Aisnon becomes what the marquis makes of her—*Madame la marquise*—Léonor, although alone, remains herself. Family, society, and nobility are saved from contamination, but the individual woman is simultaneously saved from absorption by them. If this validation of Léonor is not explicit, such paradoxes nonetheless mark the subtext of eighteenth-century fiction by women.

The "virtue" of Mademoiselle d'Aisnon and Léonor is dynamic, and its virtuoso performance accompanies the development of female identity. The manipulative ingenuity of Léonor and Mademoiselle d'Aisnon, then, by no means excludes their capacity to assume ingenuousness. In Diderot, the doxies become consubstantial: the former prostitute declares that she was essentially good all along and will be a chaste wife. Here is how, as the new marquise des Arcis, she explains to her husband that the courtesan's career may be less the mask of independence or depravity than of servitude—implicitly condemning her mother in the bargain:

Je me suis laissé conduire par faiblesse, par séduction, par autorité, par menaces, à une action infâme; mais ne croyez pas, monsieur, que je sois méchante. . . . La corruption s'est posée sur moi; mais elle ne s'y est point attachée. Je me connais, et une justice que je me rends, c'est que par mes goûts, par mes sentiments, par mon caractère, j'étais née digne de l'honneur de vous appartenir. (194)

[Weak, seduced, ordered about, intimidated, I was led to commit an infamous act; but don't think, sir, that I am wicked. . . . Corruption alighted on me, but didn't attach itself. I know myself and I do myself justice: by my tastes, my feelings, my character, I was born worthy of the honor of being yours.]

Léonor put it differently in an early letter to her confidante:

Je t'assure que, si je deviens femme de qualité, j'en saurai prendre le ton. Eh! que sais-je? Peut-être alors deviendrais-je tout à fait honnête femme. Celles qui le sont, l'auraient-elles été, si elles avaient éprouvé nos situations et nos besoins? (164–65)

[I assure you that if I become a woman of quality, I'll be able to strike the right tone. And who knows? Perhaps then I'd even become an altogether honest woman. Would those who are honest women have been so, if they had found themselves in our situations and with our needs?]

She alludes not to the fixities of birth and character that are adduced by Mademoiselle d'Aisnon, but to the possibility of change, of eventually transcending categories of good and evil. Indeed, in the question she phrases about "honest women," it is possible to hear something like a meditation on injustice.

Joachim Merlant, writing shortly after the turn of the twentieth century, sees Elie de Beaumont—just as most of her contemporaries did—as a strongly moral author. He deems her a worthy precursor of Rousseau, socially aware, happy, and well balanced like her book, which is itself an example of the best kind of "conservative liberalism." Its fundamental moral: "La vertu n'est pas affaire de mode" ["Virtue is not a matter of style"] (21–22). His sanguine and aphoristic formulation contrasts with my reading of the novel as portraying a morality more subtle and supple: the "virtue" that the era officially proclaimed as a static ideal for women can never be that, although it can come into being as an acquired quality of their humanness. In my reading, the subtext is aptly expressed in Léonor's own epigrammatic summation of the novel's extended meditation on virtue real or false, rigorous or easy, attractive or repugnant, triumphant or confounded: "La vertu," she concludes, "est affaire de circonstance" ["Virtue is a matter of circumstance"] (165).

CHAPTER 4

REMARRYING

Marie Jeanne Riccoboni

For more than a quarter century after her 1734 marriage into an Italian family of actors and playwrights, Marie Jeanne Riccoboni (1713–92) worked as an actress with the Comédie Italienne in Paris. She began publishing novels in her mid-forties, and only several years later did the proceeds enable her to retire from the troupe. Her husband (Antoine François Riccoboni), his parents, her closest companion (Thérèse Biancolelli), and her friend and correspondent David Garrick were all actors; through them and through her own work she had extensive experience with the world of theater. She also had firsthand acquaintance with the condition of the working woman.

As a professional woman of letters who had a significant stage career, Riccoboni invites comparison with Colette, even at a distance of two centuries. But while Colette would write stories about acting and writing, Riccoboni never turned for material directly to the theatrical milieu or sought inspiration in the publishing world she knew well. Fanni Butlerd, her first heroine, has some brief experience with publication when she avenges herself on her lover by placing a letter of rebuke in the "public papers," but in general these epistolary heroines write only for themselves, a lover, or a friend.

Indeed, only a few of Riccoboni's protagonists earn their living at all. Ernestine, title character of a 1765 novel, who paints miniatures, is a notable exception. The heroine of *Lettres d'Elisabeth-Sophie de Vallière*

(1772) thinks of doing needlework after she loses her protectress, but feels too dejected to go to work. When the heroine of *Histoire de Miss Jenny* (1764), in dire straits, rouses herself to become assistant to a silk merchant, she discovers that she is ill suited for success at handwork— "Mes doigts si habiles à parcourir les touches d'un clavecin, mêlaient avec maladresse les différents assortiments des soies" ["My fingers, so deft on the keys of a harpsichord, clumsily mixed the different kinds of silks"] (125)—and a turn in fortune shortly releases her from the effort.

Despite the glaring absence of theater people and of working people in general in the writings of a woman who spent so many of her younger and middle years in the company of actors, nineteenth- and early twentieth-century critics have stressed the autobiographical aspect of Riccoboni's novels, sometimes exclusively. By identifying all her heroines with the author and implicitly reducing a varied oeuvre to a monotonous autobiography, they perpetuate a stereotypical vision of the woman writer. In the only study devoted to women novelists of the French Enlightenment, Anne Louis Anton Mooij maintains that eighteenth-century women write autobiographically: "Toute oeuvre féminine tend à l'autobiographie, dans ce siècle féminin par excellence" ["Every work by a woman tends to autobiography in this century which was feminine *par excellence*"] (49). Although many novels by both men and women display such tendencies, characterizations like this trivialize. They fail, for instance, to account for Riccoboni's marked preference for depicting the leisured aristocracy, a class to which she herself did not habitually have access; her numerous heroines sometimes love as she did, and certainly write a lot, but they neither work nor act like her.

In fact, the relation between fiction and autobiography in the writing of Riccoboni is less unilateral than such remarks would suggest. Certainly, some of her novels contain elements whose source one can find in her personal experience. *Histoire de Miss Jenny,* her bleakest novel, is the story of a young woman of illegitimate birth trapped by a sham wedding ceremony, and *Lettres d'Elisabeth-Sophie de Vallière* takes for its heroine a girl deprived of her inheritance by the mystery of her birth. These plot ingredients indirectly recall a biographical fact partially concealed by Riccoboni during her lifetime: she was technically illegitimate, her father having been excommunicated for bigamy and her parents' marriage declared null.[1] Beyond those facts, however, the pathos of Miss Jenny's chronicle and the extravagance of Sophie de Vallière's experience have little in common with Riccoboni's life, although they do recall purely fictional precedents, in particular Marivaux's *La vie de Marianne*.

The personal use she made of her first novel, *Lettres de Mistriss Fanni Butlerd* (1757), complicates the relation between invention and autobiography: the love letters of Fanni Butlerd to Alfred, the man who finally abandons her, may be read as literary models for the impassioned letters that Marie Jeanne Riccoboni later addressed over a period of more than seventeen years to Robert Liston.[2] Liston, a Scottish diplomat nearly thirty years her junior, would call on her when he was in Paris, to dine and give her English lessons; and when he was home, they would exchange letters in which Riccoboni expressed not only maternal interest but also feelings more troubling to her. *Lettres de Mistriss Fanni Butlerd* reads, then, as a rehearsal for life. A few days before her fifty-third birthday, she wrote to Liston:

> J'ai désiré, oui, désiré avec passion, qu'il fût en mon pouvoir de rapprocher les temps, les lieux. . . . J'ai connu toute la folie de mes désirs, j'ai regardé mon penchant comme une extravagance, mais je l'ai conservé; je ne vous l'ai pas caché, parce que je suis vraie, même quand j'ai intérêt à ne pas l'être. (*Letters* 92)

> [I have wished, yes, passionately wished, that it were in my power to bring time and place nearer together. . . . I have known the folly of my desires, I have regarded my penchant as madness, but it is there still; I haven't hidden it from you because I am truthful, even when it's in my interest not to be.]

With its beautiful expression of impossible love, moreover, the Liston correspondence began to unfold about the time that she was sketching out another novel, *Lettres d'Adélaïde de Dammartin, comtesse de Sancerre, à M. le comte de Nancé, son ami* (1767), the story of a woman in love with a married man despite herself. It has been noted that the comic resolution

Marie Jeanne Riccoboni. Deveria/Couché fils.
Frontispiece, *Oeuvres de Madame Riccoboni*, vol. I
(Paris: Brissot-Thivars, 1826).

of this particular novelistic situation was somehow liberating for its author, permitting her to sort out the real-life plot,[3] what Riccoboni calls the "madness" and "folly" of her hopeless inclination for a man far too young and too far away. Perhaps, finally, it is possible to read in a diatribe in *Lettres de Mylord Rivers* (1777) a reminiscence of the dilemma posed by her feelings for Liston, with whom she was still corresponding regularly at the time she composed that novel: thirty-six-year-old Mylady Orrery, beguiled by a handsome young American ten years her junior, expresses anger at the version of the double standard that allows old men with withered faces to take child brides, but stigmatizes a woman who thinks of marrying a younger man (278–79).

It is not, then, the simple reflection of biographical detail which is principally of interest in Riccoboni's novels, but a more complicated relation with her life.[4] And if biographical data engage us today, it is not only for their complex mirroring in her narratives, but also because they reveal her as one of the most professional writers of eighteenth-century Europe. Beginning with *Lettres de Mistriss Fanni Butlerd,* her novels were so popular, according to one nineteenth-century account, that certain contemporary critics thought no woman could have written them.[5] While the majority of novels had only one printing, or at most elicited one or two reeditions, Riccoboni's were repeatedly reissued, and sold widely both in France and abroad; several ran to five, ten, twenty, or more editions (Martin, "Romans et romanciers," passim). Other novelists tried to ride the wave of the extraordinary vogue of her novels: the title page of a mediocre memoir-novel by Charlotte de la Guesnerie, *Mémoires de Miledi B...* (1760), announced the author as "Madame R," and the work was at first mistakenly attributed to Riccoboni.[6]

She was a major figure in the European literary world of the third quarter of the century, by far one of the era's most renowned writers, male or female. When in 1782, at nearly seventy years of age, she wrote the author of *Les liaisons dangereuses* to object to his characterization of Madame de Merteuil, he felt honored to attract the attention of the eminent Riccoboni.[7] Interest in her began to abate after the Revolution, although an edition of selected works was published by Garnier as late as 1865.

But by "professionalism," I mean something more than just her immense popularity. Marie Jeanne Riccoboni's psychological and material investment in her work and the role it played in her life, as disclosed in her correspondence, come close to a model we are familiar with today. Her own testimony and that of Thérèse Biancolelli, with whom she lived for some thirty-five years, indicate that she read widely in French and English literature, wrote slowly, revised laboriously, studied the tastes of the reading public in France as well as in England, and followed the literary and philosophical debates of the time. David Garrick and Denis Diderot engaged her by letter in discussions of theater. Letters to Garrick and to her French publisher, Humblot, and her circuitous long-distance negotiations with her English publisher, Thomas Becket, convey her concern with marketability, the difficulties she had with delayed payments, unauthorized editions, and bad translations, and the occasional disheartenment of the working woman: "L'écriture me vieillit, et me tue" ["Writing ages and kills me"], she wrote to Liston in 1767 (*Letters* 109).

It has been noted that Riccoboni's life conforms to a "modern" paradigm (Demay 12): she married unwisely at the age of twenty in order to escape a cranky mother; she learned a profession; she separated from her husband; through her work (which brought her a pension from Louis XV) she gained financial autonomy, although she contributed to the support of both mother and husband until they died; she found emotional stability and modest material security in sharing a small apartment (and occasionally collaborating on translations) with another woman, Thérèse Biancolelli, a retired actress like herself.

But if these patterns shaped her life, they do not in any obvious way shape novels peopled mostly by idle aristocrats who devote their time to love. If the novels have nonetheless been read in the first instance as implicitly autobiographical, we should consider, for example, that the very narrator of *Histoire de M. le marquis de Cressy* (1758) speaks in the first-person feminine plural, creating a sense of deep personal investment on the part of the author:

Les hommes sont cruels, ils se plaisent à voir fermenter dans nos coeurs le poison qu'ils y versent eux-mêmes: ce n'est pas de notre sensibilité, mais de l'objet qui la fait naître, que nous devons nous plaindre. L'amour ne nous causerait jamais de peine, si l'homme qui nous en inspire était digne de nos sentiments. (59–60)[8]

[Men are cruel, they take pleasure in seeing in our hearts the fermentation of the poison they have poured into them. We should complain not of our own sensibility, but of the object that gives birth to it. Love would never cause us pain, if the man who inspired it were worthy of our feelings.]

Les hommes nous accusent d'une extrême crédulité sur ce qui flatte notre amour-propre; mais quelle vanité peut se comparer à leur faiblesse? La moindre louange les séduit; à peine soufferts, ils se croient aimés. (98)

[Men accuse us of extreme credulity about anything that flatters our pride; but what vanity can compare to their weakness? The least bit of praise seduces them; even when barely tolerated they think they are loved.]

Riccoboni indicts men and champions women with something that sounds like the sincere accents of a woman spurned. The autobiographical inference that habitually attaches itself to passages like the preceding nevertheless captures our critical imagination less today than it once did, for reading patterns have changed and we tend to favor other ways of looking at texts.

As Elizabeth Heckendorn Cook suggests, late twentieth-century critics have been preoccupied with what such passages suggest about another matter, namely, Riccoboni's "feminism" (33). In the 1970s and 1980s, thoughtful essays, much-needed editions, and one short book on Riccoboni appeared, most of them written in French; the titles of several announce as an agenda a consideration of her feminism.[9] While they usually support the legitimacy of applying the "feminist" epithet to Riccoboni, they also tend to make some disclaimer about her talent.[10] In any event, the important question they pose has surely been answered, if what we mean by feminism entails a forceful statement of prevailing gender inequities and the demand that they be addressed.

Riccoboni depicts the personal and social problems women faced in society as it was organized, and she asks for an end to sexual exploitation and for an affirmation of women's rights to a decent education and life. She wants men, collectively and individually, to exercise more generosity toward women. As her narrative use of "we" indicates, moreover, she writes not just in the name of women but, like Le Prince de Beaumont, *for* women. I am interested here less in explicitly arguing or questioning her feminism once more, than in emphasizing that as early as the mid-eighteenth century, through her life and work, she was directly posing the question of the meaning of a woman's existence in a vigorous and remarkable new way.[11] She uses and violates canons of decorum to create original accounts of women's lot which had tremendous success in her day and remain highly readable in ours.

Although there is some similarity of preoccupation among her eight novels, there is also considerable difference in emphasis and execution. Two of the six letter-novels, *Histoire de Miss Jenny* and *Lettres d'Elisabeth-Sophie de Vallière,* assign a large role to bizarre accidents of fate, coincidences, and interpolated stories. The simpler novels, both epistolary and nonepistolary, were on the whole better received. I shall concentrate in this chapter on two of them: *Histoire de M. le marquis de Cressy* (hereafter *Histoire de Cressy*) and *Lettres d'Adélaïde de Dammartin, comtesse de Sancerre, à M. le comte de Nancé, son ami* (hereafter *Lettres de Sancerre*). *Lettres de Milady Juliette Catesby* (1759) will be the subject of chapter 6. Although in both theme and form *Lettres de Mistriss Fanni Butlerd* marks an important date in the history of fiction, I am for the most part leaving it aside here, both because it has already received sustained attention elsewhere[12] and because I prefer to focus on representations of marriage.

Histoire de Cressy is set in the last years of the reign of Louis XIV. The twenty-eight-year-old protagonist, handsome and ambitious, returns to court after distinguishing himself in the war with Spain. Two good women fall in love with him: Adélaïde du Bugei,[13] an ingenuous sixteen-year-old fresh from a convent school, and Madame de Raisel, a rich widow of twenty-six whose elderly and disagreeable husband has been dead two years. Cressy is aroused by Adélaïde but, given the modesty of

Madame de Cressy receives the poisoned tea
from her husband. Unsigned. *Histoire de M. le marquis
de Cressy,* in *Oeuvres complètes de Madame Riccoboni,*
nouvelle édition, vol. 2 (Paris: Volland, 1786).

her dowry, disinclined to propose marriage. He attempts instead to seduce her and, when he accidentally discovers Madame de Raisel's interest in him, abandons the girl altogether in order to court and marry the widow. Disillusioned, Adélaïde retires to a convent and takes vows. After a brief conjugal idyll, Cressy begins an affair with Madame de Raisel's protégée, Hortense de Berneil. When his unsuspecting wife learns that she is betrayed under her own roof, that her husband actually tried to seduce Adélaïde, and, further, that he is having an affair with yet another woman, she contrives to receive a cup of poisoned tea from his hands. She slips gently into death, forgiving him (and leaving him her money). Cressy repents and spends the rest of his life in regret: "il fut riche, il fut élevé: mais il ne fut point heureux" ["He was rich, he was distinguished, but he was not happy"] (108).

Lettres de Sancerre consists of the letters addressed by a young widow of twenty-six to a male friend. After an infernal youthful marriage, she is initially determined never to remarry. But she falls in love with Monsieur de Montalais, who has already entered a *mariage de convenance* with an unattractive woman. When the wife dies in childbirth, Madame de Sancerre marries him. Her two widowed friends, Madame de Mirande and Madame de Martigues, also remarry.

If these two novels are both about remarrying, they nonetheless differ substantially. In *Histoire de Cressy* an omniscient and sententious narrator tells a tightly woven story with a limited cast of characters and a tragic ending. Its court atmosphere is reminiscent of *La princesse de Clèves,* and the impression it conveys is of classical brevity and exemplary unity of action, without interpolated stories or outside intervention, and where no detail is superfluous. *Lettres de Sancerre,* on the other hand, is an epistolary novel where the writing protagonist, surrounded by a coterie of relatives and socialite friends, addresses someone outside the action whose replies we do not see. It is longer and more elaborate than *Histoire de Cressy* and recalls the letters of Sévigné in the anecdotal epistolary accounts of the pastimes of the rich. The happy ending—Madame de Sancerre's marriage to Montalais—follows upon three phases of plot: the narrative of her first marriage, the acknowledgment of her love for Montalais, and the arrival of an outrageous cousin who threatens to upset everything.

If legitimate theater is not a plot element in these stories, theatricality is thematically and psychologically crucial to both. The husbands are not just "false" but consummate social actors. Cressy is past master at controlling appearances. Even after declining the hand of Adélaïde du Bugei, he wants to continue basking in her infatuation. Grasping for a way to ask the forgiveness he has no intention of meriting, he hits on the idea of telling her *the truth* and writes an artful but more or less accurate letter flagellating himself for having been too ambitious to marry her. He speculates correctly, and this strategy where "un aveu sincère" ["a sincere confession"] (58) becomes a form of masculine guile touches the guileless Adélaïde.

Only after he nearly succeeds in seducing her does she finally see through him. His talent for manipulating the truth is even more apparent in another exquisite scene where he has to tell Madame de Raisel, whom he is now courting, about his relations with Adélaïde. His narrative is a tour de force of almost impalpable distortions. The "facts" are there: the surprise and pleasure he felt at detecting Adélaïde's penchant; his realization that he could not make her happy; his rapture at the discovery of Madame de Raisel's interest. It is difficult to locate an outright lie, though he plays loose with chronology and strings the particulars together in such a way that his forsaking Adélaïde seems to proceed from generous sensibilities and love for Madame de Raisel. And in the account that he fashions for Madame de Raisel, he describes the letter to Adélaïde in which he accused himself of being excessively ambitious, as a strategy of lies rather than of truth: it seemed the best way, he says, not to hurt her.

Since Sancerre is a comparably fine actor, his unkindnesses toward his wife are manifest to no one but her. Society takes him to be the perfect husband, noble and magnanimous: "son goût et sa magnificence surprenaient; mais il me refusait des bagatelles qui excitaient mes désirs; il me demandait compte de la petite somme destinée à mes amusements; il obligeait mes femmes à lui en dire l'emploi; souvent il le blâmait" ["his taste and the noble way he spent money amazed people; but he would deny me the trinkets I fancied; he would demand an accounting of the small sum set aside for my entertainment; he would make my maids tell him how it was used; and often he would criticize"] (63).

The man who plays in public at being generous and devoted behaves like a penny-pinching misogynist on the home front. Like Cressy, Sancerre routinely "dissimulates"—"la dissimulation et la finesse furent les seules qualités qu'il jugea nécessaire d'acquérir et de perfectionner" ["dissimulation and diplomacy were the only qualities he judged necessary to acquire and perfect"] (84)—not on the stage, but in the drawing room and boudoir, where he improvises a stunning succession of parts. Both men are adept at sizing up their female public and donning a strategic mask to induce into wedlock the wealthy women who can assure their fortunes. Cressy plays out his life as surely as does the actress Léonor in Elie de Beaumont's *Lettres du marquis de Roselle*. Indeed, like Elie de Beaumont, Riccoboni reminds us that social virtue is situational, its success residing in the quality of performance: "L'apparence des vertus est bien plus séduisante que les vertus mêmes; et celui qui feint de les avoir, a bien de l'avantage sur celui qui les possède" ["The appearance of virtues is much more attractive than virtues themselves; and someone who pretends to have them has a considerable advantage over someone who really possesses them"] (*Histoire de Cressy* 50).

Her finely drawn male characters, never wholly corrupt, illustrate a remark Riccoboni made in a 1782 letter to Choderlos de Laclos: "un homme extrêmement pervers est aussi rare dans la société qu'un homme extrêmement vertueux" ["an extremely perverse man is as rare in society as an extremely virtuous one"] (Laclos 763). Their philanderings are hardly a matter of pure desire, and in the extramarital liaisons for which Cressy and Sancerre sacrifice conjugal happiness there is more vanity than ardor. These men are manipulated by domineering women just as surely as they exploit their trustful wives. It is mostly out of inertia that Sancerre keeps his mistress—"s'il aima longtemps madame de Cézanes, ce fut avec plus de faiblesse que de véritable passion" ["if he loved Madame de Cézanes for a long time, it was with more weakness than real passion"] (85)—a woman so imperious that she becomes enraged when she suspects he is sleeping with his wife. But the man who is cowed by Madame de Cézanes dies bravely in battle. Cressy, for his part, acts out of pique, initially making love to the haughty Hortense de Berneil only because she defies him to excite her. He identifies too closely with his role, however, and the illusion he wants to create becomes reality—"Il s'accoutuma à l'entretenir d'un sentiment qu'il cessa de feindre" ["He became accustomed to speaking to her of a feeling that he no longer feigned"] (87)—and then he hasn't the courage to brave her and end a dreary romance. Despite his lies and infidelities, Cressy loves his wife and is tempted more than once to confess. One of the most effective leading men in novels by women, Cressy displays verbal dexterity and a combination of mettle, cowardice, and remorse which suggests a complex interior life. His behavior, with the pretense and the pain, the prudence and the gambles, raises the question of what is real and what is show, of the instability of appearances and of reality, especially in relations between the sexes. "Appear" and "appearance" are words that recur often in these novels.

Riccoboni's heroines, on the other hand, tend to be "sincere" and "true," and as mediocre at acting as Riccoboni herself. Worthy successors of Fanni Butlerd, her later heroines are also incapable of extemporizing, and their discourse and behavior are not calculated for effect. They are, however, extraordinarily self-aware, and if their goodwill blinds them to injustice for a time, Adélaïde du Bugei and others burn with insights when their sentimental bents or sensual inclinations are too severely violated. With heroines as candid as the men are devious, Riccoboni may appear to be far from the mentality of a Le Prince de Beaumont or an Elie de Beaumont, who extolled without irony the silent subordination of wives: "la soumission à un époux n'avilirait pas la première de toutes les femmes: ce respect, cette soumission, sont de droit divin" ["submission to a spouse would not degrade the foremost of women: such respect and submission are given by divine right"] (*La nouvelle Clarice* 1: 16).

Riccoboni's rhetoric is different; she allows her narrators as well as her characters continually to berate men. And yet, despite the fervor with which they denounce injustice, married heroines like Madame de Sancerre for the most part put quietly into practice the morality preached in novels by Le Prince de Beaumont. Riccoboni's heroines do not invoke divine right, but in a pinch their instincts are to conceal the vices of their husbands; rather than seek vengeance, they exhibit what Joachim Merlant calls "the heroism of silence" (6). Madame de Sancerre chooses to renounce her inheritance, compromise her reputation, and live in seclusion, rather than publicly repudiate the spouse who mistreats her. And when Madame de Raisel understands the deception her husband practices, she resolves never to complain.

The Guizots articulate the curious tension born of this dichotomy: "Les héroïnes de Mme Riccoboni ont en général d'assez faux principes et une très bonne conduite" ["The heroines of Madame Riccoboni in general have faulty principles and very good behavior"] (2: 197). That is to say, they think that if their husbands act unfaithfully, they are entitled to do likewise, but they don't actually do so. The sense of fictional truth that distinguishes her novels derives partly from the forceful but economical expression of these dichotomies between appearances and reality, social force and moral weakness, beliefs and actions. The situations that Riccoboni imagined to convey such complexities pose questions about the meaning of women's lives and suggest troubling moral ambivalences.

Not surprisingly, novels where vice and virtue seem to cohabit uneasily in a single character, and sometimes even in a single gesture, met with strong reactions. Indeed, in a period when heroines of fiction were mostly sedentary and passive witnesses to their fate,[14] Riccoboni's are notable for their assertiveness. When she falls in love with Cressy, Madame de Raisel takes the unusual step of expressing her feelings before she has any indication that he might reciprocate, courting him anonymously with gifts and billets-doux. Madame de Martigues in *Lettres de Sancerre* is an elegantly droll figure whose morals are excellent, but whose unconventional behavior raises questions of propriety, and her companion, Madame de Sancerre, is repeatedly obliged to defend her. For a modern reader familiar with other sentimental novels of the mid-century, one of the refreshing aspects of Riccoboni's work is the fact that her heroines usually speak their mind and are not always prim, but this did not necessarily endear them to those critics for whom one of the chief justifications of the novel was to teach and to moralize. Fanni Butlerd, who indulges in erotic fantasies and congratulates herself on having "given" herself rather than being taken by her lover, was charged with indecency of speech and action.[15] On the other hand, the plot of the second novel, *Lettres de Milady Juliette Catesby,* although constructed around the seduction-rape and death of an adolescent girl, was widely acclaimed as her most charming.

It was her third novel, *Histoire de Cressy,* which generated the most criticism. If La Harpe considered it her most appealing work (*Cours de littérature* 23: 20), Félicité de Genlis was shocked by the suicide. Genlis's objections have to do with both morality and plausibility: virtuous women neither *should* nor *would* kill themselves:

> Ce suicide est d'autant plus révoltant qu'on l'attribue à une femme douce, sensible et vertueuse; et une telle femme ne s'ôte point la vie! Madame Riccoboni a eu la première la funeste idée de vouloir rendre le suicide intéressant, et c'est un reproche grave que l'on doit faire à sa mémoire. Il n'est permis d'attribuer cet acte affreux qu'à un personnage vicieux et perverti.[16]

> [This suicide is all the more revolting for being imputed to a woman who is gentle, sensitive and virtuous; such a woman does not take her own life! Madame Riccoboni was the first to have the dreadful idea of trying to make suicide appear intriguing, and that is a serious reproach to her memory. This hideous act may be imputed only to a depraved, perverted character.]

Giving voice to the contradictions one senses in Riccoboni's writing, Julia Kavanagh quaintly judged *Histoire de Cressy* "one of her best, but also of her least pleasing productions" (2: 1). It seems, as Olga Cragg says, that in the name of conventional morality, critics expected to see vice punished in the person of Cressy rather than the disappearance of the virtuous heroine (*Histoire de Cressy,* ed. Cragg 27).

To the modern reader, however, who is somewhat inured to suicide in fiction, events in *Lettres de Sancerre* are likely to appear morally more dubious than the much criticized conclusion of *Histoire de Cressy*. In the former, the heroine finds herself in the ambiguous situation not just of loving a married man, but of waiting for the death of his first wife—a woman who has committed no other crimes than failing to be beautiful, finding herself in a *mariage de convenance*, and desiring children despite her poor health. Madame de Sancerre permits herself in the first flush of love and jealousy to speak of her rival in terms hardly becoming a sensitive woman: "Sans exagération, sa femme est odieuse. En voyant son portrait hier chez madame de Comminges, j'ai pensé crier" ["Without exaggeration, his wife is odious. When I saw her portrait yesterday at Madame de Comminges', I thought I'd scream"] (17). When the wife at last obliges by succumbing in childbirth, our heroine's pity is belatedly aroused, but she begins immediately to imagine a future for herself with the widower. Montalais himself is even more tactless; the very note in which he acknowledges her expression of regret at his wife's death includes the following heavily charged ellipses: "Me sera-t-il permis un jour? ... Oserai-je, Madame... Non, mon coeur n'ose encore exprimer que les sentiments de la reconnaissance et du respect" ["Will I some day be permitted? ... Do I dare, Madame? ... No, my heart still dares only to express feelings of gratitude and respect"] (181). In the service of exalting a *mariage d'amour* between two deserving people, Riccoboni is willing to sacrifice an innocent woman and violate norms of decorum (just as she did with the rape and premature death of a protagonist of *Lettres de Milady Juliette Catesby*). One early twentieth-century commentator, a perceptive reader of Riccoboni, found the situation indecorous at best:

> Mme Riccoboni a beau s'en tirer le plus finement du monde, donner à Mme de Montalais un caractère effacé, à demi sympathique, nous faire le plus séduisant portrait de son mari et de la jolie veuve, nous pouvons bien souhaiter qu'ils deviennent heureux mais, au risque d'en juger bourgeoisement, nous sommes surpris que ce bonheur s'arrange si facilement après un deuil qui a seulement rendu plus intéressant ce si galant veuf. (Merlant 9)

> [It is to no avail that Madame Riccoboni manages it all quite subtly, making Madame de Montalais unobtrusive, half likable, describing

in the most attractive way the husband and the lovely widow. We can very well hope that they will be happy, but, at the risk of sounding bourgeois, we're surprised that this happiness is so easily arranged after a bereavement which only makes this galant widower even more appealing.]

As surely as the suicide of a virtuous woman in *Histoire de Cressy,* aspects of the demeanor of an equally righteous woman and her respectable admirer in *Lettres de Sancerre* challenge conventions of sensibility and codes of virtue. *L'amant bourru* [The churlish lover], Boutet de Monvel's 1777 stage adaptation of the novel, in early recognition of the indelicacy of the extramarital passion and precipitate remarriage, eliminates Montalais's first wife from the plot.

The widow played an important role in French fiction: she was a useful figure because she was socially and legally freer than the unmarried girl, who depended on parents, and also freer than the wife who had to answer to a husband. Widowhood conferred a certain liberty that could help shape a heroine's drama, making her responsible for her own actions, so that the major obstacles to her happiness might be portrayed as psychological. To social and personal independence, moreover, the widow of fiction frequently joined some degree of financial stability. Pierre Fauchery notes that the figure of the widow corresponds to a historical fact indicated in statistics on premature deaths by accident, illness, and war, and the disproportion of ages so frequent in *mariages de convenance* (417). In the libertine novel, such a figure might treat herself to sexual adventure (like Madame de Merteuil in Laclos's *Liaisons dangereuses*), but in the sentimental novel she usually remains chaste.

Memorable portrayals of young widows occur in Duclos's *Confessions du comte de* *** (1741) and in the fiction of Diderot—notably, in the la Pommeraye episode of *Jacques le fataliste* and in *Histoire de Madame de la Carlière,* both of which turn on questions of betrayal and vengeance. In a story typical of Françoise Albine Benoist, whose protagonists play with illicit sexual behavior only the more dramatically to recognize their errors in the end, the thirty-one-year-old title character of *Sophronie* (1769) considers that her hard-earned reputation for virtue entitles her to some belated gratifications in her widowhood. Pretending—and almost believing—that she wants only to orchestrate a lesson for her fifteen-year-old daughter, Adelle, on how to refuse a man's advances, Sophronie tries to seduce Valzan. Mortified to discover that he is actually in love with her daughter, she does what is expedient, arranging his marriage with the girl and constituting herself his "mother." Unlike Sophronie or the widows of Diderot and Duclos who enter into extraconjugal but monogamous relations, none of Riccoboni's widows is tempted in the slightest by dalliance.

Her work is, on the whole, more sober and reflective, less outrageously *romanesque,* than that of some novelists who wrote about widows. Fanny de Beauharnais, for example, began publishing a series of novels of frenzied sensibility about a generation after Ricoboni's work started to appear. Her *L'Abailard supposé* (1780) is about a nineteen-year-old widow whose experience with an older husband is as unhappy as that of Ricoboni's several heroines and who, like them, intends never again to marry. But by pretending that he has been castrated, friends of the young marquis de Rosebelle cajole her into marriage with him, and only after the ceremony does he reveal himself as potent. (This drastic gesture is typical of Beauharnais's work: her *L'aveugle par amour* [1781] concerns a protagonist who blinds herself to express her love for a blind man.)

Despite its extravagance, the plot of *L'Abailard supposé* emphasizes the anxiety about sexuality which is a component of the diffidence many of these widows feel. They are motivated not by economic considerations, like so many of their unmarried sisters, but by psychological factors. Such factors are especially powerful, as I explained in chapter 3, in novels by Le Prince de Beaumont: the wealthy "perfect widow" in the subtitle of her *Mémoires de Madame la baronne de Batteville* seems to merit that epithet because of her refusal to remarry.

Ricoboni, of course, as Arlette André points out, had reason to realize that independent means could be crucial to independence of action,[17] and the dramas of young widows like Madame de Raisel, Juliette Catesby, and Madame de Sancerre are played out against a background of enormous wealth. In *Lettres de Sancerre,* the very possibility of marriage is tied up with fortunes that are won and lost in a matter of just a few words. In broad strokes of fate, vast sums change hands. Shortly before she marries for the first time, Madame de Sancerre unexpectedly secures a legacy from an uncle newly returned from Martinique and intent on disinheriting a prodigal son. Her marriage brings her into an even larger fortune when her husband's uncle makes her his heir. She renounces the right to this, however, when she separates from the faithless Sancerre, but at his death she regains it. Through astute management of her estates she increases her holdings further, although she nearly loses her money again when her long-lost cousin appears on the scene and demands either her hand or the money his father left her. But in the end, in a fit of generosity, he declines her wealth and allows her to marry Montalais. Meanwhile, through deaths and marriages, Montalais too has secured or lost several fortunes.

While making clear that money could make women prey to ambitious men and that marriage was in large measure a financial transaction, Riccoboni also uses their relations to wealth to underscore both her heroines' independence and their generosity. Madame de Sancerre, Juliette Catesby, and Madame de Raisel-Cressy repeatedly enlist their wealth in the service of charity or justice. Madame de Sancerre tries to give hers away to the cousin whose claim she considers greater than her own, and Juliette Catesby dowers Sara, a peasant who needs only money in order to marry the man she loves. Madame de Raisel-Cressy, for her part, makes in extremis the extraordinary gesture of bequeathing a substantial sum to the protegée who has betrayed her.

We can speculate that it was this entangling of the most noble generosity with the "hideous" act of taking her own life which so vexed readers like Genlis. The inadmissable suicide of the heroine who is depicted as magnanimous in death makes her story harder to categorize, for it seems to send mixed messages about how women may behave. (Madame de Raisel-Cressy also inspires ambivalence in the modern reader of feminist sensibilities, but for different reasons. On the one hand, there is her disconcerting internalization and expiation through death of her husband's crimes; but on the other, there is the elegant and effective way in which she bestows, along with her money, an almost suffocating guilt on the husband she leaves behind.)

But I wish to emphasize a less obvious psychological attribute of widowhood in these novels. The widow was distinguished from the orphan, who might also have the freedom to make her own choices (and for whom Riccoboni also had a predilection), principally in that she knew what to expect in marriage. While the misadventure of Fanni Butlerd is the result of her inexperience and failure to be wary of men, Riccoboni's widows act with certain knowledge of masculine arrogance and despotism. "Ma liberté m'est chère, elle m'est plus chère que jamais" ["My freedom is precious to me, more precious than ever"] (19), writes Madame de Sancerre while the memory of the late and dreadful Monsieur de Sancerre is still vivid. The decision to remarry becomes weightier in the light of what the widow knows. Having experienced marriage at its worst, she must struggle, initially at least, to imagine it at its best.

All novelists did not uniformly put the theme of widowhood to such obvious advantage. In Gabrielle de Villeneuve's *La jardinière de Vincennes,* the marquise d'Astrel is widowed at sixteen and decides against remarriage in part because her first marriage was disappointing, but also in part because she wants to ensure that her entire fortune goes to her son. In fact, among the novel's limited cast of characters, there are three widows spanning two generations, whose stories are told as interpolated narratives. All three are more or less discouraged about their marriages, although their experiences do not play a central role in the plot.

The title of the marquise de Belvo's *Quelques lettres écrites en 1743 et 1744 par une jeune veuve au chevalier de Luzeincour* [Several letters written in 1743 and 1744 by a young widow to the Chevalier of Luzeincour] (1761), a short novel in the style of *Lettres de Mistriss Fanni Butlerd,* but without the unhappy ending, seems to promise some insights into widowly love. But the heroine makes only one brief allusion to a husband who was chosen for her and whom she mourned for no more than a week. For the rest, her love letters to the chevalier might just as well be those of any young woman. Even when she notes the capacity of some husbands to be contemptible—"La vilaine chose qu'un vilain mari!" ["What a horrible thing is a horrible husband!"] (37)—she cites the experience of a friend rather than adducing her own.

Riccoboni, on the other hand, uses the highly conventional character of the widow to reconfigure scenes of marriage and remarriage. Her handling of the emotional dilemmas and economic aspects of widowhood not only disturbs, as I have indicated, certain givens of sensibility and prescriptions for virtuous living and dying, but also lends depth to familiar stories of love and suffering. In *Lettres de Sancerre,* an investigation of widowhood no less poignant for its predictable outcome, the painful knowledge acquired in the course of a first marriage not only throws a heroine's predicament into sharp focus, but also makes the risks she runs all the more sobering.

Madame de Martigues long rebuffs her suitor, Piennes, because she is repulsed by memories of her first husband to the point that "l'esclavage et un mari se présentent ensemble à son idée" ["slavery and a husband come to mind at the same time"] (107). As late as the day set for the signing of the marriage contract, she has a last-minute panic attack and runs away, exclaiming, "l'idée d'un mari me ferait fuir au bout de l'univers" ["the idea of a husband would make me flee to the end of the earth"] (172). Her pleasantries—"Le comte de Piennes a l'esprit dérangé, il veut se *marier* ou *mourir*" ["The comte de Piennes is out of his head: he wants to *marry* or *die*"] (205)—comically echo the misgivings of Madame de Sancerre. Madame de Martigues does eventually wed the faithful Piennes, but against her better judgment, and she warns: "il va faire une grande perte, j'étais son amie, je serai sa femme, quelle différence!" ["he'll suffer a great loss: I was his friend, now I'll be his wife. What a difference!"] (205).

Even if Madame de Martigues's second attempt at marriage is successful, Riccoboni suggests that marriage is by and large a terrible thing. It is what every unmarried heroine has to hope for, but in a day when married women were by no means their own masters, the institution was routinely portrayed as being as awful as it was awesome, and women novelists generated countless fictions that convey the simultaneous allure and repulsion of marriage, emphasizing in particular the grotesque unsuitability of many arranged marriages. But these points can be differently made. When the widowed protagonists of *Lettres de Sancerre* voice their reservations about remarrying and act on those reservations, they are expressing in words and gesture what other novels express allegorically: the dread of giving oneself over into the personal and legal power of a man.

In novels where the protagonist is an innocent girl who cannot be entirely sure about what to expect, the horror of marrying is differently encoded. Rather than the qualms expressed by heroines and narrator all through Riccoboni's novels about widows, there may be premonitions at the level of plot, foreshadowings of misery, symbolic warnings of doom. Two interesting stories about marriageable girls and the complexities and ambiguities, the near impossibility, of getting married, are Marie-Anne Robert's *La voix de la nature* [The voice of nature] (1763) and Madame Beccary's *Mémoires de Fanny Spingler* (1781). Any number of novels could be used to illustrate my point; I shall discuss these two because they dramatically suggest obsessions about getting married which will help to illuminate Riccoboni's approach.

In its depiction of the coquettish and sensitive heroine of apparently humble birth who captivates the son of her highborn protectress, and in a subtitle identifying the narrator as "marquise de ***," *La voix de la nature* owes a good deal to *La vie de Marianne*. In its account of fantastic adventures that take her to Africa and America, however, and episodes entailing a stupefying number of coincidences (almost including incest), it strongly recalls Prévost's *Le philosophe anglais ou histoire de Monsieur Cleveland* (1731–39). Robert's title announces the preoccupation of almost mythic proportions that shapes the novel: the similarity between the ties of blood and the forces of passion that make it so hard to get married. Adélaïde's first admirer turns out to be her brother; the aunt by marriage who adopts her, her sister Emilie; a neighbor, their father. Finally, the abbess of the convent where she is boarding and to whom she is strongly attracted is revealed to be their mother. But not before Emilie almost marries the father, and the infatuated brother kidnaps Adélaïde.

Passion is never more than a heartbeat away from incest: characters unknowingly fall in love with or try to ravish parents, children, and siblings, disaster being narrowly avoided each time. When at the eleventh hour her father recognizes that his fiancée is his daughter, he exclaims: "Les mouvements du sang sont-ils donc si semblables à ceux de l'amour qu'on puisse s'y méprendre?" ["Are the impulses of blood then so similar to those of love that one can make a mistake about them?"] (3: 4).[18] Adélaïde's marriage, like her sister's, is repeatedly postponed or aborted by dramatic encounters, so not until late in this long novel does anyone manage to get married in due form (a version of a wedding takes place in Africa, but must of course be ratified when the couple returns to Christian France). Throughout its nearly five hundred pages of small print, the almost interminable ambiguities about fraternal, filial and passionate love, the continual postponements of the marriage ceremony, the repeated abductions of the bride, the narcissistic attraction which draws parents and siblings into erotic encounters, the startling revelations about true identity—all suggest a pervasive repressed abhorrence of marriage along with an attempt to mitigate that horror by assimilating sexual attraction to sisterly or daughterly love.

In a preface to *Mémoires de Fanny Spingler,* a cross between diary and letter-novel in the style of Richardson, Beccary warns that regard for truth forces her to leave vice unpunished and virtue without reward: this is a novel with a tragic ending and different in tone from *La voix de la nature.* Fanny, a poor orphan, loves Dorblac, with whom she was raised in the country more or less as his sister. When he moves to London, he becomes debauched and alternately abuses and neglects Fanny. He seduces a domestic servant and fathers a child. He has an affair with Lady Malgarde, wife of Fanny's protector, and she spreads the rumor that Fanny is having an affair with her husband, Sir George Malgarde. Fanny takes refuge with Lady Melville, only to be propositioned by Lord Melville.

The impoverished protegée who becomes lover to the husband of her protectress is a favorite device in the novel: the husband of the marquise in Le Prince de Beaumont's *Lettres de Madame du Montier* has a protracted affair with his wife's protegée, and of course Cressy betrays his wife with Hortense de Berneil. Fanny Spingler, however, is the innocent intruder into unhappy marriages and is condemned by appearances. She eventually proves her innocence, the despicable Dorblac undergoes a conversion of sorts, and she becomes engaged to this young man who, according to Fréron's balanced review in *L'année littéraire,* has "tous les vices de Lovelace, sans avoir rien de ses grâces, sans avoir une étincelle de son esprit" ["all the vices of Lovelace, with none of his graces, without a flash of his intelligence"] (2: 55 [1781]).

Now, one might think that Fanny, who has been bafflingly constant in her love for Dorblac, is thrilled at the prospect of marrying at last. Not a bit. On the day before the wedding, she cheerlessly writes to her correspondent:

> Au milieu de tout ce qui comble mes voeux, un mouvement intérieur semble m'avertir de repousser l'enchantement dont je devrais être préoccupée. Je cache avec soin cette tristesse profonde. . . . Mais qu'ai-je donc, ma Coraly? Mes pleurs inondent ce que j'écris. La félicité ne se fait-elle goûter à l'âme que par une impression triste! (2: 188–89)

> [Amid all that gratifies my wishes, something inside seems to warn me to reject the enchantment with which I should be preoccupied. I carefully conceal this deep sadness. . . . But what's wrong with me, Coraly? My tears cover what I write. Does happiness make itself felt only through sadness?]

Her melancholy proves justified of course. At a masked ball, just hours later, Dorblac is called upon to defend her honor and dies in a duel. Fanny's own death from shock and sorrow follows. In a plot which, according to Fréron, violates rules of propriety and plausibility (2: 57 [1781]), the heroine is relentlessly subjected to loss, solitude, poverty, calumny, manipulation, humiliation, and finally death. Most of her sufferings, moreover, are caused by the fiancé and erstwhile adoptive brother whose courtship is a continual persecution, while the examples of marriage she and the reader see around her are hardly edifying. Fanny's premonition of the tragedy about to befall her, then, is something more than that. It is also a refusal of conventional premarital contentment, a writing of the trepidation she experiences at the threshold of marriage, an expression of her ambivalence. The nuptial day, Fauchery remarks, crystallizes the virgin's fears. But while Fauchery's conclusion is that shy maids in novels need to be "doucement violentées" ["gently forced"] (357), mine is that their panic issues from more than just sexual timidity—it is an otherwise unarticulated terror about everything marriage entails.

Beccary and Robert never pull far back from their narratives, so we are left to decipher for ourselves the messages of plot and symbol. But Riccoboni's epistolary and aphoristic writing expresses a sort of complicity with the reader. Madame de Martigues generalizes from her experience to explain that "se marier, cela est si sérieux, si triste!" ["getting married is so serious, so sad!"] (157), and proclaims that "le meilleur mari est... est un mari" ["the best husband is... is a husband"] (174). Such maxims are even more prevalent, and certainly less lighthearted, in *Histoire de Cressy*, due (as I mentioned earlier) to the palpable presence of the moralizing narrator who makes clear her solidarity with women.

In an appendix to her edition of *Histoire de Cressy*, Olga Cragg lists forty-three maxims that transform local experience into universal verities like the following: "Le respect cesse quand l'amour finit" ["Respect stops when love ends"] (70). The aphorisms are for the most part reflections on the inequality of the sexes. Men are seducers and impostors who join the force of social privilege to personal and moral weakness: "les êtres inconséquents qui nous donnent des lois se sont réservé le droit de ne suivre que celles du caprice" ["the inconsistent beings who give us laws have kept for themselves the right to follow only the laws of their whims"] (70). Even the best of them are occasionally reprehensible, thoughtless, unfair, weak-willed.

Through the portraits of Sancerre and Cressy and of the misery their wives suffer at their hands, these two novels constitute an indictment of marriage. As one critic has observed, the loose structure and large cast of *Lettres de Sancerre* enable Riccoboni to illustrate by several examples what marriage was for women of the time and the harm it could do them collectively (Demay 43). And yet, paradoxically, despite all their talk, in a triumph of hope, widowed heroines remarry, thereby affirming the social and fictional order of things. Despite the rhetoric, despite what they know, they are capable of behaving like neophytes when it comes to sentiment. In *Histoire de Cressy*, of course, hope proves dramatically unwarranted, but the optimistic ending of *Lettres de Sancerre* reverses the anguish of all the plot's earlier arranged marriages and asserts faith in the *mariage d'amour*.[19] This quasi-philosophical underpinning suggests, especially in light of Riccoboni's own dismal experience with the husband she freely chose, the importance of women having the freedom to make their own mistakes.

Of course, a less sanguine way of putting this is to say that, her convictions about the incompatibility of men and women and their inevitable failures of communication notwithstanding, she still subscribes in the last analysis to a certain conventional marriage plot: Riccoboni, who spent three and a half decades living happily and working productively at the side of a woman she called "Mistress Perfection," imagines no fictional fulfillment other than marriage—or, at least, none that is publishable. Despite their range of character and outlook, despite their maturity and their outspokenness, most of her heroines are ultimately confined and defined in marriage. But perhaps it is legitimate to read the last sentence of *Lettres de Sancerre*, which is constructed so that it emphasizes woman's agency—"Malgré la différence de leurs caractères, ces deux aimables femmes rendirent leurs maris également heureux" ["Despite their differences in character, these two lovely women made their husbands equally happy"] (238)—as an oblique refusal to declare the women *themselves* happy, a kind of hedging of bets about the best that even a love match can bring to a sensitive female soul. In any event, the conventional ending of *Lettres de Sancerre*, with its multiple reinscriptions of the marriage plot, is less convincing than the tragedy of *Histoire de Cressy*, a writing of woman's fate which uneasily identifies liberty with death, and makes twice clear that in marriage *le bonheur* does not reside.

CHAPTER 5

MAPPING THE QUOTIDIAN

Isabelle de Charrière

The novels of Isabelle de Charrière (1740–1805) map a different course from that of most eighteenth-century fiction, which is rife with improbable adventures, startling coincidences, and other conventional elements of plot. Even in Riccoboni's relatively sober *Lettres de Sancerre,* several unexpected inheritances are bestowed, and the dramatic return of the outlandish cousin from Martinique threatens at the eleventh hour to thwart the happy ending. Charrière's four major works display few of the genre's habitual artifices: there are no shipwrecks or attacks by pirates, no evil plotters, no disguises, transvestism, abductions, rapes, clandestine marriages, foundlings, or unforeseen legacies. These novels are fashioned instead by concern with the minutiae of daily life: the boredom of going to work every day; the problem of chilblains and the danger of slipping on ice in winter; the sadness of losing a cat; the impact of a door's closing; the consequences of dropping a package in the mud.[1]

In a body of work exhibiting the Richardsonian emphasis on domesticity that came to her via Rousseau (of whom Charrière considered herself a disciple), she distances herself, as they do, from the formulas that shaped the older, although still current, tradition of the *roman romanesque*. But Charrière goes further: she not only avoids implausible plot conceits, but also subverts the maps or masterplots to which the Richardsonian and Rousseauist versions of the quotidian are subordinated in the end. Her epistolary novels evoke closed interior spaces furnished with events that are internalized and open-ended. Charrière uses the letter-novel to describe the fleeting and the inconclusive, and it simultaneously realizes its potential as the form best suited to writing the life of a woman and to exploring the unacknowledged control exercised by domestic concerns over female psychology.

By her origins as well, Isabelle de Charrière stands apart from most of the writers considered in this book. About her position in the history of French letters, we have the testimony of Sainte-Beuve:

Née en Hollande et vivant en Suisse, [elle] n'écrivait à la fin ses légers ouvrages que pour qu'on les traduisît en allemand . . . pourtant, par l'esprit et par le ton, [elle] fut de la pure littérature française, et de la plus rare aujourd'hui, de celle de Gil Blas, d'Hamilton et de Zadig. (*Portraits* 456)

[Born in Holland and living in Switzerland, (she) wrote her slight works in the end only for them to be translated into German . . . nonetheless, in spirit and tone, (she) was pure French literature, and of the rarest kind today, that of Gil Blas, Hamilton, and Zadig.]

Isabella Agneta Elisabeth van Tuyll van Serooskerken was born to a Dutch Protestant family and became known as Belle de Zuylen, for the name of the castle in the province of Utrecht where she spent her youth. French was one of her native languages, and her earliest letters are written in French—for example, the letters to Baron Constant d'Hermenches (a Swiss colonel and the uncle of Benjamin Constant), with whom the young woman had a sort of chaste epistolary affair. Her international reputation for unconventionality and dazzling wit both attracted and unnerved suitors (a blustery but irresolute James Boswell among them), and it wasn't until the age of thirty, after years of negotiations with a gamut of potential husbands, that she was joined in an unlikely marriage to a phlegmatic Swiss tutor, Charles Emmanuel de Charrière. He took her to live with his father and sisters in his native village of Colombier, near Neuchâtel, where they remained for more than thirty years.Their temperaments were distinctly different, and she did not find her marriage fulfilling.

Belle de Zuylen (Isabelle de Charrière)
by Maurice Quentin de La Tour, 1766. Frontispiece,
Philippe Godet, *Madame de Charrière et ses amis,*
vol. 1 (Geneva: A. Jullien, 1906).

On an extended visit to Paris in 1786–87, she met nineteen-year-old Benjamin Constant, to whom she became deeply attached and whose eccentricities she encouraged. The stormy liaison between Constant and Germaine de Staël which was to arouse Charrière's jealousy began about seven years later, but she corresponded with him until her death. Indeed, it was for her relations with Boswell and Constant that, until recently, Charrière was best known. In Paris she also became fascinated by a polity moving toward revolution, an interest that motivates much of the fiction of her later years, which incorporates substantial philosophical and political commentary and explores in particular the theme of emigration. In addition to her novels and a monumental correspondence, she produced essays, plays, and verse.[2]

Her first short work of fiction, *Le noble* (1763), published when she was in her early twenties, scandalized the Dutch aristocracy in its satire of pretentions about lineage: Julie d'Arnonville not only elopes with a man whose nobility is less ancient than her own, but also stacks her ancestors' portraits to break her fall as she jumps from her window. The novels generally considered her finest, and on which I shall concentrate, appeared a little over twenty years later and also generated controversy. Both *Lettres neuchâteloises* and *Lettres de Mistriss Henley publiées par son amie* went on sale in 1784, followed in spring 1785 by *Lettres écrites de Lausanne* [Letters from Lausanne]. January 1787 saw the publication of *Caliste ou continuation des Lettres écrites de Lausanne:* a new edition of the 1785 text wove Caliste's story into the final episodes of the original plot.

Even a brief summary of the first of these novels, *Lettres neuchâteloises,* suggests the degree to which Charrière's fiction conveys not only unstylized emotions and detailed dailiness but also a delicate sense of loss and transience. Most of the volume's letters, dated between November and March and addressed by the two principal characters to correspondents who remain outside the plot, narrate the discovery of first love.

Newly arrived from Frankfort as apprentice in a Neuchâtel firm, Henri Meyer, whose enlightened education has honed his fine sensibilities, is lonely, bored, and mildly critical of the society he finds himself in. He makes his first acquaintance with an unkempt seamstress, Julianne C., whom he graciously assists when she drops, in one of the town's narrow, muddy streets, a dress she is delivering to Marianne de la Prise. Julianne and Henri have a brief affair, to which he puts an end. Meanwhile, he is falling in love with Marianne herself, whom he meets at a concert in which she is the singer and he is the accompanist. The event that paradoxically welds their affections is the discovery of Julianne's pregnancy. Rising above standard notions of appropriate preoccupations for young women like herself, Marianne makes arrangements for mother and child and in so doing demonstrates both compassion and practical sense (Julianne is sent promptly away). When Henri leaves Neuchâtel just afterward for the bedside of his ailing correspondent, he takes with him an elliptical assurance of Marianne's love.

The publication of *Lettres neuchâteloises* was greeted in some quarters with indignation: Charrière was both censured and ridiculed for the attention she lavished on Julianne C., a representative of the lower classes, while the portrayal of a certain regional narrowness rang a little too true for the inhabitants of Neuchâtel. On more than one score her fiction was accused of triviality, that very triviality of concerns in which we might see an attentive evocation of women's lives. Here the experience of love is differently textured from what we find in most contemporary works. Marianne de la Prise is aware that the story she proposes to tell her confidante is only a fluid succession of insubstantial events difficult to recount:

> Il me semble que j'ai quelque chose à te dire; et quand je veux commencer, je ne vois plus rien qui vaille la peine d'être dit. Tous ces jours je me suis arrangée pour t'écrire; j'ai tenu ma plume pendant longtemps, et elle n'a pas tracé le moindre mot. Tous les faits sont si petits, que le récit m'en serait ennuyeux à moi-même. (64)

> [It seems to me that I have something to tell you; but when I try to begin, I can no longer see anything worth telling. Day after day I've gotten ready to write you; I've held my pen for a long time without writing the first word. All the facts are so insignificant that the story would be boring even to me.]

With Charrière, the intimate letter becomes the vehicle for meditating on and communicating the consequences of evanescent feelings and occurrences—the little things, as Marianne calls them elsewhere. The apparent paltriness of Julianne's and Marianne's concerns—the price of wood, a soiled dress, the cost of a subscription to the winter's balls—encompasses and expresses not only a human but also a specifically female condition of almost inescapable subordinacy. By dint of hard work, Henri Meyer can prevail over the tedium of his first job and become self-sufficient, but Julianne and Marianne can essentially modify their circumstances only by acquiring rich lovers or husbands.

The thematics of economic considerations and their relation to female destiny pervade the *Lettres neuchâteloises*. As a poor aristocrat, Marianne de la Prise is conscious that her marriage prospects are feeble, and in letters to her confidante, she appraises the dismal state of the family's finances. At the death of her father, they will lose even their modest pension: "dans ces circonstances et avec cette fortune, il est rare qu'on se marie" ["in this situation and with these means, one rarely marries"] (64). While numerous other novelists were lauding the *mariage d'amour,* Charrière was giving voice to a corollary issue, formulating an enlightened and explicit analysis of the economics of marriageability. Economic constraints are as crucial as affective motives for Charrière heroines who, poor and genteel, are propelled to their fates in part by the need for economic survival. In her next few novels, the theme of economic contingencies becomes more pronounced, and in each case we find the winsome and doleful silhouette of a marriageable—or, alas, not so marriageable—young woman.

During a trip to Geneva in spring 1784 to arrange for a reprinting of *Lettres neuchâteloises,* Charrière became acquainted with a Swiss letter-novel that was causing a stir: *Le mari sentimental* (1783), by still another member of the Constant family, Samuel. This story of a middle-aged man whose new wife, by rearranging his house and his life, drives him to suicide, inspired Charrière to write a rigorously parallel story from the "other" point of view, and she produced the feminist counterpart, *Lettres de Mistriss Henley*—a "très petit ouvrage" as she modestly called it (*Oeuvres* 6: 559),[3] but a gripping one, with autobiographical echoes.

Six letters from a young English bride to a friend on the continent detail her cheerless marriage to a "reasonable" man and decipher not only the messages of social condition and economic status, but also the language of the most apparently mute and ordinary signs: a cat's slumber, artificial flowers, a portrait on a wall. Orphaned and without revenue at twenty-five, the heroine must marry to find financial security. She has two eligible suitors: a handsome, immensely rich, and worldly man, a lover of the arts and the good life, over whom hangs some unsavory suspicion concerning the origins of the wealth he brought back from the Orient; and Mr. Henley, a thirty-five-year-old widower of sufficient fortune, and father of an "angelically" beautiful five-year-old girl—a man whose honesty and simple mores account for both his contentment in his country estate and the general esteem he enjoys.

Her "noble" feelings struggle only briefly against the attractions of elegance and opulence, a house of her own in London and three hundred guineas a year in pin money. Months later, she explains her decision to marry the man who "touches" her but arouses no passion:

> C'était, pour ainsi dire, la partie vile de mon coeur qui préférait les richesses de l'Orient, Londres, une liberté plus entière, une opulence plus brillante; la partie noble dédaignait tout cela, et se pénétrait des douceurs d'une félicité toute raisonnable, toute sublime, et telle que les anges devaient y applaudir. Si un père tyrannique m'eût obligée à épouser le Nabab, je me serais fait peut-être un devoir d'obéir . . . En un mot, forcée de devenir heureuse d'une manière vulgaire, je le serais devenue sans honte et peut-être avec plaisir; mais me donner moi-même de mon choix, contre des diamants, des perles, des tapis, des parfums, des mousselines brodées d'or, des soupers, des fêtes, je ne pouvais m'y résoudre, et je promis ma main à Monsieur Henley. (103–4)

> [It was, in so many words, the base part of my heart that would have preferred the wealth of the Orient, London, greater freedom, more splendid opulence; the noble part disdained all that and took comfort in the delights of an entirely reasonable, entirely sublime happi-

ness, such as the angels themselves would approve. If a tyrannical father had forced me to marry the nabob, I would have perhaps accepted it as my duty to obey . . . In a word, if I had been forced to become happy in a vulgar way, I would have done so without shame and perhaps with pleasure; but to give myself over of my own choice, in exchange for diamonds, pearls, carpets, perfumes, gold-embroidered muslin, dinners, parties—I couldn't do it, and I promised my hand to Mr. Henley.]

The passage encapsulates the responsibility to self that comes with autonomy. Deprived of the crutch of the average heroine—the "tyrannical father" who exacts obedience out of fear and love—our protagonist woefully faces the dilemma of the modern woman: the obligation to choose for herself, the necessity of trying to control her own destiny, justifying her decisions, and living with the consequences. But no psychological liberation complements her freedom of choice: she is like Rousseau's Julie without her authoritarian father, but making the choice he and Rousseau would have her make. An interiorization of the paternal law and an obsession with socially inspired notions of virtue and purity distort a relatively straightforward economic and social decision into a moral dilemma.

What man, faced with a similar choice, would reject, as she does, the offer that would confer greater status, power, and freedom? Branding the wealthier suitor a "nabob," she perversely defines the predicament—nobility, exaltation, and reason over against baseness, vulgarity, and pleasure—in such a way that she cannot accept the very proposal that dazzles her. Le Prince de Beaumont's heroines, too, are perverse in their excessive virtue, in their determination to reject all that is worldly and glitters, but this seems paradoxically to liberate them in the end. Charrière suggests the impossibility of this option, a dialectical closing in of the female destiny, despite apparent choice: Mistress Henley's espousal of virtue gives rise to unhappiness and perhaps death.

"Nos noces furent charmantes. Spirituel, élégant, décent, délicat, affectueux, M. Henley enchantait tout le monde; c'était un mari de roman" ["Our wedding was charming. Witty, elegant, proper, tactful, affection-

ate, Mr. Henley captivated everyone; he was a story-book husband"]
(104). The last phrase (literally: "a husband out of a novel") connects Mr.
Henley to the novel's self-conscious staging of lives in an estate men-
acingly named "Hollowpark": "il me semblait quelquefois un peu trop
parfait" ["sometimes he seemed to me a little too perfect"] (104), she
continues. His moderation, his impassivity, the patrician ease with which
he fills the role of benevolent master, collide with his wife's sensitivity,
secret fantasies, vivacity, and occasional impatience. The incompatibility
of two well-meaning individuals is manifested in skirmishes over apparently trivial matters. His practical sense rejects for his country-bred
daughter the frills and the talents that his wife's modish education has
taught her to value. When he gently berates Mistress Henley for allowing
her cat to sleep on the heirlooms in the boudoir, he cannot understand
the intensity of her reaction. "Ce n'est pas le chat" ["It's not the cat"]
(106), she screams—a cry whose poignancy has few equivalents in the
literature of this period. But he has already left. She retaliates by having
the furnishings replaced and the picture of his first wife removed from the
wall opposite her bed, and in the commotion the cat runs away. When her
stylish chambermaid turns the head of a young farmer who is already
spoken for, Mr. Henley observes that she should never have been
brought to the country in the first place. So her mistress dispatches her
to London, only to be admonished for acting precipitately after the damage is done. Even the little daughter of heavenly beauty turns out to
be as disappointingly dispassionate as her father. The distress Mistress
Henley suffers is made subtly more acute by her meeting one day with the
woman who married the "nabob": beautifully dressed and gracious, Lady
Bridgewater has visibly accommodated herself nicely to her husband's
tainted wealth; she embodies all that might have been.[4]

But Mistress Henley, who opted in marrying for rationality over glam-
our, is now possessed with the need to emulate and win the reluctant
admiration of the man she chose. Her constant mortifications culminate
in a letter in which she says: "je veux faire mon devoir; non d'après ma
fantaisie, mais d'après votre jugement. . . . Sur ce point et sur tous les
autres, je désire sincèrement de mériter votre approbation" ["I want to do

my duty, not according to my whim, but according to your judgment. . . . In this matter and in all others, I sincerely desire to be worthy of your approval"] (118). She asks for approval rather than love, but meriting even that proves impossible, and her story resolves itself into the harrowing account of a woman always in the wrong.

Other novelists ironize in passing about an oppressive Enlightenment "reason" that controls female destiny. In Riccoboni's *Lettres de Milord Rivers,* for example, thirty-six-year-old Lady Orrery is cross after dismissing the young admirer whom she would have liked to marry. She felt she had no choice, given societal prejudice against older women consorting with younger men. A man in her situation, she complains, could have married his nubile paramour and no one would bat an eyelash. "Pourquoi cette différence? Parce que je suis femme, obligée par état d'être *raisonnable,* et qu'un homme peut se dispenser de l'être autant que moi" ["Why this difference? Because I am a woman, forced by my very condition to be *reasonable,* while a man can dispense himself from being as reasonable as I"] (278–79). Riccoboni's stress on "*raisonnable*" calls attention to its irony, sententiousness, and inequitable applications.

What distinguishes *Lettres de Mistriss Henley* is the continual nuancing of notions of reason, right, and wrong. On the day after their arrival at Hollowpark, Mr. Henley politely reproaches his wife for bedecking her stepdaughter in city finery and artificial flowers ill suited to the simplicity of their surroundings. "Vous avez raison, Monsieur," she replies, "j'ai eu tort de lui mettre tout cela" ["You're right, Monsieur, I was wrong to dress her in all that" (104)]. *Avoir tort* becomes a kind of leitmotif:

"J'avais tort, je le sais bien; c'était moi qui avais tort" ["I was wrong, I know it, it was I who was wrong"] (105);

"Ai-je eu tort, ma chère amie?" ["Was I wrong, dear friend?"] (106);

"Je déplore mes torts" ["I deplore my wrongs"] (107);

"J'avais eu plus de tort que je ne l'avais cru" ["I was even more wrong than I had thought"] (108);

"Il avait senti, je n'en doute pas, chacun de mes torts" ["I don't doubt that he had felt every one of my wrongs"] (108);

"M. Henley ne cesse de me dire que j'ai eu tort" ["Mr. Henley never
stops telling me I was wrong"] (111);

"Aurait-il raison? ma chère amie. Aurais-je eu encore tort, toujours
tort, tort en tout?" ["Could he be right, dear friend? Was I wrong
again, always wrong, wrong in everything?"] (111).

Her "wrongs" reside not in major offenses, violations of explicit or implicit contracts, but in her day-to-day commerce with her husband and
household, in questions of perspective, attitude, mood, and the priorities
one establishes in domestic life: "Ce sont de petites choses qui m'affligent
ou m'impatientent, et me font avoir tort" ["It's the little things that
distress and provoke me and put me in the wrong"] (112). Not only
economically but morally as well, Henley always, infuriatingly, has right
on his side, while she must be wrong. "Ma chère amie, des coups de
poing me seraient moins fâcheux que toute cette raison" ["My dear
friend, punches would be less annoying than all this reasoning"] (107),
she exclaims to her correspondent; and then, to her husband: "les in-
justices d'un jaloux, les emportements d'un brutal, seraient moins fâcheux
que le flegme et l'aridité d'un sage" ["the unfairness of a jealous man, the
rages of a brutal man, would be less annoying than the serene aridity of a
sage"] (116).

Whereas other husbands exploit, deceive, brutalize, and even imprison
their wives, Mr. Henley speaks softly and deliberately, and his wife becomes almost suicidal. His self-assured rationality engenders alternating
feelings of acrimony and inferiority, while the economic and social necessity of marriage finds symbolic expression in the fact that she is designated only twice by a proper name: on the title page as "Mistress Henley"
and in the signature of a letter addressed to her husband as "S. Henley."
She is accorded, at the most, an initial of a given name: her identity
appears sayable only within the context of her existence as Henley's wife.

In her last letter, Mistress Henley, now pregnant, describes a conversation with her husband where she learns that, in the question of whether
she should nurse their child, he is concerned only lest her excessive vivacity be harmful to the baby: "De moi, de ma santé, de mon plaisir, pas
un mot: il n'était question que de cet enfant qui n'existait pas encore"

["Of me, of my health, of my pleasure, not a word: all that mattered was that child who didn't yet exist"] (120). She soon discovers in addition that, preferring the peace of the country to the turmoil of politics, he has recently declined a position at court without so much as consulting her. Her intense desolation is expressed first in temporary muteness and a faint:

> J'ai voulu dire quelque chose; mais j'avais été si attentive, j'étais tellement combattue entre l'estime que m'arrachait tant de modération, de raison, de droiture dans mon mari, et l'horreur de me voir si étrangère à ses sentiments, si fort exclue de ses pensées, si inutile, si isolée, que je n'ai pu parler. Fatiguée de tant d'efforts, ma tête s'est embarrassée; je me suis évanouie. (122)

> [I tried to say something; but I had been so attentive, I was so divided between the respect that I was forced to pay to such moderation, reasonableness, and rectitude in my husband, and the horror of seeing myself so alienated from his feelings, so completely excluded from his thoughts, so useless, so isolated, that I could not speak. Overwhelmed by so much effort, my head spun and I fainted.]

Silence and a swoon acknowledge failure to share control of her world, even of its most immediate and intimate aspects. This sense of ineluctable frustration then finds a more important expression in the symbolically permanent silence on which the novel ends, as she announces to her confidante that she will write no more.

At least one modern critic, Robert Mauzi, a careful reader of questions of "happiness" in the eighteenth-century novel, sees Mistress Henley as an example of the melancholia of the soul then so much talked about:

> La vocation du malheur est si forte dans une âme mélancolique qu'elle persiste même lorsqu'il n'existe aucune condition objective du malheur. Cleveland, M. de La Bédoyère[5] ont à subir des épreuves qu'ils n'inventent pas. Mais que dire de Mistress Henley, l'héroïne de Mme de Charrière, qui vit au milieu d'une lumineuse nature, auprès d'un mari si épris et si parfait qu'elle l'appelle elle-même un "mari de

roman"? Le destin de Mistress Henley illustre le thème de l'*impossible bonheur*. Toujours froissée, aigrie, "affligée" par de "petites choses," chimérique, cultivant une solitude imaginaire, jouant à l'incomprise, elle fait cet aveu significatif: "Une femme raisonnable ne pouvait manquer d'être heureuse; mais je ne suis pas une femme raisonnable." C'est avec de "puériles (sic) chagrins" que cette femme, qui devrait se dire heureuse, se compose un destin aussi insupportable que celui, authentiquement noir, d'un Cleveland. (Mauzi, "Maladies" 479)

[The vocation of unhappiness is so strong in a melancholic soul that it subsists even in the absence of an objectively unhappy condition. Cleveland and Monsieur de La Bédoyère have to undergo trials that are not imaginary. But what can we say about Mistress Henley, Madame de Charrière's heroine, who lives in a radiant natural setting, with a husband so in love and so perfect that she herself calls him a "story-book husband"? The fate of Mistress Henley illustrates the theme of *impossible happiness*. Always huffy, sour, "distressed" by "little things," chimerical, cultivating an imaginary solitude, pretending to be misunderstood, she makes this indicative confession: "A reasonable woman could not help being happy; but I am not a reasonable woman." With "childish [*sic*] troubles," this woman, who should consider herself happy, constructs for herself a fate as insufferable as the authentically grim fate of a Cleveland.]

But surely Mistress Henley's sorrows are not inauthentic simply because they are subjective. Her misery is no willful construction of her own. And the drama of her husband's inability to relate to his wife's sensitivities is not only play-acting on her part. Her "invented" domestic problems—what Mauzi also calls her "pseudo-malheurs" (479)22— resonate more strongly than the outlandishly "authentic" trials of these other eighteenth-century heroes of fiction. And her troubles are more womanly than "childish," even if she herself self-deprecatingly applies that epithet. The cause of her suffering—like Charrière's own difficulties in marrying—is not generic but gender-specific. The network of responses characterizing her are explicitly female, and her dilemma is an aspect of the female condition.

This is no groundless melancholia to be ascribed merely to a temporary vogue of idle despondency: it is rooted in her social and personal situation, in the ideology of the "perfect" husband who is less than perfectly "in love," and in the menace of his excessive rationality. She marries with all the sincerity in the world, but she can't live his constraining version of happiness. Indeed, in an understated way the novel makes clear just how irrational by any standards many of his positions really are.[6] In this text femininity is allied with sentiment and impetuosity (consider, for example, the way she arrives at the decision to marry Henley), while masculine preeminence resides in moderation and especially in a display of "reason." Men are characterized not just by economic strength, but also by economy of feeling and expression, while women (as Mauzi makes clear) are still seen as sinning by excess—a dichotomy that takes us back nearly forty years to Le Prince de Beaumont's analysis of men and women in her *Lettre en réponse à L'année merveilleuse.*

What then, to repeat our critic's question, can we say about Mistress Henley? Above all, that her unhappiness is more the effect of provocation than "vocation." She compellingly figures woman in her status as a social, political, and economic inferior, and she is subtly oppressed by a society where, as Isabelle de Charrière had ample opportunity to find out, a financially disadvantaged woman cannot decently survive outside of marriage and a sensitive or reflective woman can only endure within it.

Her last letter and the volume conclude with the suggestion that, although she rejects suicide, her misery may make death imminent: "Dans un an, dans deux ans, vous apprendrez, je l'espère, que je suis raisonnable et heureuse, ou que je ne suis plus" ["In a year, two years, you'll learn, I hope, that I am reasonable and happy, or that I am no longer"] (122). Achieving a certain "happiness" depends on renouncing the female principles of vivacity and change and accepting reason as opposition to excess and maintenance of the status quo—symbolized, in the Henleys' case, by the heavy and somber furnishings of the boudoir she inherits from Henley's first wife, whose portrait hangs across from the bed.

The alternative to accommodating such a version of life seems to be death—which we recognize, of course, as a conventional ending to narratives of female lives and desires. The heroines of Richardson's *Clarissa* and Rousseau's *Julie,* for all these novels' emphasis on daily and domestic life, end up dead, just like the unhappy heroine of *La princesse de Clèves.* Fate intervenes and individual fates are resolved. But Charrière eschews the grand and tragic gestures familiar to her readers, and her novels characteristically fail even to conclude. Her heroines are not subjected to rape and death, like Clarissa, nor, for the most part, do they fornicate and eventually die, like Julie. Charrière's mapping of life's little incidents exhibits few distinct borders and avoids artificial, final flourishes.[7] Events are suspended in the silent space between impossible accession to male values and demise—suspended in the resounding silence of defeat.

The first half of the *Lettres écrites de Lausanne* is the (likewise unfinished) story of seventeen-year-old Cécile, told by her widowed mother in seventeen letters written to a cousin in France. The initial letter raises the troubling question that echoes unanswered through the work: "Ma pauvre Cécile, que deviendra-t-elle?" ["What will become of my poor Cécile?"] (138). The "poor" is, of course, intended metaphorically, but it is literal, too, for her mother's concern relates directly to their modest resources: the mother knows that eligible young men do not spontaneously seek out young women, even comely ones, of meager means. Her ability to show her daughter to best advantage ("il faut donc la montrer" ["so I have to show her"] 138), along with the quality of Cécile's self-presentation, is therefore crucial. Neither a great reader of books nor an enthusiastic writer, Cécile does not play the harp, knows neither Italian nor English, becomes unpleasantly flushed when she dances, is developing a thick neck, and is subject to headache and chilblains. Yet she is, with Charrière's other heroines, among the most endearing female protagonists in late eighteenth-century fiction. In an early description, her mother refuses normal novelistic categories in describing her daughter in homey phrases as a "belle et bonne fille" whose strong suits are "la santé, la bonté, la gaieté, la susceptibilité d'amour et d'amitié, la simplicité de coeur et la droiture d'esprit, et non l'extrême élégance, délicatesse, finesse, noblesse" ["health, goodness, gaiety, susceptibility to love and friend-ship, simplicity of heart and rightness of mind, and not extreme elegance, refinement, finesse or nobility"] (139). Cécile falls in love with Edward, a young English lord on the grand tour wintering in Lausanne with his tutor. He is charmed but not inspired enough to ask for her hand. For a change of scenery, and to give him a chance to think things over, mother and daughter agree to leave Lausanne for a while; and there the story halts.

Following in the tradition of the mothers of *Lettres de Madame du Montier* and *Lettres du marquis de Roselle,* Cécile's has occasion to advise her, both in conversation and by letter, about codes of behavior.[8] Two things are remarkable about the mother's account of virtue and the dou-ble standard. In the first place, she distinguishes between an ineffectual generic definition of virtue and what is specifically meant by *woman's* virtue. She makes explicit what is usually only implied: the functional meaning of the word "virtue" for women and the lengths to which a young woman must go in appearing to embody it. If society asks men to practice a combination of courage and probity, it requires something different of women: "Ce qu'on appelle *vertu* chez les femmes sera presque la seule que vous puissiez ne pas avoir, la seule que vous pratiquiez en tant que vertu" ["What is called *virtue* in women is the only one that you might happen not to have, the only one that you would practice as a virtue"] (160). A woman's virtue, she explains, has nothing to do with observing commandments forbidding murder, theft, or slander, for these interdictions are hardly likely to pose problems. Instead it signifies the preservation of virginity before marriage and of fidelity thereafter, the only things that really matter to men of the marrying sort. A girl has to marry to live, and she must remember that in the final analysis men are motivated by "le désir d'une propriété exclusive" ["the desire for exclusive possession"] (162). By maintaining exquisite control of her reactions, a marriageable girl must therefore induce potential suitors—if necessary, she must even "deceive" them—into understanding that she is ruled by neither sentiment nor sensuality.

But in a second, antithetical move, the mother undercuts the impact of this extraordinarily candid assessment of the property ethic in sexual and conjugal relations, by adding that chastity is not everything in life. Cécile should remember that if ever she did err, her mother would care about (and for) her no less. Parents in fiction do not usually talk this way. In Riccoboni's *Histoire de Cressy,* when Adélaïde du Bugei finds herself in circumstances not unlike Cécile's, her father, a "man of honor" who cherishes her, announces:

> Je vous aime, vous le savez; mais je ne répondrais pas de vous conserver ma tendresse, si vous étiez assez faible pour vous livrer encore à un penchant que vous devez rougir d'avoir laissé paraître. (57)

> [I love you and you know it; but I could not promise to continue to love you, if you were weak enough to give yourself over again to a penchant which you should blush at having betrayed.]

Charrière, on the other hand, subtly gives us to understand that maternal love, like female integrity, is finally independent of austere societal injunctions regarding female behavior. The tender and disabused characterization of virtue in the exchange between mother and daughter exemplifies Charrière's manner and her originality: she criticizes and rhetorically distances herself from inflexible social constraints and prejudices, especially as they apply to women, while she insists on their ineluctable force as norms of society.

Virtue and reason are not the only terms that are invoked in new ways in her novels. Cécile's mother comments that her daughter's guardians harass her about Cécile's upbringing, contradicting themselves and demanding the preposterous:

> Voilà comme, avec des mots qui se laissent mettre à côté les uns des autres, on fabrique des caractères, des législations, des éducations et des bonheurs domestiques impossibles. Avec cela on tourmente les femmes, les mères, les jeunes filles, tous les imbéciles qui se laissent moraliser. (138)

> [That is how, with words that can be strung one after the other, they invent characters, laws, educations, and impossible domestic happi-

ness. And with them they torment women, mothers, girls, all the imbeciles who listen to their moral lessons.]

It is hard to think of a more eloquent eighteenth-century expression of men's concatenation of menacing words, of their almost conspiratorial complicity in notions like morality and reason. The passage crystallizes some of the most important aspects of Charrière's fictional enterprise. Like *Lettres de Mistriss Henley,* this novel lays bare "domestic happiness" as a verbal construction, a notion invented (like laws and education) by sermonizing men and imposed on tractable women. Genuine happiness, maternal love, an honest education—these reside elsewhere.

Neither Cécile's story, Marianne's, nor Mistress Henley's ends conventionally. More than one contemporary was critical of this: for La Harpe, writing in February 1788, *Lettres écrites de Lausanne* begins well enough, but the love affair between Cécile and the English lord, initially so promising, goes nowhere: "c'est une conception avortée" (*Letters to the Shuvalovs* 306). A few years later, Germaine de Staël complained in a letter to Charrière: "je me suis intéressée vivement aux lettres neuchâteloises, mais je ne sais rien de plus pénible que votre manière de commencer sans finir" ["I was intensely involved in *Lettres neuchâteloises,* but I know of nothing more distressing than your way of beginning without ending"] (Charrière, *Oeuvres* IV: 162).

In the middle of the next century, Julia Kavanagh, whose elegant remarks are frequently probing, expressed a similar objection: "it is unfinished, imperfect, like a glimpse from the great drama of reality. It begins, but does not end" (2: 111). Can we even call these stories? Henri Meyer leaves Neuchâtel with no more than an inference of Marianne's feelings for him. Will they marry? Their relation seems hopeful, but their future is uncharted. And what of Mistress Henley: will she become "reasonable" or die? What *will* happen to "poor" Cécile? The last letter of each of these narratives calls attention to the absence of finality while the blank space that follows signifies both rupture and the possibility of continuance. In an exceptionally open enciphering of plot, these novels abandon their heroes and heroines to the indefinite.

The case is different for the second part of *Lettres écrites de Lausanne,* which, like *Lettres de Mistriss Henley,* is set in England. Here William, Edward's forlorn tutor and traveling companion, sends Cécile's mother his own story and that of Caliste, the woman he loved. This is the romanticized, novelistic version of Cécile's story:[9] the mother's admonition to her cousin—"Mais songez que ma fille et moi ne sommes pas un roman" ["Remember that my daughter and I are not a novel"] (149)—contrasts with the opening of William's narrative: "Mon histoire est romanesque" ["My story is romantic" (literally: novelistic)] (189). While Cécile's mother conceals their last name in her letters, fearing that postal accidents may compromise them, Caliste has only an assumed name taken from the role she played in her one stage appearance.[10]

We learn that her destitute mother had taken advantage of Caliste's beauty and talents to put her on the stage at an early age; after her debut, she was sold to an English nobleman who made her his mistress, but also gave her a convent education in the arts and letters and treated her with discreet consideration. After his death, Caliste falls in love with William. In spite of her irregular past, she is worthy of William both morally and intellectually, but he never summons up the resolve either to make her his mistress or to defy his father and marry her.[11] In the end, he marries a flighty young widow of his father's choosing. Caliste marries instead a basically good man who cannot tolerate her love for William. By the time William's written account of their story is completed, Caliste has died an exemplary death at her husband's side, and even William's father has realized his error: "qui pouvait croire," he asks rhetorically, "qu'il y eût tant de différence entre une femme et une autre femme?" ["who would believe there could be so much difference between one woman and another?"] (225). In Lausanne, William castigates himself and compulsively expresses futile regrets about having failed to do what was "natural," about always waiting until "too late." His obsessive repetitions of *j'aurais dû* ["I should have"] structure his grief, just as Mistress Henley's reiterated *j'ai tort* ["I am wrong"] organizes hers:

Il me semble que je n'ai rien fait de ce qu'il aurait été naturel de faire. *J'aurais dû* l'épouser sans demander un consentement dont je n'avais pas besoin. *J'aurais dû* l'empêcher de promettre qu'elle ne m'épouserait pas sans ce consentement. Si mille efforts n'avaient pu fléchir mon père, *j'aurais dû* en faire ma maîtresse, et pour elle et moi ma femme, quand tout son coeur le demandait malgré elle, et que je le voyais malgré ses paroles. *J'aurais dû* l'entendre, lorsqu'ayant écarté tout le monde, elle voulut m'empêcher de la quitter. Revenu chez elle, *j'aurais dû* briser sa porte . . . L'ayant retrouvée *j'aurais dû* ne la plus quitter . . . J'ai été sans courage pour prévenir cette perte; je suis sans force pour la supporter. (231, my emphasis)

[I seem to have done nothing of what it would have been natural to do. I should have married her without asking a consent that I didn't need. I should not have let her promise not to marry me without that consent. If no amount of effort could bend my father, I should have made her my mistress and in our own minds, my wife, when with her whole heart she was begging me in spite of herself, and I could see it in spite of her words. I should have listened to her, when after sending everyone else away, she tried to keep me from leaving. When I came back, I should have broken the door down. . . . Once I found her, I should never have left her again . . . I didn't have the courage to prevent this loss; I don't have the strength to endure it.]

An obvious precursor of Benjamin Constant's indecisive Adolphe, William also resembles Cécile's would-be suitor Edward in *Lettres écrites de Lausanne*. Less able to liberate themselves from social prejudice, they love less courageously and more regretfully than the women. Edward manifests strong interest in Cécile when she is in the sights of other men; but he is unable to sustain such interest with intensity. And his friend William, despite sparks of ardor, betrays an occasional disturbing passivity and a sort of morbid inertness at the end. Cécile and Caliste are caught in a social order that produces men like Edward and William, incapable of directly expressing their sentiments, more or less incapable of "doing" anything at all.

But the system also denies women the right to take matters into their own hands. Their affective and material subordination are, moreover, as Starobinski points out, paralleled in the narrative form: Cécile's story is told by her mother and Caliste's by William. In both cases the heroine is "ce dont on parle" ["that which is spoken of"] (134). But Caliste's tale has a tragic ending with a cautionary value for the unfinished story of Cécile. With its melodrama and amorous death, *Caliste* was embraced by critics and readers alike, and this "most conventional, least threatening of her works" (MacArthur, "Devious" 17) became Charrière's most popular.

The shape of *Caliste,* doubly closed, by the conclusiveness of the heroine's death and by its insertion within another story, sets it apart from Charrière's earlier works. But in theme and content, it rejoins them. When William asks Caliste if she never thought of leaving the man who bought and educated her, but saw no point in marrying her, she responds that she considered it, but was struck with the ingratitude of such an idea: "je me crus la dupe d'un fantôme qui s'appelait la vertu, et qui était le vice, et je le repoussai avec horreur" ["I thought myself the dupe of a ghost called virtue, but which was in fact vice, and I repulsed it in horror"] (201). Virtue fails Caliste even more dramatically than it did Mistress Henley, who is desolate in marriage despite her virtue, or Cécile who, despite hers, may be unable to marry at all. Charrière intimates the near bankruptcy of virtue as a usable commodity for women. Her (partly unconscious) response to the Richardsonian/Rousseauist program of moral regeneration through (female) virtue is decisive and lucid.

Charrière confers an almost Balzacian attention on the trifling and potentially desolating incidents of daily life, although she displays none of his impulse to make them monumentally important. She is a kind of historian of mentalities, whose subtle descriptions plot the circumstances of an era, a locale, and a class. Her stories are shaped by the implications of speech and habits of the mind and heart for an assessment of women's lot. Appearing a generation or more after the novels of Riccoboni, Elie de Beaumont, and Le Prince de Beaumont, those of Charrière may be seen as standing in a quasi-dialectical relation to the earlier ones, where there is vigorous action and clear resolution of plot, and where chastity and silence are often self-determining. For Le Prince de Beaumont and Elie de Beaumont, in particular, virtue as a concept appears adoptable by women and (for Le Prince de Beaumont, at least) opposable to reason, whereas

Charrière's novels suggest that virtue, like happiness and reason, may not be viable, or at least may need redefining as it applies to women. With Charrière, female destiny is sometimes tragic, sometimes uneasy, and sometimes just uncertain—precisely because, as Starobinski suggests, there seems to be no one capable of imposing energetic action on a hushed and terrible world.[12]

CHAPTER 6

ECONOMIES

Marie Jeanne Riccoboni and
Isabelle de Charrière

Eighteenth-century fiction offers plenty of seductions of adolescent girls by insouciant young men and countless variations on the theme of result-ing pregnancy. I propose now to consider in more detail the conse-quences of seduction in a novel by Riccoboni and in one by Charrière. Neither is really "about" seduction: the episodes that I shall analyze are subsidiary to the primary plot and have no villains. In each of these novels, the hero's fitful dalliance makes him a father, and his very fornica-tion becomes the occasion for a display of integrity. In fact, the main stories turn chiefly on requited love and the possibility of marriage. But the seduction scenes are crucial to plot resolution, as are the relations of the secondary (seduced) female characters with the chaste principals. A comparison of the two works will illuminate, I think, a certain continuity of concerns among eighteenth-century women writers as well as the vari-ety of their novelistic practices.

Lettres de Milady Juliette Catesby à Milady Henriette Campley, son amie (hereafter *Juliette Catesby*) appeared in Paris in 1759; *Lettres neuchâteloises* was printed in Switzerland and published in Amsterdam in 1784. De-spite their separation by almost a quarter of a century and by differences of nation, culture, and class, seducers in both novels ultimately behave according to the dictates of honor, and each story has a happy ending. But in Riccoboni's fictional universe, where most of the characters are quite rich, economic realities emerge in sweeping, general strokes, while a more precise thematics of social and financial status and of its relation to marriageability and survival pervades the novels of Charrière.

I am interested here in examining the different ways in which sex, text, and economic and marital exchange come together to demonstrate the relativity of honorable arrangements and of endings based on marriage. By considering how minor episodes and characters may clarify the ethos of fiction, I also wish to suggest how misleading it is to speak of a monolithic "female destiny" in the eighteenth-century novel.

Juliette Catesby is set in England; it is Juliette's account in letters to her confidante of her relations with Lord d'Ossery. Once engaged to the young widow Juliette, d'Ossery unaccountably abandons her for Jenny Montfort. When Jenny dies about a year later, he resumes his courtship of a now perplexed and disgruntled Juliette, who, in order to avoid his attentions, flees from London to the country house of a friend at Winchester. Eventually, he writes her a long letter explaining why he married the less comely Jenny: after drinking too much during dinner at the home of Jenny's brother, he seduced her; she became pregnant, gave birth, and died of consumption a few months later. Now Juliette relents, and the two wed. Jenny Montfort never speaks directly, and d'Ossery himself speaks only through Juliette's letters to her confidante: his story appears in quotation marks, transcribed by Juliette.

Of all of Riccoboni's widely acclaimed novels, *Juliette Catesby* was the most popular: there were at least half a dozen editions in the first year alone.[1] Contemporary reviewers were enthusiastic and especially noticed the pivotal role of d'Ossery's letter to Juliette. The *Correspondance littéraire* of April 1759 discreetly avoids explicit reference to seduction or pregnancy, but admires the artfulness of the letter: "Cette aventure, qui fait tout le fond du roman, était bien difficile à conter; et c'est le chef-d'oeuvre de madame Riccoboni" ["This adventure, which constitutes the entire background of the novel, was very difficult to relate, and it is Madame Riccoboni's chef d'oeuvre"] (part 1, 2: 402).[2]

Like Riccoboni's novel, Charrière's is, in part at least, about the separate educations of young men and women. We recall that Charrière focuses on Henri Meyer, a bourgeois German working in Neuchâtel, and

Marianne de la Prise, a resident of the town. Shortly before meeting Marianne, Henri Meyer has a brief affair with a tailor's assistant, Julianne C., who becomes pregnant. When Marianne learns of Julianne's plight, she intervenes to help work out a suitable arrangement, which is to send Julianne for her confinement to Henri's uncle in Germany. This unlikely gesture on the part of a "proper" young lady becomes part of her education in the broad sense of the term.

Charrière was brought to task for the episode's audacity, just as the review in *L'année littéraire* had faulted Beccary's *Mémoires de Fanny Spingler* for a similar episode: after learning that her fiancé has seduced a young woman named Claire, Fanny intervenes on behalf of her rival: "Les développements sur cette matière sont trop embarrassants, de la part d'une jeune fille bien élevée, et je crains bien que la pudeur de Fanny n'ait beaucoup à souffrir dans cette explication" ["Expanding on this subject is too awkward for a well-brought-up girl, and I fear that Fanny's modesty will greatly suffer in the discussion"] (2: 67 [1781]). As far as the critics were concerned, nice girls of fiction didn't get involved in the affairs of unwed mothers. Charrière's sensitive rendering of the theme, which becomes a far more integral part of the plot than in *Mémoires de Fanny Spingler,* is an aspect of her originality.

In both Riccoboni and Charrière, the hero's dalliance with a secondary character and his subsequently honorable conduct toward her galvanize the affections he feels for another woman. But at the same time, despite the exemplary postcoital behavior of the men, the victims are sacrificed to economic urgency and textual economics. That is to say, the primary love interest requires that the unhappy rival be disposed of. So in Charrière's novel the tailor's assistant has her confinement subsidized, on condition that she give up the child and disappear from the scene; and in Riccoboni's, although the young lady's honor is salvaged through marriage and her daughter legitimized, she herself must die.

These plot elements disclose different fictional systems and suggest the determining mental and social habits of bourgeois and aristocratic societies. They are, moreover, crucial for any assessment of female roles in fiction by women: the love (-and-marriage) experience of the primary female characters in these novels may in fact be made possible, on the one hand, by an original writing of male sexuality (to which I shall return shortly), and, on the other, by the pitting of one woman's fate against another's. Women characters are defined not only with respect to men, but also in their relations with each other, and one woman's bliss is another's devastation.

Meaning no harm, d'Ossery offhandedly seduces a sweet young noblewoman of average face and middling fortune, of whom the worst one can say is that she is imprudent. Henri Meyer, on the other hand, dallies with a sexually alert working woman. Her letters convey a luminous picture of her sense of self, her lack of formal education (words are misused and grammar is faulty), and her strategies for survival in a cruel world with a rigid class system. When she gingerly details her sexual experience and lays claim to a messy sort of honor, she simultaneously reveals the agility of her reasoning and the flexible boundaries of her moral world. Writing to her aunt in the provincial dialect for which the author was both applauded and criticized, Julianne speculates about whether someone has told Henri Meyer that she is not "une honnête fille" ["an honorable girl"]: "et pourtant" ["and yet"], she muses:

> Si ce n'était ce vilain maître horloger chez qui j'ai servi, et qui était pourtant un homme marié, il n'y aurait pas eu une plus brave fille que moi dans le Val-de-Rus: car pour avoir quelquefois badiné avec les garçons à la veillée ou pendant les foins, les autres filles en faisaient autant que moi; et je ne sais pas si un Monsieur penserait pour ça qu'on n'aurait pas été une brave fille. (71)

> [If it weren't for that nasty master clockmaker I worked for, and who was even a married man, there wouldn't have been a better girl in the Val-de-Rus: as for fooling around with the boys a little in the evenings or at straw-gathering time, the other girls did it just as much as I did; and I don't think that would be enough to make a gentleman think that a girl hadn't been good.]

The beguiling mesh of frankness and footwork that Julianne marshals to attenuate the meaning of integrity and the author's almost palpable sympathy for her working-class character are responsible in no small measure for the book's charm. Julianne's conception of honor is enlarged by practical notions about the nastiness of certain men in authority and the behavior of her peers: she counts a lapse of virtue for little if everyone else is doing it, too.

The turn Henri Meyer puts on her experience is also, in its own way, devious. "Une jeune ouvrière, que je n'ai pas séduite, dit être grosse" ["A young working woman, whom I did not seduce, claims to be pregnant"] (82), he writes to his uncle: what he presumably means by not having seduced her is that he was not her first (thus implying that she offered no resistance); he takes no account of his educational advantages, higher social rank, and greater wealth.

In any event, Henri is less a cad than d'Ossery, whose justifications for abusing a naïve adolescent are wine and circumstance. But in both novels the hero proves less a scoundrel than he might. For one thing, neither hesitates to own up to his paternity, although d'Ossery and Jenny have made love just once, and Henri and Julianne C. only twice. And d'Ossery, of course, goes so far as to marry the young woman. Moreover, both men are made to seem inexperienced virgins before the incident and afterward adopt a scrupulous chastity. Since Henri Meyer and d'Ossery are less rakish than other men, we are prepared to read their misdeeds more indulgently. Meyer is so shaken by his own act that he writes, "Je pleure; je suis inquiet: une nouvelle époque de ma vie a commencé" ["I weep; I worry: a new era of my life has begun"] (58).

In a reversal of convention, the female virginity or chastity normally emphasized as a moral and social value in the heroines of sentimental fiction is here taken for granted, while the virginity of the male protagonists which will eventually make possible their transcendence becomes the object of discreet textual insistence. D'Ossery insinuates his virginity when he notes that before meeting Juliette, "ma sagesse paraissait ridicule" ["my good conduct appeared ridiculous"] (140). He alludes later to his unwitting violation with Jenny Montfort of laws that he had always held sacred. After his unwanted wedding, he apparently never, as he puts it, fulfilled all of his conjugal duties. Henri Meyer is likewise inexperienced, reminding his confidant that before Julianne, women were strangers to him.

The men's claim to inexperience is a significant token in the textual systems of exchange: because the heroes are made to appear sexually innocent, the heroine and the readers can accept the elimination of the rival woman, thus expediting resolution of plot. Once d'Ossery has revealed both the sordid details of his "story" and his redeeming self-sacrifice, Juliette sheds a tear or two for poor dead Jenny and marries the contrite survivor. The ending of *Lettres neuchâteloises* is less conclusive, as is typical in Charrière's novels, but signs point to happiness for Henri and Marianne.

For the pregnant young women, however, the perspective differs substantially: the sins of the men are visited on their sexual partners without regard to their degree of guilt or guile. For Julianne, a financial arrangement suffices. This is a novel that goes into the circumstances of Marianne's father's modest pension and the monetary details of Henri Meyer's employment and of his arrangements with his uncle. The uncle is paying thirty louis for Henri's board and a half-louis each month for laundry and is giving him a quarterly allowance of ten louis in pocket money, in addition to paying for his lessons and clothing during his first year in Neuchâtel. We learn later that after his first visit to Julianne's room, Henri gives her two louis to buy wood. The vocabulary of financial transactions especially pervades the section dealing with the discovery and disposition of Julianne's condition: "Je donnai ma bourse" ["I gave over my purse"] (81), writes Henri Meyer at the end of the long letter to his confidant recounting how he learned of the pregnancy. And in the following letter, addressed to his uncle, he specifies, "j'ai de quoi subvenir en ce moment à ses besoins" ["I have enough to provide for her needs at this point"] (82). The uncle's response—"Faites partir la fille . . . j'en paierai les frais" ["Send the girl . . . I'll pay her expenses"] (82)—is accompanied by a bill of exchange for fifty louis. Henri Meyer rapidly writes his compliance: "La fille est partie" ["The girl has left"] (83). The damage control around Henri's lapse and the intrusive child is frighteningly skillful: when Julianne goes off to Germany to bear the child,

Henri's conscience is soothed, the claim on his wallet is reduced, and Marianne is unburdened. And Julianne, it seems, is comfortably provided for.

So in a novel where fiscal concerns appear nearly as crucial as affective motives, Henri Meyer hands over his purse. D'Ossery, caught in a similar plot in a differently ordered novelistic world, tenders his hand. He considers only briefly the possibility of paying Jenny Montfort off:

> Je formai mille projets; ma raison les détruisait à mesure qu'ils s'offraient à mon imagination; je voulais aller trouver Montfort, lui apprendre mon malheur, abandonner à sa soeur la moitié de mon bien, tout même. . . . Mais de quel front proposer à mon ami une réparation qu'en pareil cas je n'aurais point acceptée! Après l'avoir offensé, devais-je l'insulter? risquer de devenir l'assassin d'un homme dont j'avais déshonoré la soeur? (152–53)

> [I thought of a hundred schemes; my reasoning mind destroyed them as fast as I thought them up; I thought of going to see Montfort, of telling him of his misfortune, of surrendering to his sister half of my wealth, even all of it. . . . But what presumption to offer my friend amends which in a similar circumstance I myself would not have accepted! After having offended him, was I to insult him and risk causing the death of a man whose sister I had dishonored?]

The final rhetorical question reinforces the concern with honor that is central to a nobleman's behavior and a noblewoman's requirements. The very idea of reparation in the sense of compensation or indemnity is rejected as soon as it arises: it is not through a pecuniary but a connubial settlement that d'Ossery can compensate the genteelly undowered Jenny.

While in Charrière's novel the circulating medium is money, in Riccoboni's it is matrimony. D'Ossery and Jenny wed and she gives birth to a baby girl, whom he names for Juliette. But Jenny soon dies of illness exacerbated by a broken heart, for d'Ossery, with uncalculated cruelty, neglects his rueful young wife to pine for Juliette Catesby. Jenny is a figure of unmitigated pathos, her life narrowly circumscribed by her schooling, seduction, wedding, and confinement. She is not the only secondary female character whom Riccoboni eliminates so that an irreproachable husband can marry someone else: there is also the first wife of Charles Arundel in *Histoire de Miss Jenny* and the first Madame de Montalais in *Lettres de Sancerre*. But Jenny is the earliest and most poignant of these devoted wives of frail health and middling beauty who conveniently die.

While Julianne's future, like her past, is a little murky, Jenny Montfort's fate is as unambiguous as her fault. It neatly illustrates the intertwining of marriage and death, generation and destruction, the indispensable items of currency in Riccoboni's universe—as, indeed, in most of the period's fiction. When in the end destiny conspires richly to reward d'Ossery and Juliette Catesby, it does so precisely through a series of fortuitous premature deaths—those of Juliette's older brother and d'Ossery's two older brothers, and of course that of Jenny Montfort herself. These deaths make possible the marriage of the protagonists, simultaneously conferring on them independence, wealth, and rank. Riccoboni is said by Sylvain Menant to have described "le meilleur des mondes" ["the best of worlds"] in a novel whose end is "providential" (Desjonquères ed., preface ix–x). Yet that ending depends on a sacrificial lamb whose undoing and demise are essential to the disconcertingly happy outcome.

Let us turn again to that crucial fall from grace, both metaphorical and literal. As d'Ossery describes the episode for Juliette, Jenny has been home from boarding school only one day, her mother is absent, and her brother, his friends, and her governess are all inebriated. Jenny and d'Ossery, each trying to escape the dining-table noise, inadvertently end up in the same room. Jenny accidentally knocks over a small table holding the only candle, and they laughingly stumble around in the dark:

> Malheureusement elle s'embarrassa dans la table qu'elle avait renversée et tomba rudement. Sa chute entraîna la mienne; bientôt de grands éclats de rire me prouvèrent qu'elle ne s'était point blessée. L'excès de son enjouement me fit une impression extraordinaire; il m'enhardit: l'égarement de ma raison passa jusqu'à mon coeur. (149)

[Unfortunately, she tripped over the table that she had overturned and she took a good fall, pulling me down with her. Soon great bursts of laughter proved that she wasn't hurt. Her extraordinary playfulness excited and emboldened me: the disorder in my head went to my heart.]

A drunken d'Ossery takes advantage of the confusion and Jenny's naïveté to deflower her: "Un mouvement impétueux m'emporta; j'osai tout, j'abusai cruellement du désordre et de la simplicité d'une jeune imprudente, dont l'innocence causa la défaite" ["Impulse got the best of me; I risked everything, I took cruel advantage of the confusion and simplicity of an imprudent girl, whose innocence was her undoing"] (149–50). Jenny tumbles amid childish laughter, but as she rises with a muddled sense of her undoing, her laughter turns to tears: "Miss Jenny revenue à elle-même, remplissait l'air de ses cris, gémissait, fondait en larmes" ["When she regained her senses, Miss Jenny filled the air with her cries and moans and dissolved into tears"] (150). The fall becomes a wedge between two periods of her life. In Riccoboni's universe of economic and rhetorical excesses, which pits chastity against confusion, so serious a "fall" implies death.

In Charrière the theme of falling and dropping (*tomber/laisser tomber*) is even more pronounced and pervasive; but events and tropes are scaled down, and consequences are more psychological than physical or moral. The first instance occurs at the start of the story, where Julianne relates to her aunt how she dropped the dress she was sent to deliver to Marianne de la Prise:

Comme je descendais en bas le Neubourg, il y avait beaucoup d'écombres, et il passait aussi un Monsieur qui avait l'air bien genti, qui avait un joli habit. J'avais avec la robe encore un paquet sous mon bras, et en me retournant j'ai tout ça laissé tomber, et je suis aussi tombée; il avait plu et le chemin était glissant: je ne me suis rien faite de mal, mais la robe a été un petit peu salie . . . Mais j'eus encore de la chance: car le Monsieur, quand il m'eut aidé à ramasser toutes les briques, voulut venir avec moi pour dire à mes maîtresses que ce n'était pas ma faute. (47)

[As I was going through the lower town, there was a lot of rubbish, and a gentleman who looked very nice in a handsome suit was passing by, too. I had another package under my arm along with the dress, and as I turned I dropped everything and fell down with it. It had rained and the road was slippery; I didn't get hurt, but the dress got a little dirty . . . But still I was lucky, because the gentleman, when he had helped me to pick it all up, decided to come along to tell my mistresses that it wasn't my fault.]

The nice gentleman in the handsome suit who turns her head and loosens her grip is, of course, Henri Meyer, newly arrived in Neuchâtel. He thus at once symbolically rescues from the gutter the new dress of a young woman with whom he will soon fall in love, and excuses Julianne's "faute," which may be read as a simple slip of the foot and hand or, in its stronger sense, as an anticipation of her later "tumble" with Henri Meyer himself.

Just as he is the unintentional cause of Julianne's dropping the dress and falling, he will make Marianne herself behave clumsily the first time he sees her: recognizing the dress she wears at a recital, he stares so hard that she drops her music. Lacking this time the presence of mind that he had when he picked up the dress, he is paralyzed by the spectacle of the fallen scores and merely gawks. A few weeks later, Henri and Marianne take a walk in the snow and ice and come across Julianne, besieged by snowball-throwing boys. Once again, he intervenes kindheartedly on her behalf, explaining: "elle était dans un véritable danger; elle aurait pu tomber contre une borne, contre le coin d'une maison" ["she was really in danger; she might have fallen against a corner-post, against the corner of a house"] (73). Things fall (apart) here, but falls are not fatalities: people do not die much in Charrière's novels.

The schematic differences that I have attempted to identify in the stories of Jenny Montfort and Julianne C. reflect two different societies. Charrière's is Swiss provincial, Calvinist, and predominantly middle-class; Riccoboni's, Catholic and aristocratic, set in an England the author had never seen, an England of pure convention. In spite of the irregularity of Riccoboni's own birth and marital situation, in spite of the marginality of her original profession and her apparent disinterest in religious questions, her fiction espouses the values and captures the tone of the French Catholic aristocracy. In her book, the wages of sin is death. In Charrière's, Julianne's is banishment and, literally, wages. In both cases, of course, the only grave sin at issue is woman's fall from virtue.

The various falls and near-falls in these novels[3] ring even more allegorically when one takes account of the class differences at stake. Jenny Montfort is victim not just of her brother's errors of judgment in exposing her to his carousing friends, and of d'Ossery's wantonness, but also of an entire social and educational system which Riccoboni in fact criticized in her personal letters. Jenny's misfortune results as much from social structures that empower her brother and an education that inadequately prepares her for life, as from the extinction of the candle that creates the obscurity (both extenuating circumstance and symbol) favorable to her fall. Indeed, although the accident occurs in her own home, she is, fresh from school, as much a stranger there as d'Ossery. After their inadvertent romp, she is implacably caught in a system based on absolutes, which admits no accommodation short of marriage, just as, in the rules of the fictional machine, no outcome short of death is proportionate to her dilemma and incidentally conducive to (another's) happy ending. Through the trauma to which she hardly gives knowing consent, she becomes a sort of martyr to society, unrewarded by any compensating spiritual fulfillment.[4]

Questions of honor, promises, death, and inheritance as they relate to marriagiability echo through a brief "peasant" episode in *Juliette Catesby*—an episode whose resolution throws into relief, by contrast, the very possibilities that are in some ways closed to the upper classes. Strolling with her maid one morning by the river, Juliette Catesby notices a young flower-seller named Sara.[5] Juliette engages her in conversation and learns that she is disheartened because her engagement has just been broken off. Since her fiancé came into a small inheritance on the death of a sister, his avaricious grandfather, a Winchester farmer, is demanding a larger dowry, and Sara's mother, insulted, refuses to negotiate. Juliette is able to set everything right in a way unavailable in her own aristocratic circles:

The peasant Sara tells her story to Juliette
Catesby and her maid. Unsigned. *Lettres de Milady Juliette
Catesby,* in *Oeuvres complètes de Madame Riccoboni,*
nouvelle édition, vol. 1 (Paris: Volland, 1786).

with 150 guineas, she dowers Sara and hosts the wedding, complete with fireworks and masked ball.

In the case of Charrière's Julianne, we have a poor but economically viable character in a bourgeois Calvinist community which, despite its strict moral code, foregrounds a language of transaction applicable to her situation. Isabelle de Charrière, although Dutch by birth, had lived in a village near Neuchâtel for twelve and a half years before the publication of the novel. In 1804 she would write that she had learned from reading the Dutch novel *Sara Burgerhart* how, "en peignant des lieux et des moeurs que l'on connaît bien, l'on donne à des personnages fictifs une réalité précieuse" ["by depicting places and customs one knows well, one can give fictional characters a priceless reality"] (6: 558). Her household and street scenes, rich in local color, anchor both characterization and intrigue, and the society she portrays is that of Neuchâtel, where pregnancy out of wedlock was punished with exile (the author herself protected a pregnant unmarried maid who declined to name the father). Charrière convincingly evokes the mentality of a Calvinist social and legal system, and, as Starobinski says, the mentality of a commercial town at a time when financial prestige overshadows nobility of birth (130).

It is as if this smallness of scale and mentality were reflected in the way events are minimized. Henri Meyer and Marianne de la Prise characteristically understate their situation, as when he says that there are things it would be ridiculous or even wrong to write about, or when she speaks of relating what she calls "un assemblage de si petites choses que je ne saurais comment te les raconter" ["a collection of such petty things that I wouldn't know how to tell you about them"] (64). Letters render the fragile immateriality of apparently insignificant things, the "trifles" whose effects, especially on women's lives, may be vastly disproportionate to their supposed importance.

By contrast, Juliette Catesby uses a more typical rhetoric of inflation: she nearly dies from disillusion, then becomes incoherent with happiness; d'Ossery nearly dies from guilt and then again from disappointment. Only once, at the end, does Juliette admit that her original heartbreak was incommensurate with Jenny Montfort's tragedy: "j'ai pleuré," she concedes, "et Lady d'Ossery est morte" ["I cried and Lady d'Ossery died"] (167).

Insofar as the unborn are concerned, the plot structure and the rhetoric of the two novels coincide. In Riccoboni, Jenny is the central enigma on which the story turns, and it is clarified for Juliette and the reader at the same time. In Charrière, where events are more muted, Henri's discovery of Julianne's pregnancy is the culminating event. The conception of a child is in each case a nasty surprise, the unfortunate sequel or result (*suite*) of what would otherwise be a relatively incidental narrative. "Je commençais à regarder mon aventure comme une faiblesse dont le souvenir pouvait se perdre, lorsque ses funestes suites me la rappelèrent avec force" ["I was beginning to regard my adventure as a moment of weakness which could be forgotten, when its fatal results brought it forcefully back to mind"] (151), writes d'Ossery. And Henri Meyer, to his confidant, before he knows that Julianne is pregnant: "C'est une longue histoire que je te raconterai peut-être quelque jour, si elle a des suites; ce qui, j'espère, n'arrivera pas" ["It's a long story which I may tell you one day, if it has a sequel, which I hope it won't"] (53). The "moment de misère, de honte et de malheur" ["moment of misery, shame, and misfortune"] (80), when it does happen, is like d'Ossery's "aventure fatale" (143). And in the end both offspring are definitively separated from their other, occulted "cause"—the natural mother.

While *Juliette Catesby* and *Lettres neuchâteloises* share common structures emphasizing love, sexuality, and circumstance, they are shaped by different codes of language, gesture, and custom. Riccoboni assembles exclamations, moral reflections, excoriations of men, coquettish meditations on love and society, short interpolated stories, and at least one major surprise, whereas Charrière's novel, more pictorial, takes its form from a subtle weave of occurrences and more or less chronic conditions—bad weather, high prices, frugal suppers—belonging to the realm of everyday life. The prose follows two different economies, one understated and the other emphatic, and these differences correspond to the economic and social milieus that propel the secondary female characters to paradigmatically different destinies.

Although the European novel had undoubtedly evolved in the quarter century separating the two works, the differences between them should not be understood as simply a matter of timing. Consider once again the case of Beccary's *Mémoires de Fanny Spingler* (1781), a grimmer novel than either of these, more or less contemporary with *Lettres neuchâteloises,* but far more bombastic. Here the heroine-narrator discovers that Dorblac (her adoptive brother, sometime fiancé, the continuing object of her affections, and a more cold-hearted seducer than Henri Meyer or d'Ossery) has impregnated Claire, his social inferior. Fanny gives her what help she can, and after Dorblac takes responsibility for the child, Fanny pardons him. The reader, however, is little inclined to indulgence, for Dorblac has consistently behaved odiously. Fanny's intention is to lavish love on his daughter (why are these illegitimate babies almost always daughters?), but she and Dorblac both die before she gets the chance. In a novel whose tragic ending is overdetermined from the start, Claire is expendable. The tainted woman doesn't need to be sacrificed, since no one will be happy anyway.

On the other hand, Juliette Catesby and Marianne de la Prise enjoy similar fates: a forgiving and slightly chastened Juliette Catesby marries d'Ossery, and Marianne de la Prise, having grown in stature, exonerates Henri Meyer and will perhaps marry him. Juliette and Marianne are among the earliest and most fortunate heroines of Riccoboni and Charrière. But in each case, as corrective to that macro-narrative of happiness, we read a micro-story of a young woman's misadventure, and the texts seem to remind us that if certain social (and narrative) conventions work to the advantage of some women, it may be at the cost of others.

CHAPTER 7

WEDDING NIGHTS

Isabelle de Montolieu

Typically, eighteenth-century sentimental fiction either begins with marriage—be it of love, convenience, or obligation—and traces the ordeals of conjugal life (for example, *Lettres de Madame du Montier, Mémoires de Madame la baronne de Batteville, Histoire de Cressy, Lettres de Mistriss Henley*); or else it takes as heroine the marriageable woman and plots the events leading up to marriage (*Lettres de Milady Juliette Catesby, Lettres de Sancerre*) or to its frustration (*Lettres d'une Péruvienne, Lettres écrites de Lausanne, Mémoires de Fanny Spingler*).[1] We are accustomed, then, on the one hand, to novels that bear the protagonists to the point where marital schemes are either realized or foiled and, on the other hand, to those that pick up on them subsequent to that moment.

Although the passage into womanhood functioned both as social signpost and as psychological turning-point, that precise pivot from "fille" to "femme," from "Mademoiselle" to "Madame," was, for the most part, shrouded in verbal and literary reticence: it seemed not to be describable in any fiction that was not licentious. How was a novelist—and a woman novelist—to talk about it?[2]

Throughout the century, representations of the wedding ceremony itself tend to be commonplace, but the night that follows repeatedly becomes the locus of a barely articulated spectrum of phantasms, as authors explore ways of representing conjugal duress without violating conventions of discretion and decency. The *nuit de noces* is a recurring, if generally understated, motif.

Consider, for example, Le Prince de Beaumont's *Mémoires de Madame la baronne de Batteville,* in which the heroine's reservations about the old baron chosen for her by her mother are insinuated in the briefest notation after the wedding ceremony: "L'étendue des devoirs que j'allais m'imposer m'effraya" ["The breadth of the duties I was about to take on frightened me"] (99). She is speaking in a general way about subscribing to a spectrum of conjugal obligations, but her words also suggest anxiety about sex with a man she doesn't want to marry.

La comtesse de Mortane, originally published in 1699 and frequently reprinted during the eighteenth century, was the first work of Catherine Durand Bédacier, who was to become known for her renditions of fairy tales. One early scene in this otherwise silly novel nicely exemplifies the reserve that typically cloaks the moment of nuptial and sexual awakening, while also making an unusually explicit statement about conjugal "horrors." The protagonist, forced to wed a moral monster, gingerly alludes to the abhorrence she felt for him:

> Je pâlis tout à coup à la fin de la cérémonie, et prenant le prétexte d'un corps qui me serrait trop, on se hâta de me faire monter en carrosse pour m'emmener. Je ne vous dirai point l'horrible douleur que je sentis lorsqu'on me déshabilla pour me mettre au lit; vous la devez comprendre pour peu que vous soyez capable de haine et d'amour. Oui, Madame, je la comprends, interrompit Madame de Marigue, tirons le rideau sur le reste de cette aventure, et continuez, s'il vous plaît, votre récit. (1: 36)

> [I paled at the end of the ceremony; using the pretext of a bodice that was too tight, they hurried me into a coach and took me away. I won't tell you about my horrible suffering when they undressed me to put me to bed; if you are at all capable of hatred and love, you surely must understand it. Yes, Madame, I understand, interrupted Madame de Marigue, let us draw the curtain on this part; please go on with your story.]

The paraleipsis ("Je ne vous dirai point. . .") rhetorically points to what novels conventionally seclude: the carnal passage to womanhood. At that moment, the "curtain" of narration, like the bed curtain, is expeditiously drawn (incidentally reversing the anticipatory effect of the undressing), and the narration is strategically suspended.[3] Madame de Mortane will "go on" with an account of the next day.

Other authors grapple differently with the wedding night and imagine varieties of intimate arrangements to tame the nuptial act or circumvent its necessity, displacing, palliating, or metaphorizing it, symbolically differentiating it from other rituals, and making of it a social commentary. Supposedly "translated from the Greek" (according to its subtitle), *Le triomphe de l'amitié* (1751) by Marianne Agnès Falques (or Fauques) is a novel of relentless adventure—it teems with startling coincidences, sea voyages, shipwrecks, disguises, kidnappings, and last-minute rescues—loosely structured around successive postponements or modifications of the great event. Agenor and Ismène, madly in love, pretend to be brother and sister so that the pirates who have kidnapped them will leave them together by day and by night until they can be really wed; Arsés and Cloé, meanwhile, married under duress after a shipwreck, prefer to remain chaste, but later get married in due form. The nuptial moment is thus gradually stripped of its fearfulness as well as its decisiveness.

In Françoise Albine Benoist's *Lettres du Colonel Talbert* (1767), the wedding night is also aborted. Her heroine, Hélène, a French version of Clarissa, is tricked, sequestered, and nearly ravished by Talbert, who is determined to make love without marrying her. Trying to escape, she falls from a ladder. Talbert agrees to marry her on her deathbed, so Hélène dies a wedded virgin.[4]

In *La destinée féminine dans le roman européen au dix-huitième siècle*, Pierre Fauchery writes: "si l'héroïne, comme on l'a vu, parvient quelquefois à prolonger *avant* le mariage le 'temps des faveurs,' en revanche il est à peu près sans exemple qu'elle obtienne un sursis à sa *consommation*" ["if the heroine, as we have seen, sometimes succeeds in prolonging the 'time of favors' before marriage, on the other hand it is almost unprecedented for her to obtain a postponement of its *consummation*"] (359). As a "very rare" exception to the rule, he cites Louisa in Henry Brooke's *The Fool of Quality,* who succeeds in getting her husband to sleep apart for the first few nights.

In fact, however, more than one novel by a French woman writer turns coercion into fantasy precisely by featuring a husband who consents to a platonic relationship, either provisional or permanent. The heroine of Le Prince de Beaumont's *La nouvelle Clarice* gets her husband to agree to postpone the consummation of their marriage for months, until she can secure the express approval of her mother and thereby feel "truly married" (1: 319). Adélaïde de Souza's *Adèle de Sénange* (1794), which I shall discuss in my next chapter, is another version of this theme: although Adèle's septuagenarian spouse exhibits a husband's jealousy, he claims none of the usual prerogatives. Similarly, Riccoboni's *Lettres d'Elisabeth-Sophie de Vallière* interpolates the story of Henriette d'Alby, a young bride who is terrified shortly after the marriage ceremony when an officious friend provides rather too much detail about what awaits her after dark. Moved by her distress, Monsieur de Monglas, the elderly groom, revises his anticipated delights and, to her relief, they spend the night talking (she begins to call him "father").[5]

Isabelle de Montolieu (1751–1832) likewise uses the figure of a husband who sacrifices his own pleasure to his young wife's preferences. Montolieu showed her originality in finding a way to write at length about sexual reluctance and nuptial repugnance while still respecting the convention of reticence. In *Caroline de Lichtfield* (1786), marriage functions as both beginning and closure, effectively defining an entire fiction in terms of the temporal space between the marriage ceremony and its consummation, that space normally "curtained off" from narrative.[6] This text marks off a mostly uncharted space, metaphorizing the anxieties, hopes, fantasies, and energies that furnish it. Montolieu's novel is an important part of a process of discreet disclosure, allowing the sharing and examination of the experience of women's institutionally sanctioned sexuality.

The novel begins at the Prussian court where the fifteen-year-old heroine learns from her ambitious father, the baron of Lichtfield, that he has promised her hand to the king's favorite. Initially delighted by the prospect of marriage, Caroline is understandably taken aback at the first sight of her intended, a man twice her age and with an altogether beastly countenance: stooping, bald, emaciated, jaundiced, and one-eyed, Count

Walstein also limps and has a horrific facial scar. Her father cajoles her into going through with the wedding, but the ceremony is barely over when she petitions for the right to live apart. Walstein, whose appearance belies his goodness, consents, and only after three years (during which Caroline falls in and out of love with his best friend, the dashing young Lindorf) is the couple reunited. Not only has her husband's merit by now been made clear, but he has also become unexpectedly dashing, thanks to diet, rest, regrowth of hair, and an artificial eye. The facial scar has even faded, and he has learned to stand up straight. After numerous misunderstandings, the marriage is consummated.

Caroline de Lichtfield was the first work of Isabelle Polier de Bottens, a resident of Lausanne who was born into an aristocratic Swiss family and married Benjamin Adolphe de Crousaz in 1769. He left her a widow at twenty-four. She became baroness of Montolieu by her second marriage a little over a decade later and began publishing not long after that. She survived her second husband, who died in 1800, by over thirty-two years. She was a friend of Gibbon and for years a correspondent of Félicité de Genlis, whom she had met when Genlis visited Lausanne in 1775 and took lodgings with her. Later, Montolieu sent her the manuscript of the novel for a critique.[7]

The novel adapts and substantially elaborates a seventy-page German story by Antoine Wall which appeared in 1783 in the periodical *Les bagatelles*.[8] Initially published anonymously, Caroline's adventures saw several editions in the first year, and others appeared regularly through the next quarter-century. Wrote André Chénier, twenty-four years old at its publication:

> C'est un de ces ouvrages charmants qui vous rendent la vertu si aimable et vous affermissent dans le voeu d'être homme de bien. Je me rappellerai toujours avec plaisir les émotions douces et délicieuses que m'ont fait éprouver mille détails pleins de vérité, de naïveté, de grâce, de délicatesse.[9]

> [It is one of those charming works that make virtue appealing and strengthen one's resolve to be a good man. I shall always remember

with pleasure the sweet and delicious emotions that I experienced on reading a thousand details full of truth, naïveté, grace, and delicacy.]

The novel was thought in some quarters to be the best since *La princesse de Clèves*.[10] Germaine de Staël in *Essai sur les fictions* names it along with a handful of choice works worthy of admiration for the delicate principles they propose for female conduct, in which women's very mistakes form a more "moral" and more "severe" picture than the spectacle of virtue itself.[11] Montolieu was to live nearly forty-six years after *Caroline de Lichtfield* and publish over a hundred additional volumes, including translations and adaptations of French, English, and especially German works;[12] but she never quite duplicated her initial success.

I read the plot as a version of *La Belle et la Bête:* it is difficult to imagine a novel corresponding more richly to Le Prince de Beaumont's 1757 classic rendition of the tale, which was intended as a lesson for girls. Montolieu reproduces the myth's essential outline and innumerable details, yet neither she nor any of her critics seems to have noticed the resemblances. We usually associate with *La Belle et la Bête* the moral that looks are not everything. But neither is wit. When Beauty comments that, although she finds Beast quite ugly, she believes him to be good, he replies with a play on the word *bête*:

> —Vous avez raison, dit le monstre; mais, outre que je suis laid, je n'ai point d'esprit: je sais bien que je ne suis qu'une bête. . . . j'ai le coeur bon, mais je suis un monstre.—Il y a bien des hommes qui sont plus monstres que vous, dit la Belle, et je vous aime mieux, avec votre figure, que ceux qui, avec la figure d'homme, cachent un coeur faux, corrompu, ingrat.—Si j'avais de l'esprit, reprit la Bête, je vous ferais un grand compliment pour vous remercier; mais tout ce que je puis vous dire, c'est que je vous suis bien obligé. (44)

> [—You're right, said the monster; but not only am I ugly, I have no wit: I know perfectly well that I am only a stupid beast. . . . I have a good heart, but I am a monster.—Many men are more monstrous than you, said Beauty, and I love you better, with the face you have, than those who, with a man's face, hide a heart that is false, corrupt,

and ungrateful.—If I had any wit, replied the Beast, I would make you a fine compliment by way of thanks; but all I can say is that I am much obliged.]

When Beauty's two wicked sisters eventually marry, one chooses a handsome man whose looks eclipse her own and whose vanity proves insufferable. The second weds a clever fellow who drives everyone crazy. Beauty assimilates these lessons and in the end opts for her beast. Because she learns to prefer goodness to both good looks and wit, she lives happily ever after.

The tale has been read by Bruno Bettelheim as a story about sexual anxiety, about the adolescent who must resolve oedipal ties and eventually learn to accept sex, symbolized in its apparent fearfulness by the countenance of the beast. Beauty must be persuaded to give a positive answer to Beast's nightly question as to whether she will have him. Bettelheim's generalization is complicated by a symbolic difference in detail which Jacques Barchillon points out (9) between the early version by Gabrielle de Villeneuve and the classic rendition by Le Prince de Beaumont: in the original tale, each evening after dinner, Beast implores: "La Belle, voulez-vous que je couche avec vous?" ["Beauty, do you want me to go to bed with you?"], but Le Prince de Beaumont attenuates the crudity of the question and shifts the emphasis to the institutional union: "La Belle," asks her Beast, "voulez-vous être ma femme?" ["do you want to be my wife?"]. *Caroline de Lichtfield* may be read as a third version, an attempt to arbitrate between those two formulations, between becoming a man's wife and going to bed with him.

"As the culminating event in most folktales and in life, marriage . . . displays the victory of patriarchal culture itself," writes Karen Rowe (251). A tale of the type of *La Belle et la Bête,* then, comments not only on the heroine's subordination to men and her assimilation of the virtues of "passivity" and "self-sacrifice" (239), but also on her "*imaginative* assent to the proposition that marriage is the best of all possible worlds" (251). But with its improbable social and psychological dimensions (not to mention the physiological ones), *Caroline de Lichtfield* subtly transforms the fairy-tale prototype. Montolieu uses what Rowe calls "the allure of romance" (237) to emphasize not passivity but female power and creativity. For if *Caroline de Lichtfield* resembles *La Belle et la Bête* in that both are stories of integration, the novel parts ways with the model by suggesting the creative force of female assertiveness and resourcefulness. What Rowe calls the "victory" (251) of the marriage narrative may then be seen as belonging not so much to patriarchal culture as to the heroine herself.

If, as Bettelheim notes, the rose that Beauty's father picks for her in Beast's garden represents loss of maidenhood (306), Caroline is symbolically associated early on with a rapid succession of images suggestive of a transition from virginity to sexual function. Her father's announcement of her engagement (he takes care not to describe the count's appearance) sends her to her piano, where she plays quadrilles and waltzes for half an hour.

> Il lui vint tout à coup à l'esprit, en les jouant, que le comte les répéterait avec elle, et qu'il serait assez doux d'avoir toujours un danseur à ses ordres. . . . Ce fut donc en formant un projet de danse continuelle dans son nouveau ménage, qu'elle courut au jardin, cueillir son bouquet pour la soirée; tout en le cueillant, elle vit voltiger autour des fleurs quelques beaux papillons, elle s'échauffa longtemps à les poursuivre, n'en prit pas un seul, et se consola en pensant que le comte serait peut-être plus leste qu'elle et saurait mieux les attraper: quand nous serons deux, dit-elle en sautant, il y a bien du malheur s'ils nous échappent. (1: 12–13)

> [It suddenly occurred to her while playing that the count would practice them with her, and that it would be very nice always to have a dancer at her disposal. . . . And so, while planning a marriage of continual dance, she ran to the garden to pick a bouquet for the evening; while she picked, she saw some lovely butterflies flitting about the flowers; she pursued them vigorously for some while, didn't catch a single one, and consoled herself with the thought that the count would perhaps be more nimble than she and better able to catch them: when there are two of us, she said, jumping up and down, we will have to be very unlucky for them to get away.]

Dance as a metaphor for marriage connotes physical convergence and rhythmic, aesthetic/erotic movement; picking flowers anticipates virginity lost. The butterfly episode allegorizes even more pointedly her sexuality, her innocence, and her desire for compensatory expertise. Back in her room, finally, she daydreams about the jewels and finery she will wear as ambassador's wife, the emblems of her accession to a new social status: "enfin le bonheur conjugal de Caroline, fondé sur la danse, les papillons et la parure, lui parut la chose du monde la plus assurée" ["in short, Caroline's conjugal happiness, founded on finery, butterflies, and jewels, appeared to her the most certain thing in the world"] (1: 13–14).

The aesthetic qualities of dance, butterflies, and dress as foundation for happiness are tied to the force of another word: "il est le *favori* du roi, lui avait dit son père, or ce mot de *favori* emportait beaucoup de choses dans l'idée de Caroline. . . . le *favori* d'un roi devait certainement être le phénix de [son espèce], et le plus beau, et le plus aimable des êtres" ["he is the king's *favorite*, her father had told her; now the word *favorite* entailed many things in Caroline's mind. . . . the king's *favorite* must surely be the phoenix of [his kind], and the handsomest and most amiable of creatures"] (1: 14). Her sexual élan—an aesthetic reaction to a new experience—will be challenged by the empty specificity of the courtier's language, for *favori* carries none of the guarantees of beauty with which she invests it. She discovers that the man whom she imagined chasing butterflies and dancing from dawn to dusk limps and has only a single eye in his livid face. Caroline emits a piercing scream and runs away. She will be obliged eventually to re-create a "favorite" in her own image.

The baron exhorts her to be reasonable, paternalistically pleading for an adjustment of passionate feelings to the claims of reason. But her first protestation of love is now made not to Walstein but to her father, and she implores him, just as Beauty does hers, to allow her to remain with him forever. As in the case of Beauty, this filial attachment will eventually account for her very willingness to give herself over into the hands of the beast. Beauty's father is literally threatened with death unless a daughter sacrifices herself in his place; Caroline's crafty parent claims that he will suffer political disgrace, the equivalent of death for a courtier, unless she consents to the marriage he has in mind:

Qu'est-ce que vous feriez, ma fille, si la vie de votre père était entre vos mains?—Votre vie! Je la sauverais aux dépens de la mienne! En pouvez-vous douter? . . .—Je n'en attendais pas moins de vous, ma chère enfant, et vous venez de décider de votre sort et du mien. Oui, mon existence, ma vie dépendent de vous seule; n'espérez pas que je survive un jour à ma disgrâce, et elle est assurée si votre union avec le comte de Walstein n'a pas lieu. (1: 20)

[What would you do, my daughter, if your father's life were in your hands?—Your life! I'd save it if it cost me my own! Can you doubt it? . . .—I expected no less from you, dear child, and you have just decided your fate and mine. Yes, my existence, my life depend on you alone; don't expect me to live a single day in disgrace, and my disgrace is certain if your wedding with Count Walstein doesn't take place.]

Caroline assigns literal value to the baron's hyperbolic evocations of death. The mythical force of her purity and the paradoxical generosity of her self-concern will "save" not only herself but her father and Walstein, too.

Caroline de Lichtfield seems, at the outset, to contain the familiar phallocentric topoi. But in counterpoint to the female sexual anxiety, which the novel metaphorically analyzes, there is a pervasive male fantasy, a topos dating back to the role of Agnès in Molière's *L'école des femmes,* of the young woman raised in ignorance of the world who makes the perfect wife. The ideal woman, according to this theory, is the blankest of pages on which the male can imprint and admire his own image. A woman's hesitancy in the face of sexual demands contrasts, then, with a man's fantasy of unlimited gratification, of the narcissistic privilege of making love to his own creation. Weaving logical formulations with images of penetration and gratitude, Walstein explains to Lindorf his "system" for finding a wife:

Vous connaissez mon système, c'était sur cette ignorance du monde et de l'amour qu'il était fondé. Je saurai bien, me disais-je, pénétrer dans ce jeune coeur, et me l'attacher, sinon par l'amour, du moins

par une amitié si vive, et une reconnaissance si tendre, qu'elles pour-
ront m'en tenir lieu. (2: 70)

[You know my system. It was founded on this ignorance of society
and of love. I'll surely be able, I said to myself, to penetrate this
young heart, and attach her to me, if not by love, at least by friendship so strong and gratitude so tender that they can take the place of
love.]

Caroline's father, moreover, has had her raised in isolation precisely
with a view to keeping her innocent, the better to guarantee both her filial
obedience and her desirability as a wife. But neither Walstein nor the
baron "reads" her correctly, and her willfulness astonishes them at the
ceremony's end, when she sends her written request for independence:
"Il y a de l'énergie dans ce caractère" ["There's energy in that character"]
(1: 32), the king marvels—transformative female energy that discredits
simple male "systems." At the novel's end Walstein recognizes the seductiveness of Caroline's maturity: "je crois qu'il n'y a rien de plus doux, et de
plus flatteur, que d'être le second objet de l'attachement d'une femme
délicate et sensible" ["I think there is nothing sweeter and more flattering
than to be the second love of a delicate and sensitive woman"] (3: 81–
82). Walstein's final credo revises a pattern of the novel of sensibility and
the fairy tale alike, for he challenges the mentality that exalts first love and
valorizes woman's virginal impressionability. The Pygmalion myth fails
here, since Caroline's allegiance to herself as value lends her the creative
power to change Walstein, fiction, and the world.

Another reversal in *Caroline de Lichtfield* may be described in terms of
narrative organization. The wedding that traditionally closes a fairy tale is
transferred, as I have indicated, to the novel's opening pages. It does not
end, but on the contrary begins, the heroine's dilemma. Immediately
after the wedding she leaves Walstein's house and reenters a sort of
gynaeceum characterized by creativity and aesthetic pursuits: Caroline
sings, paints, and has a pavilion built and dedicated to friendship. It is the
country estate where she was raised by the kindly but extravagant canoness of Rindaw, once in love with Caroline's father, now an elderly woman

addicted to novels. Fiction is the norm by which the canoness measures reality, so that she is determined, for example, to find Caroline a husband comparable to the most sublime heroes of romance. For the canoness has not been told about the marriage to Walstein (the king has decreed that it be secret, and the canoness is notoriously indiscreet). Her own competing "system" reveals a philosophy at once romantic and disabused:

> A ton âge on voulut aussi me marier sans me consulter, mais je m'aperçus à temps que mon futur louchait horriblement, et je n'en voulus plus entendre parler. . . . Mon grand système à moi, c'est qu'il faut s'aimer à la passion quand on se marie; il n'y a que cela qui puisse faire supporter les peines de cet état. (1: 43–44)

> [At your age, they wanted to marry me off, too, without asking my opinion, but I noticed in time that my fiancé was horribly cross-eyed, and I refused to have anything more to do with him. . . . My own system is that you must be passionately in love when you marry; that's the only thing that can make the burdens of marriage bearable.]

Caroline gradually forgets the nightmare of Walstein, as though it were only a distant dream. In the course of the summer she meets their new neighbor, Lindorf, twenty-five years old, an excellent horseman, gallant, and musical: precisely the *mari de roman* that the good canoness would wish for Caroline. Lindorf sings the high-voice part to Caroline's favorite song about the anxieties of a young shepherdess who both "fears and desires" love (1: 65).[13] He is abashed when he finally learns that Caroline is his best friend's wife, and at this point he sends her a portrait of a younger, handsomer Walstein and an account of how he himself had disfigured Walstein for protecting a young peasant named Louise whom Lindorf was trying to seduce. The count forgave him ("un ami tel que vous le serez toujours pour moi, mérite bien d'être acheté par la perte d'un oeil" ["a friend such as you will always be for me, is well worth the loss of an eye"] (1: 186) and they began planning Lindorf's marriage to Walstein's sister Matilde. By means of the highly conventional portrait and letter, Caroline comes to understand that her husband is at heart neither beastly nor monstrous. In *La Belle et la Bête,* the reason for the hero's enchantment is never clarified, but as Bettelheim points out, the hero in similar European tales is bewitched in punishment for the seduction of a helpless victim (306). Walstein's bestial appearance echoes such stories, except that the lust is Lindorf's.

Caroline's increasing affection for Walstein is partly a process of maturation as she grows sophisticated and resilient. As her imagination charts the intersections of reason, passion, beauty, and happiness, Walstein, although separated from her, seems to feel the effects. Midpoint, the reader learns that Walstein himself has been undergoing a metamorphosis precisely during the period when Caroline begins to "see" him differently. We now learn that he is a man of eloquence and wit, who speaks tastefully and amiably, without pretention or pedantry. And his appearance has gradually become harmonious with his discourse:

> Ses cheveux, que la fièvre avait fait tomber alors entièrement, étaient revenus en abondance, parfaitement bien plantés, et toujours arrangés avec soin; le temps et un peu d'embonpoint avaient presque effacé les traces de sa cicatrice, et lui donnaient un air de santé, de jeunesse, bien différent de ce teint jaune, de cette maigreur effrayante qu'il avait lors de son mariage; un oeil d'émail, fait avec tout l'art possible, remplaçait celui qu'il avait perdu, au point qu'on pouvait à peine s'apercevoir d'une légère différence; un peu d'attention sur lui-même lui avait fait aussi redresser sa taille; elle n'était plus remarquable que par une attitude aisée et négligée, bien préférable à la raideur; il boitait encore, il est vrai, mais on ne marche pas toujours, et il marchait peu: on peut donc imaginer qu'avec de très belles dents, et beaucoup d'expression dans la physionomie, le comte de Walstein, alors âgé de 32 ans, n'était pas un objet bien effrayant. (2: 78)

> [His hair, which had fallen out during his earlier fever, had grown back lush and was always carefully arranged; time and a little weight had almost erased the remains of his scar, and gave him a look of health and youth quite different from the yellowish skin and frightful emaciation of the time of his marriage; an artificial eye, very

artfully made, replaced the one he had lost, so that the difference could hardly be seen; he had learned to stand up straight, and he looked easy-going and relaxed, which is better than looking stiff; he still limped, it's true, but one doesn't walk all the time, and he walked little: you can imagine then, that with beautiful teeth and a lively facial expression, Count Walstein, then thirty-two years old, was not at all a frightful sight.]

Caroline herself is the indispensable observer of the changes, just as she is the judging listener of his conversation; she is the synthesizing audience without whom his eloquence and elegance, like the whole language of masculine taste, reason, and knowledge, would be pointless. Even from afar, in a sense she both recognizes and creates his real amiability, his fitness for being loved.

Their restoration to each other entails a symbolic physical recuperation. In *La Belle et la Bête,* Beast becomes sick almost unto death when after three months Beauty seems to have abandoned him. Caroline falls deathly ill at the emotion of an unexpected meeting with Walstein, whom she now loves. Poor Walstein thinks that her illness comes from her horror at seeing him again, but can't help reaching out to and for her during her delirium: "il passait à chaque instant ses mains tremblantes ou sur le sein ou sur la bouche de Caroline, pour s'assurer qu'elle respirait encore" ["he constantly ran his trembling hands over Caroline's breast or mouth, to make sure she was still breathing"] (2: 144). She retains a delicious threshold awareness of these anguished demonstrations, and her long convalescence exploits the ambiguities of physical intimacy in a hothouse atmosphere; her first experience of passion occurs, like her sexual anxieties, at the level of her unconscious.

When she has recovered, she remains under Walstein's roof. But still their cohabitation excludes consummation, a singularity of which Caroline is only dimly aware: "enfin, disait-elle, il ne tenait qu'à lui de rester, nous aurions encore un peu causé, un peu lu, un peu fait de musique; et demain à mon réveil, j'aurais eu le plaisir de le voir tout de suite. Ne pourrait-il pas dormir dans ma chambre comme dans la sienne?" ["after all, she would say, he could very well have remained, we could have chatted a bit longer, read a little, made some music; and when I awaken tomorrow, I could have had the pleasure of seeing him right away. Couldn't he sleep in my room as in his own?"] (3: 19). Although the passage humorously proclaims her unaltered ingenuousness, it also translates a subliminal readiness for sex in terms of her emotional and intellectual sureness. Caroline's evolution, then, is parallel to Beauty's, who also thrives on supper exchanges with Beast and grows lonely in his absence—lonely for conversation:

> Tous les soirs la Bête lui rendait visite, l'entretenait pendant le souper avec assez de bon sens, mais jamais avec ce qu'on appelle esprit dans le monde. Chaque jour, Belle découvrait de nouvelles bontés dans ce monstre; l'habitude de le voir l'avait accoutumée à sa laideur, et loin de craindre le moment de la visite, elle regardait souvent à sa montre pour voir s'il était bientôt neuf heures; car la Bête ne manquait jamais de venir à cette heure-là. (45)

> [Every evening the Beast would visit her, speaking rather sensibly to her during supper, but without what society calls wit. Each day, Beauty discovered more kindness in this monster; seeing him often had accustomed her to his ugliness, and far from fearing the hour of the visit, she would often look at her watch to see if it would soon be nine o'clock, for Beast never failed to come at that time.]

Doubts and timidity keep Caroline and Walstein at bay for a while. Their one hundred twenty pages of chaste cohabitation represent the symbolic nurturing of speech as preparation for greater intimacy. In contrast to the usual asymmetry, Walstein and Caroline learn to speak their love at the same time. It is, however, Caroline's initiative that brings about the dénouement: when she asserts her love unequivocally, the enchantment ends, just as Beast's is over when Beauty speaks her willingness to marry. Redeemed by the force of love and the power of words, Walstein has become almost his former handsome self: "Il est vrai qu'il ressemblait tous les jours plus à son portrait" ["It's true that he looked daily more like his portrait"] (3: 36).

Finally, after hundreds of pages of anticipation, the story comes to its sexual climax. It is nonetheless self-consciously relegated to the traditional realm of the unsayable:

> Le manuscrit ne dit point si la force de l'habitude le fit retirer dans un autre appartement, d'abord après le souper: on laisse au lecteur le soin de le deviner. Le lendemain matin, Caroline fit promettre au comte qu'ils reviendraient bientôt dans cette charmante terre, qu'elle aimerait toute sa vie, ajouta-t-elle, en baissant les yeux et la voix. (3: 56)

> [The manuscript doesn't say if force of habit made him retire to another apartment right after supper: we leave the reader to guess. The next morning, Caroline made the count promise that they would return soon to that charming spot, which she would love all her life, she added, lowering her voice and eyelids.]

This modest display indicates Caroline's satisfaction, although it "curtains off" its explicit expression.

As in *La comtesse de Mortane,* a chaste hiatus deposits the reader in "le lendemain." Caroline and Walstein set off for Dresden to see his sister Matilde, who is known to be pining for Lindorf. They stop en route at an inn but discover that its only two guest rooms are engaged by a young couple. The jovial innkeeper is nonetheless persuaded that everyone can be accommodated, if the earlier arrivals will only share a bedroom: "ils ne se quittent pas un instant de tout le jour: eh bien, ils ne se quitteront pas de la nuit, et malgré leur micmac de deux chambres, je crois qu'ils n'en seront pas fâchés" ["they're never apart for a minute during the day: so let them not be apart at night, and despite their nonsense about two rooms, I think they won't mind"] (3: 61). The couple turns out to be Matilde and Lindorf: he has transferred his passion from Caroline and they want only Walstein's permission to wed. The innkeeper's amusing characterization of "le micmac de deux chambres" cannot but recall Walstein and Caroline's long ballet now being repeated by their alter egos.

For in *Caroline de Lichtfield*, weaknesses of style and composition[14] are redeemed by force of plot, which comprises a series of simple, powerful actions in the Aristotelian sense: unifying psychic patterns to which every detail contributes. This plot, moreover, constantly reformulates itself in its component parts, as the same problems—sex, speech, reticence— work themselves out at different psychological and social levels. Lindorf's and Matilde's experience reiterates and modulates that of Caroline and Walstein, and Lindorf's unwitting rivalry with Walstein for the affections of Caroline is repeated in two other episodes: the contest for Louise between Lindorf and another young man, and Lindorf's competition for Matilde's hand with her other suitors. His psychological growth inflects Caroline's. Her dilemma is in turn made more acute by the lack of maternal guidance: Caroline's mother is long dead and the canoness is not a serious substitute; nor does either of the other female protagonists, Louise and Matilde, have a mother. This maternal absence, corresponding to the lack of mothers in the tales of the "animal-groom cycle," of which *La Belle et la Bête* is the best known (Bettelheim 284), focuses the reader on the heroine's inherent certainty about what her development requires.

Montolieu's originality has partly to do with her frames. She adopts the most popular fictional forms of the day: the "German" tale (enthusiasm for Germany ran high in late eighteenth-century France), the "gothic" novel or *roman noir* (the heyday of the macabre in French fiction occurred in the 1780s and 1790s), and the pastoral (which also continued in popularity throughout the 1780s). But she manipulates them to her own ends. The German setting of *Caroline de Lichtfield* provides an exotic locale for the eroticism of what is more or less a fairy tale. Caroline's pastoral paradise, the Rindaw garden, is not a banal metaphor for happy innocence (as bowers, birds, and flowers frequently are), but functions as liminal, self-created freedom, through which inner power is achieved. And, finally, the hero's disfiguration and deformation (standard fare in the *roman noir*) turn out to be reversible.

The narrative discourse that establishes these frames is punctuated by phrases like "le manuscrit ne dit point" and by expressions of equivocation such as "je ne sais," "peut-être," and "sans doute":

Cette morale peut paraître étrange dans la bouche d'un père; celui-ci sans doute avait des raisons pour être aussi coulant. (1: 11)

[This moral may appear strange in the mouth of a father: he must have had his reasons for being so accommodating.]

Peut-être aussi feignit-il de le croire; on ne sait trop sur quoi compter avec les courtisans, ils savent dérouter l'historien le plus exact. (1: 16–17)

[And maybe he was just pretending to believe it; one never knows what to think with courtiers, they can throw the most rigorous historian off the track.]

Such disclaimers of the possibility of historical accuracy are often imitated in comic fiction. Here they call attention to fictionality, with an undermining of textual authority corresponding to the undermining of other "systems"—social, sexual, nuptial. The ironic use of the sweet tears of sensibility[15] (the very tears that the canoness sheds over Walstein when she discovers how like a novel his story is) and the humorously casual allusions to ghoulish detail—"son grand oeil noir était assez beau; mais hélas; il n'en avait qu'un," ["his big dark eye was very handsome; but unfortunately he had only one"] (1: 15)—facilitate the construction of haunting patterns and liberate the narrative from expected meanings.

Montolieu's writing of the wedding night is made possible by the allegorization of hallowed and hackneyed codes, so that doubt is cast on public and social forms (weddings, history, the court), while the value of private experience is stressed. She explores an important aspect of the collective female unconscious—one that must have been all the more crucial in an era when women married early and unprepared and were often given no choice in the matter. She treats familiar themes—arranged marriages, masculine inconstancy, spouses' disparity, female timidity—and weaves them into a female fantasy of luxury, liberty, music, art, literature, and love, of fulfillment in every sensual and intellectual respect and satisfaction of every esthetic instinct. The esthetic (song, dance, dress, appearance) precedes the sexual. Caroline finds her voice and uses it to say "no" in a first moment of individuation. Her narcissism initially protects her undeveloped psyche; later, her esthetic self-concern humanizes the beast.

With pervasive humor, ironic enlistment of commonplace fictional themes, and self-conscious recognition of the distance between reality and romance, *Caroline de Lichtfield* is a fable of improbable social and psychological dimensions. While it explores, like traditional myth, the basic facts of gender differentiation and the politics of speech and image, it also resolves the conflicting social, sexual, and psychological tensions that are the very stuff of the female novel of the era, and transforms coercion and victimization into self-assertion and gratification. *Caroline de Lichtfield* is a fantasy of domesticated passion.

CHAPTER 8

GILDED CAGES

Adélaïde de Souza

From Sainte-Beuve, who implicitly likened her work to "quelque belle eau pure qui guérisse nos palais échauffés" ["lovely pure water that can restore our overheated palates"] (*Adèle de Sénange* i), to Laurent Versini, who qualified her novels as "delicate" and "pale" (*Laclos* 32; *Roman* 189), commentators on the writing of Adélaïde de Souza (1761–1836) have emphasized her exquisite seemliness. Although my own reading of Souza's work, and in particular of her first novel, is different from theirs, I propose to begin by summarizing the plot of *Adèle de Sénange ou Lettres de Lord Sydenham* (1794) in such a way that it fulfills the decorous expectations of these critics.

In a series of fifty-one letters to a friend whose responses we never see, a twenty-three-year-old traveling Englishman chronicles his love for a sixteen-year-old French girl. They meet by chance when her carriage overturns and he, Lord Sydenham, rushes to her aid. He learns that Adèle is sadly leaving the convent where she grew up. A few days later he happens upon her wedding and watches her descend the chapel steps followed by a handsome man and a gouty septuagenarian. Sydenham bristles at the thought of her being sacrificed in a marriage of convenience with a young man she probably hardly knows. When he meets them at the opera a few days later and discovers that the young man is in fact her brother, while the invalid is the husband, his indignation only increases, compounded this time by the spectacle of Adèle's cheerfulness.

But it turns out that old Sénange married Adèle to save her from being forced to take the veil and to give her financial security. Mollified, Sydenham seeks them out again and later accepts an invitation to spend the summer with them in Neuilly. He falls in love with his hostess, but also grows devoted to the husband she reveres. It develops, moreover, that Sénange long ago knew and loved Sydenham's grandmother in England. This history strengthens their ties, and Sénange declares that he will be a father to his guest. After Sénange's death in the fall, there is a skirmish between the lovers and Adèle's money-hungry mother, but the last letter announces their marriage. I shall return to details of plot which, although they in no way contradict this general outline, might nonetheless be read as subverting the novel's straightforwardness and suggesting a configuration of energies rather more seamy than seemly.

Adèle de Sénange was written by Adélaïde Marie Emilie Filleul, comtesse de Flahaut, who later became marquise de Souza by a second marriage to a Portuguese statesman and scholar. Published in London while France was in the grip of the Terror, the novel shows no explicit trace of the cataclysmic events of the preceding few years that sent her first husband to the guillotine and forced her and her young son into exile.[1] In tone and plot it seems to exemplify an earlier period; indeed one critic, writing in 1800, located its success partly in its failure of literary timeliness:

> Il parut dans le temps où nous étions inondés de ces sombres productions des romanciers anglais, qui croient plaire avec des spectres et des horreurs, et comme il n'a rien d'un si lugubre appareil, comme tous les ressorts en sont simples, il reposa agréablement de ces compositions tristes et convulsives. (Legouvé 46–47)

> [It appeared at a time when we were inundated with those somber productions of English novelists who think to please with ghosts and horrors, and since it is not at all so lugubrious, since all its means are so simple, it was a pleasant respite from those sad and convulsive compositions.]

This is an epistolary novel of sensibility, then, and one of many inspired by *Julie ou la nouvelle Héloïse,* where the relations of the three protagonists center on love, arranged marriage, incest, and adultery. In Souza's version, the older husband and the young lovers are as essentially virtuous as are Rousseau's, but whereas the tormented Julie dies in the end, the trials of Souza's lovers have a shorter term and they are united after the death of the husband.

Her next novel, *Emilie et Alphonse* (1799), written in letter form, is more pessimistic, the story of a young woman who enters into an ill-starred *mariage de raison* in order to satisfy her dying mother. The novels that followed during the next few years, although in journal form, more closely resemble *Adèle de Sénange*. Both *Charles et Marie* (1801) and *Eugène de Rothelin* (1808) tell the story of a young man's love for a spirited young woman who initially seems unavailable. Souza's novels of the first decade of the nineteenth century reproduce not only the essential themes of *Adèle de Sénange,* but also its polish and allure, and they were comparably successful.[2]

During the last years of the Ancien Régime, Adélaïde de Souza (then Madame de Flahaut) presided over a salon in the Louvre that played an important role in politics and in the dissemination of ideas; her lovers at this time included Talleyrand and Gouverneur Morris. For Marie Joseph Chénier, her novels seem to suggest the luster and breeding of the successful *salonnière:* they offer "un style orné avec mesure, la correction d'un bon livre et l'aisance d'une conversation fleurie" ["a style embellished with moderation, the propriety of a good book, and the ease of elegant conversation"] (214). From Sainte-Beuve's vantage point, *Adèle de Sénange* recalls the wholesome fiction of a bygone era, and he is moved by the stunning simplicity of plot, the sober sentimentality of tone, the laudable decorum:

> Une jeune fille qui sort pour la première fois du couvent où elle à passé toute son enfance, un beau lord élégant et sentimental, comme il s'en trouvait vers 1780 à Paris, qui la rencontre dans un léger embarras et lui apparaît d'abord comme un sauveur, un très vieux mari, bon, sensible, paternel, jamais ridicule, qui n'épouse la jeune fille que pour l'affranchir d'une mère égoïste et leur assurer fortune et avenir; . . . un babil innocent, varié, railleur ou tendre, traversé

d' éclairs passionnés; . . . la plus difficile des situations honnêtes menée à fin . . . avec une aisance qui ne penche jamais vers l'abandon, avec une noblesse de ton qui ne force jamais la nature, avec une mesure indulgente pour tout ce qui n'est pas indélicat; tels sont les mérites principaux d'un livre où pas un mot ne rompt l'harmonie. (*Adèle de Sénange* ii–iii)

[A girl taking leave of the convent where she has spent her childhood; a handsome, elegant, and sentimental lord, like those to be found in Paris around 1780, who meets her when she is in some difficulty and first seems to her a savior; a very old husband, good, sensitive, paternal, never ridiculous, who marries the girl only to free her from an egotistical mother and to secure her fortune and her future; . . . innocent prattle, sometimes bantering, sometimes tender, punctuated with passionate outbursts; . . . the most difficult of decent situations carried to its conclusion . . . with an ease of manner that is never undisciplined, a nobility of tone that never does violence to nature, and with moderate indulgence for everything that is not indelicate: such are the principal merits of a book in which not a single word disrupts the harmony.]

Elsewhere in the same essay Sainte-Beuve extols the freshness, calm, limpidity, and restfulness of Souza's work. Jean Larnac strikes a similar note, paraphrasing Chénier:

Mme de Souza, elle aussi, s'était formée à l'école des moralistes du siècle passé. Ses romans révèlent une charmante finesse d'esprit. En vain y eût-on cherché une profonde étude du coeur humain. Mais leur style correct et orné avec mesure rappelait les conversations fleuries du régime disparu. Mme de Souza était un fin pastelliste à la manière de Mme Vigée-Lebrun. Elle continuait cette lignée d'esprits charmants que le dix-huitième siècle avait produits en abondance. (169–70)

[Madame de Souza, too, was trained in the school of the moralists of the previous century. Her novels reveal a charming delicacy of mind. One would look to them in vain for a profound study of the human heart. But their style, proper and embellished with moderation, recalled the elegant conversations of the bygone regime. Madame de Souza was a delicate pastel painter in the manner of Madame Vigée-Lebrun. She carried on the line of charming minds that the eighteenth century had produced in abundance.][3]

Mooij likewise remarks that the novel awakens "les couleurs et les parfums de cette époque" ["the colors and perfumes of that era"] (34). For Michel Mercier, writing in 1976, *Adèle de Sénange* is notable because "tout y concourt à l'apologie du mariage dans un ordre social consacré" ["everything contributes to an apology for marriage in an established social order"] (172). The emphasis of Souza's critics is on surface, refinement, restraint, and moderation: in the best tradition of French moralists, Souza writes stylishly and keeps within prescribed fictional and social bounds, overstepping no limits and encouraging nostalgia for a congenial past.[4]

Adèle de Sénange, which reminds us of the author's convent education in Paris and adolescent marriage to the much older comte de Flahaut, reworks the standard marriage plot. This particular version is doubtless notable, as Sainte-Beuve suggests, for the poetry of everyday love. Indeed, at some level it answers Souza's ambitions which are expressed in a foreword:

> Cet ouvrage n'a point pour objet de peindre des caractères extraordinaires: mon ambition ne s'est pas élevée jusqu'à prétendre étonner par des situations nouvelles. J'ai voulu seulement montrer, dans la vie, ce qu'on n'y regarde pas, et décrire ces mouvements ordinaires du coeur qui composent l'histoire de chaque jour. . . . J'ai pensé que l'on pouvait se rapprocher assez de la nature et inspirer encore de l'intérêt, en se bornant à tracer ces détails fugitifs qui occupent l'espace entre les événements de la vie. (1)

> [This work does not have as its object to portray extraordinary personalities: I am not so ambitious as to try to create surprise with new situations. I have tried only to show what one doesn't look at in

life, and to describe the ordinary movements of the heart that make up the story of each day. . . . I thought that one could stay close to nature and yet inspire interest, just by outlining the fleeting details that occupy the space between life's events.]

Her narrative strategies include the repudiation of novelty and, like those of Charrière, the effort to characterize the ordinary and the fleeting. Souza also expresses the desire to show what is not normally seen, to throw into relief those details that furnish "the space between life's events."

But what resides in the space between the major events of liberation from the convent, marriage, widowhood, and remarriage seems to me precisely the female element that critics have failed to "look at" ("ce qu'on n'y regarde pas") in the plot. This is a novel emanating from a woman's consciousness where violations of social and moral prohibitions are metaphorically expressed in delicately resonant language that itself violates no codes. Potentially disruptive energies that threaten society's basic organization (and that traditionally nourish the novel) here seem linguistically nullified. A close reading suggests that the very language of sensibility admired by Chénier, Sainte-Beuve, and Larnac is also a discourse about incest, adultery, patricide, and mariticide—interdictions that are at one and the same time endorsed and violated with impunity. In fact, the novel's "charm" is ultimately the sign of flirtation with the illicit.

For *Adèle de Sénange* may be read alternatively as the story of a genial but amoral and unpredictable young woman. After his first encounter with Adèle, Sydenham voices the same Pygmalion fantasy as Walstein in *Caroline de Lichtfield:* that of shaping to his own ends a young woman raised in ignorance of the ways of the world:

Certes, si j'eusse pu deviner qu'il existait parmi nous une jeune fille soustraite au monde depuis sa naissance, unissant à l'éducation la plus soignée l'ignorance et la franchise d'une sauvage, avec quel empressement je l'eusse recherchée! . . . Dans sa simplicité, peut-être aurait-elle cru que mes défauts appartenaient à tous les hommes; tandis que son jeune coeur n'aurait attribué qu'à moi seul les biens dont elle jouissait. (9–10)

[Certainly, if I could have guessed that there existed among us a girl separated from society from birth, joining the finest education to the ignorance and candor of a savage, with what eagerness I would have sought her out! . . . In her simplicity perhaps she would have thought that my faults were those of all men, while her young heart would have been grateful to me alone for the good things she enjoyed.]

But Souza's heroine is no more susceptible to being imprinted in a man's image than was Montolieu's, and Sydenham soon realizes that she is not reducible to ordinary moral categories: "elle fait simplement le bien, franchement le mal, et ne s'étonne ni d'avoir raison ni d'avoir tort" ["she does good deeds with simplicity, bad deeds openly, and is surprised neither when she is right nor when she is wrong"] (60). She vexes her conventional elderly husband and exasperates her stodgy young English admirer because she can be as frivolous and flirtatious as she is affectionate. When the three meet at the opera shortly after her wedding, Sydenham rankles to discover in her not a sacrificial lamb but a radiant young woman. While Adèle has adjusted to her new situation, Sydenham interprets her refusal of the status of victim as a perverse capriciousness calculated to annoy him: "Ah! si elle était victime de l'ambition, de l'intérêt! Si elle avait été sacrifiée! ... Que je la plaindrais! ... Mais sa gaieté! Cette gaieté vient tout détruire" ["Ah, if she had been a victim of ambition, of avarice! If she had been sacrificed! ... How I would pity her! ... But her gaiety! Her gaiety ruins everything"] (24). He would like Adèle to give a captivating display of instinctive delicacy and silent submission to a miserable fate, but throughout the story she escapes his attempts, as admirer to control her, as letter-writer to classify her.[5] Souza's heroines are neither cowed by her narrating heroes nor defined by the feelings of guilt that normally attend latent infringements of certain behavioral codes in sentimental fiction.

Sydenham at first tries to inspire in Adèle his own disgust for her marriage, but she resists. When he makes a heavy-handed allusion to the symbolism of a pearl bracelet that she received as a wedding gift and has just broken, she matches his sarcasm with her own: "Elles ont coûté bien cher, dis-je en regardant Adèle, qui me répondit en prenant à son tour l'air du dédain: elles sont sans prix" ["They cost dearly, I said, looking at Adèle, who answered with a disdainful look of her own: they're priceless"] (24). With an oppressive mother lurking in the background, Adèle is cast between a clinging old man and a handsome younger one, forbidden and disapproving. Resisting pressures to conform, she not only manages to retain her innocence, but also, like Caroline de Lichtfield and the heroines of fairy tales, winds up with everything: money, status, sex, autonomy.

Thus *Adèle de Sénange* is a less bland work than it has appeared. It expands the novel of sensibility and revises the idea of the sentimental heroine; partly owing to the very characteristics Sainte-Beuve admires, it is a more ambiguous text than critics have allowed, turning on unspoken taboos, half-concealed energies, and the subversive power of language. A subtextual discussion centers on the allure of the forbidden, all the more forceful for being articulated in a vocabulary of virtue and obedience. While exalting the sanctity of marriage and the authority of the family, especially of the father/husband, the novel betrays drives and emotions that go against respect for these institutions, deviously introducing female autonomy, disruption, and dissolution. This novel of sensibility, which has appeared to critics no less paradigmatic for being a holdover from the pre-Revolutionary era, may be read as a discussion of sexual and nuptial rites that masks latent incest and oedipal rivalries as filial devotion and forgetfulness, and the temptation of adultery as innocent affectivity.

Marriage within and among families of two nationalities over a period of several generations is portrayed as an economic transaction. Adèle, initially destined for the convent by a mother intent on securing the family inheritance for her son, is saved by Sénange, a man who can assure her his fortune *only* through marriage (his own father, in the futile hope of perpetuating the family line, had decreed fifty years earlier that Sénange would inherit when he married). Her later marriage to Sydenham becomes possible only when she placates her mother by giving that inheritance to her brother.

In the background of this "limpid" and "restful" story, then, are murky questions of money and caste, and the plot evolves in a subtle atmosphere of relations that are symbolically incestuous. The young man whose hand the bride clasps as she descends the chapel steps turns out to be her brother, and he acknowledges the situation, as Sydenham says, "d'un air si embarrassé, que bientôt après il nous quitta" ["with such an embarrassed look that he left us soon after"] (22). The brother's embarrassment at being the apparent husband of his sister is so keen that he exits from the theater and from the text, never to be seen again. Moreover, Adèle's husband in name only is a (grand)father figure who, as her educator and guide, fills in for the unmentioned father. Finally, Adèle is married to a man who has loved her while trying to behave like a brother, and who is morally adopted by her husband/father. In this complicated pattern, maternal meanness frames a text that interweaves sisterhood, brotherhood, and fatherhood, both real and metaphorical, in a series of replacements and displacements—of fortunes, of confinements, of family roles and functions, of generational relations, of marital consummation.

The action occurs in three principal locations: Adèle's convent in Chaillot, Sénange's Paris manse, and his Neuilly estate; or, to borrow the terminology of Tony Tanner in *Adultery in the Novel*, temple, city, and field, for the locales through which the three characters progress approximate the "topographical model" of the novel of adultery he outlines with its "alternation of realms" (23). From the convent parlor with its grill, to the garden of the Paris mansion, to the streams and thickets of Neuilly on the Seine, each location is charged with social connotations, injunctions, and behavioral patterns. Each locus acknowledges certain kinds of discourse, imposing restrictions or, alternatively, allowing special liberties of speech and action.[6]

The convent appears as a symbol of struggling or "disturbed consciousness" (23), in Tanner's expression, but it is also symbolic both of innocence, on the one hand, and of coercion and sequestration, on the other. It is a point of passage, either of entry into society or of retreat from the world. At Sydenham's first meeting with her, Adèle weeps because she misses the convent and the nuns, and a few pages later the convent is the setting for the wedding recession—one of the novel's most visually powerful scenes. During the summer, Adèle enjoys visiting there and even taking Sydenham with her; she describes for him her "court-ship" by Sénange in the convent parlor. Finally, after her husband's death, she spends her mourning there, visited by Sydenham, who de-clares his love as he clasps her hand through the grill. During this second residence in the convent, Adèle builds up the strength to face her mother, who wishes to marry her off to a relative.[7]

Interpolated in the story is the tale of one of the nuns, Sister Eugénie, the convent's youngest recruit, whose dejection is associated with the grating of iron bars and locks. She sends Sydenham a letter a few days after his visit explaining that she took vows because it seemed the only way to survive. But no sooner had she pronounced them than she regretted her decision, and now she begs him to help her escape. He rescues her the same night and sends her off to England, proud of his good deed. Eugénie's story is a variant of Adèle's: here is what might have happened if Sénange had not rescued her by marriage.[8] The entire Eugénie episode and, indeed, the convent allusions in general, are couched in ambiguous rhetoric that suggests various opposing symbolisms of women's lives.

The convent seems to localize both moral plenitude and void. Adèle cries because she must leave and because she must marry; Eugénie, because she may do neither. The convent is at the same time the site of girls' preparation for social life and that of other women's eternal renun-ciation of that same life. The discourse of the mother superior exemplifies charity and wisdom, but at least one of her charges, Eugénie, is desper-ately unhappy, and the superior acknowledges her powerlessness to inter-vene.

Sydenham, meanwhile, alternately shares the contagious gaiety of the young lodgers and the sadness of Sister Eugénie. He is able to visit her there only because of a massive crack that forms in the garden wall (Adèle explains that a bizarre convent protocol allows men to enter when fate opens such a breach). The rift also provides Sister Eugénie a unique opportunity to embrace the outside world through sight: she spends all her daylight hours staring through the opening, and then, recognizing a unique opportunity for escape, she writes the hasty plea to Sydenham the day before the wall is restored.

In eighteenth-century French fiction, the convent, like the garden, is an almost constant metaphor. It functions as one term of the polarity or dialectic between physical and psychological withdrawal and the free play of the imagination that I have emphasized in other chapters. The novels of Le Prince de Beaumont stress the paradoxically satisfactory nature of seclusion (the widowed baroness of Batteville does not take vows, but does go to live in a convent), while Souza's first novel, like Montolieu's, emphasizes an imaginative wholeness that seems not exclusively literary, the simultaneous enjoyment of parks, nature, and chastity. But even in *Adèle de Sénange* the convent remains a visible alternative to worldly fulfillment. The convent wall is itself, of course, the most tangible metaphor of withdrawal. Here, however, that element is ritualized and becomes a fantastic motif, a self-subverting convention that helps account for the novel's ambiguities. It is both the image of the tomb and a rhythmically opening and closing barrier, like the garden walls and bird cages, at times keeping men out, and at others teasingly allowing them within.

As for Sister Eugénie, there is an afternote to her story of liberation. In one of the last letters, Sydenham announces that he has received news of her:

> Pour achever de me mettre mal avec moi-même, le docteur Morris m'écrit que cette jeune religieuse se désole, passe ses jours dans les larmes, fuit le monde et repousse les consolations. Sa santé s'affaiblit d'une manière effrayante; et la mort qui, dans son couvent, lui paraissait être la fin de ses peines, ne lui semble plus, aujourd'hui, que le commencement de ses maux. Il ajoute: "Que celui qui n'a pas l'âme assez forte pour se soumettre à son état, quel qu'il soit, ne sera jamais heureux dans quelque situation qu'on le place." Si cela était vrai, la plus douce récompense d'un bienfait serait perdue.—Que je hais ces tristes vérités! On cherche à les apprendre, et on désire encore plus de les oublier. (171–72).

> [As if to make me thoroughly displeased with myself, Doctor Morris writes me that this young nun grieves, spends her days in tears, flees from company, and refuses to be comforted. Her health is

becoming frightfully bad; and death which, in her convent, seemed like it would be the end of her sorrows, now seems to her only the beginning of her troubles. He adds: "Whoever is not strong enough to accept his condition, whatever it is, will never be happy in any other condition." If that were true, the sweetest reward for a good deed would be lost.—How I hate these sad truths! We try to learn them, but we want even more to forget them.]

The story of Eugénie tells "sad truths" about physical and psychological imprisonment, about the ambiguities of desire and liberation, about the irrationality of fantasies of fulfillment and anxieties of loss.

On the other hand, the opposition between Paris and Neuilly more schematically locates the rhetoric of constraint and abandon, convention and originality, culture and nature, civilization and wilderness, the domestic and the foreign. Paris is the realm of strict social conventions, whereas Neuilly allows forgetfulnes and the free play of fantasy.[9] Sydenham, with an eye for the elegant and an occasional taste for the antique, is the foreigner whose alien presence in the married couple's Paris and Neuilly residences disrupts household and marriage. On the day he first meets Adèle, as he rides his horse through the Champs Elysées, he notices a coach on the road from Chaillot:

> Je m'étais promené à cheval dans la campagne, et je revenais doucement par les Champs-Elysées, lorsque je vis sortir de Chaillot une énorme berline qui prenait le même chemin que moi. J'admirais presque également l'extrême antiquité de sa forme, et l'éclat, la fraîcheur de l'or et des paysages qui la couvraient. De grands chevaux bien engraissés, bien lourds; d'anciens valets, dont les habits, d'une couleur sombre, étaient chargés de larges galons: tout était antique, rien n'était vieux; et j'aimais assez qu'il y eût des gens qui conservassent avec soin des modes qui, peut-être, avaient fait le brillant et le succès de leur jeunesse. (3–4)

> [I had gone for a ride in the country, and I was returning unhurriedly by the Champs-Elysées, when I saw an immense coach leaving Chaillot by the same road. I admired the extreme ancientness of its

shape about as much as the brilliance and newness of the gold and landscapes painted on it. Large, heavy, well-fattened horses; elderly valets, whose dark uniforms were covered with wide braids: everything was antique, nothing was old; and I liked knowing that there were still people who carefully kept up the styles that had perhaps made their youth brilliant and successful.]

Sénange's coach is the image of its owner, venerable in its age and its links to a brilliant, bygone era. And Sydenham's emphasis on the beauties of the past may be seen as emblematic of the novel itself, as critics have traditionally read it.

Sydenham judges their Paris garden with the same artistic and foreign eye with which he prized the coach, but this time his aesthetic sense condemns it as quintessentially French and old-fashioned. When Adèle asks him to admire her aviary, he says only that it goes well with the rest, secretly noting its gilding as an example of the worst possible taste. The garden itself strikes him as frightful, an immense terrain that has been made to look horribly small: "c'est l'ancien genre français avec toute son aridité; du buis, du sable et des arbres taillés" ["it's in the old French manner with all its aridity; boxwood, sand, and pruned trees"] (33–34). He describes for Adèle the wilderness of his garden in Wales, where the birds fly free: "Elle m'entendit, et pria son mari de tout changer dans le leur, et d'en planter un autre sur mes dessins" ["She understood me, and begged her husband to change everything around in theirs, and to plant another according to my plans"] (34).

Sydenham has suggested nothing specific, but Adèle has "understood" his disdain for the very antiquity and tradition that in the coach he found so appealing, "understood" his scorn for the French notion of order and his endorsement of something wilder, larger, without cages, especially golden ones. Sénange resists the proposal to redo the garden, but he offers Adèle instead an island of forty acres (reminiscent of Julie's Elysée) on his estate in Neuilly, where she may do as she pleases. Her imagination conjures up "cool grottoes," and she renounces the sandy aridity associated with her husband for the lush and humid foliage extolled by the young Englishman. The garden scenes in the Paris estate turn on seminal questions: the preoccupation with planting and flora is the symbolic expression of tensions opposing the familiar and the foreign, the new and the old, the free and the structured. Although his discourse is not overtly subversive, Sydenham's garden talk sows in Adèle's unconscious mind both desire and an imaginative means of fulfillment, removal to the country.

As the threatening interloper, Sydenham is contained in the enclosed Paris garden, less controlled and more threatening in the fertile English garden. On the rambling Neuilly estate, what Tanner calls the "absoluteness of law" (19) seems to obtain less strictly. Here Sydenham and Adèle are free to liberate nature and rearrange their own relations. Neuilly offers escape to the river, where open fields, flowing waters, and islands mitigate the force of obligation. Garden scenes frequently localize seduction episodes; in *Histoire de Cressy,* for example, young Adélaïde du Bugei is nearly seduced in the garden. But while Adélaïde's experience leaves her feeling the guilt and mistrust that drive her to take religious vows, Adèle's psychological seduction causes no such psychological damage.

Sydenham does not make love to Adèle in Neuilly, or even propose it; only in the absence of any such explicit act are critics able to vaunt the work's sobriety and sentimentality. But while guarding a strict innocence of action and most of the proprieties of language, the two engage in verbal confidences and gestures of collusion that disturb the old man. Sydenham extracts from Adèle the assurance that he is her "only friend." Like the duc de Nemours in *La princesse de Clèves,* he surreptitiously "borrows" her portrait (an act he confesses as Sénange lies dying) and goes into a jealous depression when she dances and flirts with another young man.[10] He also makes declarations no less misplaced for being uttered in the language of sensibility and accompanied by gentle sighs: "je n'existais que pour vous! daigneriez-vous partager une si tendre affection? pouvez-vous seulement la comprendre?" ["I existed only for you! Won't you deign to share such tender affection? Can you even understand it?"] (124). And when he makes a contribution to the convent in her name, he chooses, for reasons he does not examine, to use her maiden name.

One morning while Sénange sleeps, in an episode that plays as crucial a role as the lake scene between Julie and Saint-Preux, the young pair makes an unauthorized excursion to her island. Alone with Adèle on the river, Sydenham has the feeling that "il n'y avait plus dans l'univers que le ciel, Adèle et moi! et j'avais oublié l'une et l'autre rive!" ["all that was left in the universe was the sky, Adèle, and me! And I had forgotten about both river banks!"] (107). They are free from the conscious realization of obligations to husband and society, although the expression of their affections and affinities takes the form of conversation about the goodness of Sénange. But a stern reception awaits them back at the house, where Sénange reproaches them for forgetting him and forgetting themselves; he speaks sometimes like a wounded husband and sometimes like a disapproving father. *Oublier* and its reflexive form, *s'oublier,* recur in this passage to suggest their neglect of time, place, and people, the undermining of duty, the obliteration of physical and moral realities. Sénange insists on responsible memory and respectability.

The ambiguity of Sydenham's position is elucidated by a lengthy flashback, an important stroke of memory on the part of Sénange. Early in their stay at Neuilly, Sénange describes for Sydenham a youthful adventure of his own, namely his love for Sydenham's grandmother. On his first trip to England, he met young Lady B. and her husband and children during a storm at sea, and he proffered words of reassurance and consolation, just as Sydenham had met and consoled Adèle when her carriage overturned. Like Sydenham, too, Sénange was invited, in gratitude, to come visit, and like him he stayed on to fall in love with his hostess, whose behavior prefigured Adèle's: chastely devoted to her husband, she made no declaration of love. But it is easy to surmise that she reciprocated, albeit unconsciously, her admirer's feelings.

The crucial difference in the two stories occurs when Lord B. vigorously intervenes and expels the foreigner. But not before Lady B. has made Sénange promise that if ever one of her sons should find himself alone in France, he would act as friend and guide. He vows to acquit his obligation on the grandson and invites Sydenham to depend on him as he would on a father. Sénange concludes by evoking the death of Lady B.—

"A peine Adèle a-t-elle été dans cette petite barque . . ."
["Hardly was Adèle in that little boat . . ."]. Staal/Massard.
Frontispiece, *Oeuvres de Madame de Souza* (Paris:
Garnier [Bibliothèque amusante], 1865).

we can only guess from a broken heart—and he explains that he has never told any of this to Adèle. This reluctance to tell his young wife about a woman who was "virtue itself" (87) is perhaps a recognition of the impure and illicit impulses that may lurk in even the chastest of passions.

Fifty years after the English episode, Sénange finds himself in turn threatened, but either too old or too weak to take decisive action. He reprimands Sydenham, broods a good deal, and falls ill, but never suggests that the interloper leave. Once Sydenham himself becomes aware of the nature of his sentiments for Adèle, he is disturbed by the constant awareness that he *should* depart:

> Je puis être son ami; et si jamais elle était libre!... Ah! je m'arrête: l'amour n'est pas encore mon maître, et déjà je pense sans regret au moment où ce bon, ce vertueux monsieur de Sénange ne sera plus! encore un jour, et peut-être désirerais-je sa mort!... Non, je fuirai Adèle, j'y suis résolu. (78)

> [If I can be her friend; and if ever she were free!... Ah, I must stop: love is not yet master of me, and already I am thinking without regret of the time when the good and virtuous Monsieur de Sénange will be no longer! One more day, and maybe I'd wish him dead!... No, I'll flee Adèle, my mind is made up.]

But his resolution never quite carries him out of the house. The English model is reversed; the husband dies and the lover stays to marry the widow. The literary pattern that the novel follows is likewise modified, for Adèle's enjoyment of the happy everafter is the antithesis of Julie de Wolmar's conscience-plagued death.

Sydenham's implicit guilt for the death of Sénange is problematic; if he did not actively wish it, he did somewhat complacently anticipate it. Sénange's demise is the disintegration of a failing man portrayed from the outset as gouty and debilitated. Yet the actual occasion of his death brings together the text's ambiguities. When Adèle and Sénange learn indirectly about Sister Eugénie, they assume that Sydenham's intentions were dishonorable, and Adèle joins to her disapproval an indistinct feeling of jealousy. After Sydenham produces the nun's letter he is reinstated in their graces. Adèle then finds a particular thrill in contemplating his generous deed, excitedly proclaiming that she herself feels capable of doing good just for the pleasure of telling him about it. Too excitedly:

> A ces mots, soit que monsieur de Sénange ait aperçu pour la première fois le sentiment d'Adèle, soit qu'en effet quelque douleur soudaine l'ait saisi, il s'est levé en disant qu'il souffrait. (150)

> [At these words, Monsieur de Sénange, either because he perceived Adèle's feelings for the first time, or because he actually experienced some sudden distress, rose saying that he was not well.]

Thus it seems clear that the "elegant conversation"—to quote both Larnac and Chénier—in which two young people compete in expressing delicacy and generosity paradoxically helps precipitate Sénange's last illness and death. Four days later, he is gone, done in by the language of sensibility, Sainte-Beuve's "innocent prattle." Sydenham's "good deed" in liberating Eugénie contributes to her death and Sénange's as well. But it is also he who nurses Sénange in his last illness, sheds "sincere tears" at his disappearance, and needs to believe in the soul's immortality in order to cope with that loss. Sénange leaves his fortune to Adèle but, appropriately, leaves the Neuilly house to Sydenham. The novel thus rejects a solution of renunciation, often represented by the convent with all its negations, for a total opening to money, privilege, nature, and fulfilled sexuality.

The poetry of *Adèle de Sénange* has to do with these connections between tenderness and murderous impulses, freedom and confinement, city and country, economic realities and fairy-tale solutions. Marriage is written as a coded condensation of various female fantasies: liberation from parents and society; postponed, and thereby heightened, sexual gratification; possession of and by the father with a simultaneous violation of his laws; the rhetorical legitimization of adulterous pleasure; a happy resolution of the contradictions between property obligations and passionate urgings. Unlike Rousseau's novel, however, this text published during the turbulent years of the Terror plays itself out as a guiltless fantasy of impossible plenitude and impossibly enduring innocence. The emphasis of critics of the last two hundred years on the novel's slick and genteel surface, its observance of social and fictional boundaries, and its evocation of an ineffable eighteenth-century charm, takes no account of the configurations of Souza's allegory of crime and innocence.

When Sainte-Beuve speaks of "lovely pure water" and "our overheated palates," his first-person plural is gender- and period-specific: "our" palates are as masculine and post-Revolutionary as the water is feminine and old-world. His remark exemplifies a tendency to construct a cage around the consciousness of eighteenth-century women, although its bars, like those of Adèle's French bird cages, are benevolently gilded.

CHAPTER 9

BRAZEN DESIRE

Sophie Cottin

Claire d'Albe (1799) is set in the familiar conjugal universe of the young wife whose chastity is tested, the universe of Adèle de Sénange and count-less other heroines. Rousseau's *Julie ou la nouvelle Héloïse* codifies the particular version of the *ménage à trois* that organizes many of these novels: a young woman and the older husband to whom her family has married her off are joined on their estate by a younger man. At twenty-two, Claire d'Albe has been married for seven years and has borne two children to a man forty years her elder. When the novel begins, they have just moved to the countryside near Tours where he owns a manufactory. Frédéric, a nineteen-year-old relative, comes down from the Cévennes mountains to be the husband's foreman. Claire and he fall in love, but Claire, determined to remain faithful to her husband, sends him on an extended visit to her cousin and confidante, Elise. Monsieur d'Albe, how-ever, a pathetic latter-day version of Wolmar, is aware of the attraction between them and masterminds a plan that he urges on Elise. They will divide Claire and Frédéric by persuading each that the other is fickle. Claire is undone by the thought of Frédéric's inconstancy and falls fatally ill. When Frédéric discovers the truth, he rushes back to find her in the garden late at night, meditating at an altar containing her father's ashes. There he frenetically "possesses" her for the first and last time. A febrile and repentant Claire dies the next morning, and the novel concludes with a brief description of her burial and of Frédéric's vow to follow her.[1]

This story is told in the form of forty-five letters and a postface; the preponderance (thirty-two) of the letters are written by Claire to Elise; the remainder are exchanged between Claire and Frédéric or written by Elise to d'Albe. Elise is also the author of the postface describing the final events of the heroine's life as Claire related them on her deathbed.

Sophie Ristaud (1770–1807)—she was baptized "Marie" but called "Sophie"—was born to a Protestant family in Paris and raised in Tonneins, a manufacturing town in Gascony. She was married at nineteen, two months before the fall of the Bastille, to Paul Cottin, a Parisian banker. Four years later, he died at thirty. Suspected of aristocratic sympathies, she was obliged to go into hiding with her cousin Julie Vénès Verdier. The rest of her short life was not tranquil. She moved around a good deal, a rejected suitor killed himself practically on her doorstep, and she later fell in love with a second-rate philosopher who declined to marry her because she could not have children. She was in her late twenties and financially strapped when she published her first novel, *Claire d'Albe*.[2] In her anonymous preface she says she wrote the book in a couple of weeks; proceeds from its publication were supposedly earmarked for a friend under political suspicion who had to flee the country. Between 1802 and her death from breast cancer in 1807 she published three more somber novels of passion and destruction, *Malvina* (1801), *Amélie Mansfield* (1803), and *Mathilde* (1805), as well as a more optimistic novel on filial devotion, *Elisabeth ou les exilés de Sibérie* (1806). A short, sentimental love story of biblical inspiration, *La prise de Jéricho* [The capture of Jericho], first appeared in 1803. All had great success in France and throughout Europe.

If *Claire d'Albe* captivated the public, voices nonetheless raised questions about taste and morality, and the sex scene between Claire and Frédéric was judged in some quarters to be intolerably explicit. In a letter of 1803 to Benjamin Constant, Julie Talma criticized Cottin's work for its representations of frantic, immoderate passion, faulting her in precisely the area where critics have found Souza so much to be recommended: moderation (quoted in Gaulmier, 6). Félicité de Genlis, whose objections I shall discuss at greater length in my next chapter, censured *Claire d'Albe* for its "revolting" immorality and for cynical love scenes that no woman

"Claire et Frédéric." Deveria/Masson. *Claire
d'Albe,* in *Oeuvres complètes de Mme Cottin,* vol. 1
(Paris: Ménard and Desenne, fils, 1824).

should have written (*De l'influence* 346, 350), while Julia Kavanagh would consider it one of Cottin's "most objectionable works" (2: 176). The introduction to the 1831 edition of the novel, signed only "H.D.," expressed the following reservations:

> La fable n'en est pas très heureuse, et pourra paraître un peu commune. L'union d'une jeune femme avec un vieillard prête trop au ridicule pour intéresser bien vivement. Peut-être madame Cottin a-t-elle voulu faire voir le danger de ces sortes de mariages, mais alors son but n'est pas assez fortement marqué. Le dénouement de *Claire d'Albe* est ce que l'on peut blâmer avec le plus de raison dans ce roman. Un jeune homme, quelque passionné qu'il soit, est toujours inexcusable de choisir le moment où une femme est à moitié morte pour satisfaire son amour. (8)

> [The subject is not really satisfactory and may appear a bit common. The marriage of a young woman and an old man has too much potential for ridicule to be of much interest. Perhaps Madame Cottin wanted to show the danger of this sort of marriage, but in that case her intention is not sufficiently clear. The dénouement of *Claire d'Albe* is what is most objectionable in the novel. A young man, however impassioned, is always inexcusable to choose the moment when a woman is half dead to satisfy his desire.]

This assessment is remarkable indeed. If the last sentence (about Frédéric) is hardly unfair, H.D. seems nonetheless to have missed what a modern reader must take to be the point: what H.D. calls the "fable" (what I have translated as "subject") reads indeed like a fable in the sense of an anecdote purporting to convey a lesson. The commentator does not impugn its plausibility but criticizes its conventionality. The subject, the imbalance in a *mariage de convenance* between two people of vastly different ages, is undeniably "common," as H.D. maintains, in eighteenth-century life as well as in literature: Cottin needed to look no further for an example than her favorite cousin, Julie, who had been married before she was twenty to a man in his sixties. Cottin's severe handling of the familiar motif is what makes the novel original. More puzzling is H.D.'s hesitation about whether Cottin "meant" to criticize this sort of marriage. My reading can only suggest a scathing indictment, however satisfactory Cottin's own brief conjugal experience may have been.[3]

Expanding on the novel's ending, H.D. goes on to specify that when Frédéric outtalks and overpowers Claire, he evinces a kind of brutality: "Il est pénible d'employer ce mot, mais il y a réellement là une brutalité qui fait mal" ["It hurts to use the word, but we have here a truly distressing brutality"] (8). But the "brutality" of the conclusion is not, it seems to me, disconcerting in a novel where sexual and social brutishness is precisely what is at issue. Here is a story pitting nature against civilization, a story about uncouthness and devouring passion. Warmly embraced by the turn-of-the-century public, it is marked more sharply than *Adèle de Sénange* by a cleavage between the sentimental vocabulary in which the story is largely told and social and behavioral realities—a discrepancy that explains how, while continuing the sentimental tradition, it also inaugurates (as Genlis complains) a new form of writing: the "roman passionné." In objecting to the portrayal of a heroine who is supposed to be "vertueuse, religieuse, angélique" in a wild and criminal love (*De l'influence* 346), Genlis implicitly identifies a pivotal dichotomy between sentimental discourse and the underlying thematics. It did not escape her notice that when a penitent Claire moralizes on her deathbed about her errors, the words ring hollow in comparison with the intensity of her experience of adultery. Claire proclaims rather oddly that "il est des crimes que la passion n'excuse pas" ["there are crimes that passion cannot excuse"] (177): but what crime *can* passion excuse if not illicit sex? It is worth adding that the exemplarity of the lover and especially of the husband, a construction of Claire's own stylized writing, is also implicitly refuted by the events she narrates. So the reader must uncover the sense of the novel by considering two levels of "truth": this is a book confronting culturally mandated language with "brutal" realities.

Claire never criticizes her husband. Emphasis on his goodness and her esteem for him permeates her letters. While d'Albe indulgently styles himself "un bourru bienfaisant" ["a beneficent churl"] (53), he is characterized by his young wife as an excellent man, a worthy husband, the truest and best of men: "Toute son ambition," she exclaims, "est d'en-treprendre des actions louables, comme son bonheur est d'y réussir" ["His whole ambition is to undertake praiseworthy actions, just as his whole happiness is to accomplish them"] (30). Nonetheless, while she *says* that d'Albe is all goodness, her epistolary narratives reveal him as jealous, overbearing, and quick to anger.

Tension is born of this disjunction between Claire's judgments of her husband and the words and actions she reports, such as his expression of anger when an elderly employee breaks a mechanical model; his comment that their baby daughter doesn't know her mother from the servants, except when she's nursing; his jealous response to Claire's affection for Elise. Add to this his shortsightedness in insisting that his lonely wife become the mentor of a handsome young man and, finally, his crass and crazy scheme to set things right by weaving a web of lies around Claire and Frédéric. Words like "excellent" turn corrosive as Claire portrays life at the side of a peevish, judgmental husband.

Claire writes of d'Albe in terms similar to those she marshals to evoke her dead father, another "best of men," and the explanation she gives for her marriage is worth considering: she lost her mother as an infant, and adolescent veneration for a dying father motivated her to accept d'Albe's hand. Here is what she tells Frédéric about her father:

> Sous cette tombe sacrée . . . repose la cendre du meilleur des pères. . . . je joignais pour lui, à toute la tendresse filiale qu'inspire un père, toute la vénération qu'on a pour un dieu. Il me fut enlevé comme j'entrais dans ma quatorzième année. Sentant sa fin approcher, effrayé de me laisser sans appui, et n'estimant au monde que le seul M. d'Albe, il me conjura de m'unir à lui avant sa mort. Je crus que ce sacrifice la retarderait de quelques instants, je le fis: je ne m'en suis jamais repentie. (58–59)

> [In this sacred tomb . . . lie the ashes of the best of fathers. . . . with all the filial tenderness that a father inspires, I also felt for him all the veneration one has for a god. He was taken from me as I entered my fourteenth year. Feeling the end approach, frightened of leaving me

unsupported, and having no esteem for any but Monsieur d'Albe, he beseeched me to be joined to him before he died. I thought this sacrifice would delay his death by a few moments and I accepted it: I have never regretted it.]

The fact that no explanation is offered of why her father esteems only d'Albe and no mention is made of d'Albe's own motives makes only more striking the almost mythical force of the "sacrifice." Claire's marriage is a conspiracy between two men. The father's sentimental blackmail ensures that Claire will pass from the hands of one old man to another.

D'Albe treats her more like a child than a helpmeet. He dislikes her easy laughter (shades of Charrière's Mr. Henley), and Claire reigns it in. He refuses discussion of her feelings for Frédéric, until she is on her death-bed. Like her father he decides what is best for her. It costs her life. Claire, caught between father and husband, cannot own herself. When she describes herself as "une femme qui ne s'appartient pas" ["a woman who does not belong to herself"] (83), she "means" to say, of course, that she is married, but the literal sense captures her plight. She is the object of repressive reparenting, and her dispossession is compounded by her father's and husband's disposal of her "virtues," her "charms," her laughter.

Even God plays second fiddle to the male characters in this text, where Claire reveres her father like "a god" and, persuaded that she has offended her husband "more than God," worries at the end less about God's forgiveness than about d'Albe's. The mingling of sentimental religiousness and sexual urges helps define this novel, in which God seems to be useful at most for taking up where passion leaves off. When Claire turns to religion as she pines for Frédéric, Elise begs d'Albe to indulge his wife in all the acts of piety she chooses, explaining, "le vide terrible que l'amour . . . laisse ne peut être rempli que par Dieu même" ["The terrible void . . . left by love can be filled only by God himself"] (166). We learn of d'Albe's response to such requests only indirectly, for his words, like God's, are always mediated: he is the only one of the four principal characters whose letters never appear.

The story begins in spring—the season when Claire, like so many heroines, has a touch of fever.[4] In her first letter to Elise, she declares, "je suis heureuse" ["I am happy"], but the next sentence qualifies her happiness: "oui, je suis heureuse de la satisfaction de M. d'Albe" ["yes, I am happy in Monsieur d'Albe's satisfaction"] (20). By her third letter, still congratulating herself on having so good a husband, she nonetheless expresses some reservations about her chances for real happiness. She nuances her own perceptions of "happiness," from contentment in duty to sexual fulfillment. Watching the awakening of nature, she concludes that love alone leads to *bonheur* (which by this point has taken on a more specifically sexual meaning), explaining: "je soupçonne que mon sort n'est pas rempli comme il aurait pu l'être: ce sentiment, qu'on dit être le plus délicieux de tous, et dont le germe était peut-être dans mon coeur, ne s'y développera jamais, et y mourra vierge" ["I suspect that my life is not so full as it might have been: that feeling, which they say is the most delectable of all, and the seed of which was perhaps in my heart, will never develop there, and will die virgin"] (27). Words like "full," "seed," and "virgin" overcharge Claire's sense of *bonheur*. Much more explicitly than *Caroline de Lichtfield* or *Adèle de Sénange*, this is a novel about woman's sexuality and its connection with being, becoming, and making "happy."

While d'Albe is associated with mundane commercialism (he invents and produces "mechanical models"), Frédéric is a kind of savage. One of the first things Claire notices about him is the litheness and agility of his body. Emerging from the mountains, he displays (like Voltaire's *ingénu*) "toute la piquante originalité de la nature" ["all the piquant originality of nature"] (35) and has no notion of social niceties. In his youthful certainty that no woman will ever suit him and his later haggard and wind-blown despair, he is a precursor of Chateaubriand's René, who was to appear three years later. But whereas René represents melancholy and passivity, more the contemplation of freedom than its exercise (he is more or less incapable of *doing* anything at all), Claire admires in Frédéric a "franchise crue" ["crude directness"] (31) which goes hand in hand with verbal and physical aggressiveness. He insults her, declaring that her baby daughter is ugly and smells of sour milk, abandons her on a long walk, holds no doors, begins eating before her at table, asks indiscrete questions.

He is uncivilized, unpolished, pure energy. And once he has declared

"Claire coupable" ["Claire guilty"]. Deveria/Masson.
Claire d'Albe, in *Oeuvres complètes de Mme Cottin,* vol. 1
(Paris: Ménard and Desenne, fils, 1824).

his desire, he never misses an opportunity for touching, whether it is to fondle her when she has passed out or to stroke her from behind and pretend it was her son. When he learns that Claire is dying and that they have been lied to, he is ferocious: "nulle force ne peut le retenir, il écrase tout ce qui s'oppose à sa fuite" ["no power can restrain him, he crushes everything that stands in his way"] (168), and when he joins her at the end, his very boldness overwhelms her.

But the passion between Frédéric and Claire, rendered in these images of potency and savagery, derives simultaneously from sentimental defer- rals and detours. Frédéric's initial attraction is toward her husband, whose praises he sings as cloyingly as does Claire. His own father dead, he loses no time in deciding that d'Albe can replace him. Charmed by his adulation, d'Albe responds with self-satisfaction:

> Vous aimez donc beaucoup ma femme, Frédéric? lui a-t-il dit.— Beaucoup? non.—La quitteriez-vous sans regret?—Elle me plaît; mais je crois qu'au bout de peu de jours je n'y penserais plus.—Et moi, mon ami? Vous! s'est-il écrié en se levant, et courant se jeter dans ses bras, je ne m'en consolerais jamais. C'est bien, c'est bien, mon Frédéric, lui a dit M. d'Albe tout ému. (37–38)

> [You like my wife a great deal, then, Frédéric? he said.—A great deal? No.—Could you leave her with no regrets?—I like her; but I think that after a few days, I'd think no more of her.—And me, my friend?—You! he cried, getting up and running to embrace him, I would never get over it. That's fine, fine, my Frédéric, said M. d'Albe, very moved.]

D'Albe proposes to make Frédéric "un heureux" ["a happy man"] and find him a woman like Claire.

Even as she grows increasingly interested in Frédéric, Claire insists for a while that their shared tenderness for d'Albe is the tie that binds them. The novel charts a crossing of desire, for while Frédéric is at first extrava- gantly admiring his adoptive father, Claire's own instinct draws her to Elise. Their attachment reminds us of Rousseau's "inseparables," Julie d'Etanges and her cousin Claire d'Orbe, as well as of Cottin's lifelong affection for her cousin Julie. Indeed the most lyrical of the love letters Claire d'Albe composes is addressed not to Frédéric but to her recently widowed cousin. In her first letter, she writes: "tu profiteras de ton indépendance pour ne pas laisser divisé ce que le ciel créa pour être uni; tu viendras rendre à mon coeur la plus chère portion de lui-même" ["you'll take advantage of your freedom to reunite what heaven created to be one; you'll come and restore the dearest part of myself"] (22).

Frédéric's protestations of exclusive love for d'Albe smack of silliness and stridency, but in Claire's fondness for Elise we hear accents of authenticity despite the clichés of love. Indeed, as Claire explains, d'Albe was once jealous of Elise. There is a break in Frédéric's affectivity, a kind of coming of age when he transfers his emotions from d'Albe to Claire; in contrast, Claire demonstrates simultaneous desire for cousin and lover. In death she displays the complexity of her attachments to the others, squeezing the hand of Elise, looking at her husband, but speaking Frédéric's name.

A fast talker and excellent singer, Frédéric represents the seductiveness of voice, whereas d'Albe, scientific and rational, incarnates the aspects of the male mystique critiqued by Le Prince de Beaumont—silence and order. In her husband's house, isolated from society, Claire lives a constricting version of domestic happiness, punctuated by frustration and longing. At the start of the industrial era, Claire is thus situated between progress and wilderness, order and chaos, old age and youth, duty and passion, silence and speech. The confluence of her husband's civilized duplicity and her lover's wild tenacity leaves her little room, except the imaginary space of the letters in which she lives.

Claire d'Albe endorses the age-old convention according to which passion leads to death. The novel stands apart not for its subtlety or stylistic elegance but, as Fauchery suggests, for the temerity of its distinct linkage of extramarital intercourse with death (802). Near the end Elise describes, in words the reader assumes were borrowed from Claire on her deathbed, the latter's experience:

> Elle l'a goûté dans toute sa plénitude, cet éclair de délice qu'il n'appartient qu'à l'amour de sentir; elle l'a connue, cette jouissance délic-

ieuse et unique, rare et divine comme le sentiment qui l'a créée: son
âme, confondue dans celle de son amant, nage dans un torrent de
volupté; il fallait mourir alors; mais Claire était coupable et la puni-
tion l'attendait au réveil. (173)

[She tasted in all its fullness that fire of delight which belongs only to
love; she knew that delicious and unique ecstacy, rare and divine as
the feeling that begat it: her soul, merging with her lover's, swam in
a torrent of pleasure; afterward she had to die; but Claire was guilty
and punishment awaited her at dawn.]

Rarely does a heroine of this period (except in pornography) enjoy sex so
keenly or suffer its consequences so swiftly and inexorably. Whereas the
death of Rousseau's Julie and of Charrière's Caliste ennobles them,
Claire's humanizes her: she dies not transcending her love but succumbing to it. And unlike those who live for years after their fall from virtue,
Claire survives for only a matter of hours.

There is exaltation and voluptuousness in the love scene, beginning
when an impious and half-mad Frédéric cries that he must have her at any
price: "qu'elle m'appartienne un instant sur la terre, et que le ciel m'écrase
pendant l'éternité" ["let her be mine for an instant on this earth, and let
heaven crush me for all eternity"] (172). Of course, it is not unusual for
adultery or fornication to take place during a moment when the woman is
only half-awake: this was an old device for abrogating or at least at-
tenuating responsibility. But Claire is *literally* near death: Frédéric recognizes the "seal of death" on her face (170). And if there is unusual emphasis on the violence of his actions, there is also indication both of
Claire's reluctant acquiescence and of the "divine" pleasure she takes in
adulterous love.

The glorification of virtue and religion, the rhetoric of righteousness
and Claire's encomia of her husband must be read against this powerful
figuring of the passion that is her short-lived happiness. The final irony is
perhaps her abashed husband's attempt to summon his dying wife back
to life: "Claire, lui dit-il, votre faute est grande sans doute, mais il vous
reste encore assez de vertus pour faire mon bonheur" ["Claire, he tells

her, your sin is doubtless great, but you still have enough virtues to make me happy"] (177). To the end, he confuses "happiness" and "virtue," *his* happiness and *her* virtue.

Modern studies of Cottin have tended to stress the intersections in her novels of romanticism with notions like pathos, passion, and *"pudeur."*[5] But in giving priority to the "romantic" or "preromantic," they have sometimes failed to give play to the audacity of her portrayals of violent love and lovers which break so drastically with the sentimental tradition and thus so shocked Genlis.[6] *Claire d'Albe* is rich in symbolic detail, dramatizing the tensions and the revolt that characterize a tradition of novels by women and proposing a nuanced vision of female sexuality as integral to personality, diametrically opposed to the notion advanced by Restif and others of female sexuality as justifiable mainly in terms of social utility.

Frédéric, this man of words and actions who, covered with sweat and dust, makes impetuous love on the ground, is a new sort of hero. There had been examples of males capable of remarkable acts of sensibility despite a tendency to licentiousness or debauchery. But the case of Frédéric is different: he is simultaneously virtuous and violent, feeling and coarse; and his savagery in no way compromises his purity.[7] This fissure of identity establishes Cottin's new man as a creature of his time, the embodiment perhaps of a paradox of the Revolutionary period. Frédéric's natural force, egoism, refusal of manners, and devotion to a harsh sort of honesty suggest the Revolutionary attempt to ground a structure in the rejection of all existing, constraining structures. It is important to realize that the social and political upheavals of the Revolutionary period failed to replace the public's literary taste toward the end of the eighteenth century; the popularity of the sentimental novel continued in force in the 1780s and 1790s, as my discussion has indicated.

Henri Coulet explains that many novelists went on setting their stories in pre-Revolutionary France in order to exploit characters and situations consecrated by tradition; they continued to write about orphans making their way in an antiquated society, about sensitive souls, egotistic aristocrats, and munificent lords, about thwarted love and forced vocations, "comme si la Révolution n'avait pas radicalement changé les rapports de la noblesse et du peuple et fermé les couvents" ["as though the Revolution had not radically changed the relations of the nobility and the people and closed the convents"] ("Quelques aspects" 28).[8] But Coulet is also doubtless right in asserting that the fact of the Revolution itself, even when it is not specifically mentioned, often affected the meaning of novels in half-hidden ways: the very silencing of the great event characteristic of a tragic novel like *Claire d'Albe* may be the recognition that the Revolution has "changed everything," opening wounds, unleashing fears, and transforming ways of thinking and acting.[9]

Indeed, in the first paragraphs of a short preface, Cottin explains how she came to write *Claire d'Albe,* alluding obliquely to the turmoil of an era during which she had seen friends and relatives disappear: "le dégoût, le danger ou l'effroi du monde ayant fait naître en moi le besoin de me retirer dans un monde idéal, déjà j'embrassais un vaste plan qui devait m'y retenir longtemps" ["Disgust, danger, and fear of society having awakened in me the need to retire into an ideal world, I was already embracing a vast project that would hold my attention for a long time"]. But an unforeseen circumstance, she says, takes her to the countryside near Rouen, where she is moved by the beauty of the woods and the water and meets someone who played a role in the events of *Claire d'Albe.* She asks permission to write the story down and finishes it in two weeks.

The preface loosely incorporates the standard claims of eighteenth-century fiction. Like Rousseau's, Cottin's original impulse is to seek refuge in an "ideal" world, but chance modifies her plan and she ends up writing a story different from the one she intended. We are given to understand that it is a "true" story—told to her by one of the principals—and at the same time a story that speaks, like the landscape in which she found it, to her "imagination" and her "heart."

For L. C. Sykes, therefore, *Claire d'Albe* is "un rêve éveillé" ["a waking dream"] (144), while Janine Rossard comments that Cottin turned to literature to forget the cruelty of her fate and "sans doute, revivre le bonheur passé" ["doubtless relive past happiness"] (*Pudeur* 17). Fauchery takes Cottin's description at face value, assimilating her account of the novel's creation to what he sees as the "typical" experience of women novelists—novel-writing as a form of escape from reality:

> Pour bien des romancères, comme pour un Rousseau, la création littéraire n'est-elle pas une façon de se détourner d'un monde qui les blesse? Une Mme Cottin, par exemple, nous confie qu'elle a commencé un roman pour satisfaire son "besoin de [se] retirer dans un monde idéal." C'est l'éternelle tentation de la vie suspendue, laissée derrière soi, passée du plan du vécu au plan de la contemplation, et qu'au sein même de la fiction romanesque, satisfont les innombrables narratrices de leur passé, ces femmes "retirées du monde," en qui la littérature s'affirme comme l'occupation typique de la retraite sentimentale. (685)

> [For many women novelists, as for Rousseau, isn't the literary vocation a way of turning aside from a world that afflicts them? A Madame Cottin, for example, confides in us that she began a novel to satisfy her "need to withdraw into an ideal world." It's the perpetual temptation of suspended animation, leaving life behind, passing from reality to contemplation, which countless female narrators of their past—those women "in retirement from society," for whom literature is the typical occupation of sentimental withdrawal—indulge from within romantic fiction.]

His remarks faintly echo the stereotypical notions of Mooij: "Mécontentes de leur destinée en général, ces femmes-auteurs ont cherché un refuge idéal dans des fictions aimables" ["Unhappy with their fate in general, these women authors sought an ideal refuge in these pleasant fictions"] (50). Sentimental withdrawal? An ideal refuge? Pleasant fiction? Daydreams? Such epithets may in some ways be applicable to *Adèle de Sénange,* but they hardly suit Cottin's novel of adultery, wrath and death. From her idyll of passion, Cottin may well have derived, as these critics suggest, as much pleasure as she gave. But, apart from the fact that the literary vocation was, for the widowed writer trying to survive in a dramatically changing society, a way of earning money as well as a possible means of "sentimental withdrawal," it is also surely worth noting that she abandons a real world that inspires "fear" to create a fictional universe where the morbid resolution of events is hardly less daunting.

In my reading, the elliptical prefatory anecdote suggests an inevitable incompatibility between an ideal world and lived experience; the dichotomy between the frequently florid vocabulary and Claire's ordeal reproduces that rift. Her mythical escape from a world that "afflicts," to use Fauchery's term, takes her to a harsh place indeed. In the familiar rural landscape that nourishes Julie de Wolmar, Mistress Henley, Caroline de Lichtfield, and Adèle de Sénange, Claire d'Albe is caught in a brutish plot representing a fierce confrontation of sexuality and virtue.[10] The father and the husband play God, and God himself is less severe.

But perhaps we can read the ending as also suggesting a kind of transcendence. By Claire's final, adulterous act, she avenges herself for the social and sexual isolation of the life imposed on her and she controls the destiny of her husband and of her persistent lover. Without overtly challenging the authority of the "excellent" husband before whom she remains submissive, Claire subjects him to a profound humiliation, cuckolding him through the agency of his adoptive son. The adultery/ incest takes place not only on the husband's property, but on the tomb of Claire's father, at the altar where she kneels to pray. Here at the last, even while she worries about eternity, she acknowledges having made Frédéric her "god." Sacred, patriarchal spaces are thus defiled in the sacrifice of her fidelity. While she is to some extent being violated, Claire manages simultaneously to violate her husband, her father, and God, and to bequeath to her lover a fatal dose of remorse. By the force of its association with paternity and sex, her sacrificial death is also an attack on the ideology of fatherhood and phallus.

CHAPTER 10

MORALS

Sophie Cottin and
Félicité de Genlis

Félicité de Genlis (1746–1830), one of the most productive and controversial writers of her time, excoriated the work of Sophie Cottin, and most of all her first novel, *Claire d'Albe,* for the brazenness of its portrayal of carnal pleasure and adulterous love. Genlis included her censure in a volume written a few years after Cottin's death, *De l'influence des femmes sur la littérature française* (1811), a compendium of biographical and critical reviews of literary women from the time of Charlemagne, preceded by "réflexions préliminaires" of a more general nature on women's place in literary history. The latter constitute both a justification of and a prescription for writing by women.

I do not intend to discuss extensively *De l'influence des femmes sur la littérature française,* which deserves much closer study than I can give it here.[1] I do propose, however, to use Genlis's remarks on Sophie Cottin both as a way of emphasizing the originality and daring of Cottin's first novel and as a point of entry into Genlis's own fiction of the closing years of the eighteenth century.

The last article of *De l'influence des femmes sur la littérature française,* devoted to Cottin, is unusually long. Genlis dispenses in a few paragraphs with each of Cottin's later novels, published in the early years of the nineteenth century, in which she finds redeeming qualities of style or content. But she lavishes twelve bitter pages on *Claire d'Albe.* She describes it as a pioneering novel, "le premier roman dans *le genre passionné*" ["the first novel in *the passionate genre*"] (346), but also decries it as the very image of the terrible period during which it was written. Its portrayal of love is of a piece with the insanity and ferocity of the reign of Robespierre. She criticizes the "incorrection de style, phrases ininintellig-ibles" ["incorrect style, unintelligible sentences"] (357), the silly metaphors, and the clichés of the kind of writing *Claire d'Albe* both inaugurates and represents, including phlegmatic husbands and women speaking profanely of eternity as they kneel before tempestuous lovers.

The very prose in which Genlis expresses these objections bears the marks of her hostility. Whereas elsewhere in *De l'influence des femmes sur la littérature française* the writing is sober, here it is alternately frantic and clipped. There are successions of short paragraphs, sometimes comprising a single sentence; occasionally Genlis's only commentary on a passage she finds repugnant is transcription in italics of the offending lines with the addition of an exclamation point.

Like the suicide in Riccoboni's *Histoire de Cressy* that Genlis condemns, the plot of *Claire d'Albe* is judged intolerable on the score of both propriety and plausibility. In the case of *Histoire de Cressy,* Genlis maintains that suicide is incongruous with the otherwise commendable demeanor of Madame de Raisel. In *Claire d'Albe,* she finds the heroine's language and behavior consistently incompatible with virtue and concludes that it is improper and offensive to call her virtuous. Thus, on grounds of taste and decency, Genlis is outraged that, despite the criminality of her passion, the other characters of the novel regard Claire as a virtuous, angelic woman.

Its success notwithstanding, *Claire d'Albe* is not just an absurdity, but a "monstrosity," and no part of it more so than the description of the sexual scene. Genlis quotes part of the passage, only to suspend her quotation with the notation: "Il est impossible de ne pas supprimer ici huit lignes" ["I cannot avoid deleting eight lines here"] (354). The censored lines are these:

> [Frédéric] la serre dans ses bras, il la couvre de baisers, il lui prodigue ses brûlantes caresses. L'infortunée, abattue par tant de sensations, palpitante, oppressée, à demi vaincue par son coeur et par sa fai-

blesse, résiste encore, le repousse, et s'écrie: Malheureux! quand l'éternité va commencer pour moi, veux-tu que je paraisse déshonorée devant le tribunal de Dieu? Frédéric! c'est pour toi que je l'implore. (172)

[Frédéric holds her tight, covers her with kisses, and lavishes on her his burning caresses; the poor woman, undone by so many feelings, quivering, subjugated, almost gives way to love and weakness, but still resists, pushes him away, and cries out: You wretch! when eternity is about to begin for me, do you wish me to appear dishonored before the tribunal of God? Frédéric! it is for you that I implore Him.]

This is, of course, the culminating moment of the novel, when the disparity is most remarkable between Cottin's palpitating heroine and numerous vapid and vaporish predecessors; Claire is prey here not to the usual excesses of sentimental imagination, but to explicitly sexual impulses. For Genlis, this disgusting mélange of sensual fever and religious fervor derives its scandalous energies as much from "extravagance" as from "impiété" (354). Most incomprehensible of all, this narrative is drawn from a manuscript written after Claire's death by her supposedly prudent cousin Elise—for the eventual instruction of Claire's daughter! Lamentably, the novel would give rise to a deplorable new school of writing: this "coupable et misérable production" ["guilty and miserable work"] (356) is therefore both climactic and originary.

Paradoxically, Cottin herself (like Rousseau) held all novels to be reprehensible—perhaps in tacit acknowledgment of the problematic view of virtue that her own embodied—even while she went on writing them. Genlis, on the other hand, considered novel writing as consonant with woman's duties, provided the writing was moral and modest. Genlis read Cottin against her own standards of the admissibility of certain innovations in fiction and the "impossibility" of others, concluding that Cottin violates the basic duty of the writer, especially the woman writer, the obligation to write morally.

In order to understand Genlis's pedagogical and moralistic stance and her dismay at the account of Claire d'Albe's adultery as a lesson for the next generation, it is useful to review her career briefly. She was tutor to the children of the duc de Chartres (her lover and the future Philippe-Egalité) and the first woman to be accorded the title of royal *gouverneur*. She also raised her own children, several adoptive ones (some of whom were rumored to be her illegitimate offspring), and a niece. With political opinions as strong as her literary convictions, she spent the century's most turbulent decade in exile, shepherding various royal protégés and other assorted young people.

During this period—when she was, incidentally, assisted by Isabelle de Montolieu and censured by the normally indulgent Adélaïde de Souza— she thought more than once of publishing or reissuing certain works as a way of raising funds to support her itinerant little band. First and foremost, she considered herself an educator, and she devoted much of her enormous energy to perfecting ways of inculcating morality, ethics, religion, etiquette, and music, among other things. She continued writing almost until her death as an octogenarian on the last day of 1830, the year of the ascension to the French throne of Louis-Philippe, who had been her pupil.[2]

Starting in the 1780s, Genlis published hundreds of volumes, mostly didactic fiction: "J'ose croire que mes romans sont *des traités de morale,* ainsi je me flatte que l'on voudra bien leur pardonner de n'être pas tout à fait aussi frivoles que tant d'autres" ["I dare say that my novels are *moral treatises,* and so I flatter myself that people will forgive them for not being quite so frivolous as so many others"] (*Mères rivales* 3: vi). Her first novel, *Adèle et Théodore* (1782), is indeed largely a treatise on education.[3] The second volume contains an interpolated story, supposedly translated from the Italian and rather different in tone from the rest. Entitled *Histoire intéressante de Madame la duchesse de C**** (hereafter *Histoire intéressante*), this novel within a novel was reissued separately the following year, running to 109 pages. A reading of this inaugural tale may illuminate both the nuances and the contradictions of Genlis's position vis-à-vis Cottin.

The story is told in the first person by an Italian noblewoman who at age fifteen falls in love, unbeknown to her parents, with the sensitive young Belmire. But shortly thereafter she is married by her authoritarian father to Belmire's wealthy and sinister thirty-six-year-old uncle, the duke of C***, who coincidentally becomes the younger man's guardian. The duke learns from his wife's correspondence of her love for another man, and some months after the birth of their daughter takes her to his castle outside Naples. Unable to extract the name of the man she loves, he drugs her, stages her death, and keeps her for nine years in a subterranean prison on a diet of bread and water. At his death, Belmire himself discovers and liberates the duchess. Now twenty-seven years old, she refuses the hand of her faithful admirer; five years later, she decides he will marry her daughter.

Like *Claire d'Albe*, *Histoire intéressante* belongs to a line of novels by women which, far from conforming to a stereotypical notion of the sentimental novel as an ongoing account of the persecuted virgin, offer instead an account of the awkwardness of specifically *conjugal* virtue. It is also similar to *Claire d'Albe* in its triangular structure—young wife and mother, older husband, husband's relative and protegé—and both are stories about arranged marriage and (real or implied) adultery. But whereas in Cottin's story the whole movement is toward the climactic final scene and the "virtuous" heroine's guilty death, *Histoire intéressante* resolves itself in the heroine's gradual acceptance of living martyrdom in marriage as just retribution.

But retribution for what? Unlike Claire d'Albe, the duchess of C*** was not adulterous. But the transgression she committed, it seems, was just as bad—failing to confide in her mother:

Tous mes malheurs sont mon ouvrage; j'ai manqué de confiance en ma mère; en cessant de la consulter, je me suis égarée: fille ingrate et coupable! le ciel, pour me punir, aveugla mes parents dans leur choix; l'époux qu'ils me donnèrent ne pouvait faire mon bonheur. (68)

[All my trials are my own doing; I lacked confidence in my mother; when I stopped seeking her counsel, I strayed: ungrateful, guilty daughter! In order to punish me, heaven blinded my parents in their selection of a husband for me; the one they gave me was incapable of making me happy.]

This explicit moral is remarkable. Like numerous other stories by women, *Histoire intéressante* uses the social and economic ritual of marriage as a vehicle for fantasy and protest. It conveys an intense portrait of a version of married life and a denunciation of arranged marriages and economically motivated parents. But nowhere is such a denunciation explicit. The heroine does not rebuke her parents; she throws herself into their arms after her ordeal comes to an end, and they proffer not a syllable of apology for their own stupidity. The duchess reproaches only herself: through her parents' choice of a spouse for her, God punished a filial sin of omission. She duly reports that the greatest misfortune that can befall a girl is failure to regard her own mother as confidante and true friend. So while the plot seems to say one thing, the "moral" makes a different point.

A brief "editor's preface" to the 1783 edition indirectly recognizes these disparities in its acknowledgment that the separate publication came about because the anecdote was judged "out of place" in *Adèle et Théodore,* a work destined for young people. It goes on to make various traditional claims, including novelty—"on ne voit rien de nouveau sous le soleil, est une phrase vulgaire qu'inventa l'ignorance, et que répète la paresse" ["There's nothing new under the sun is a phrase invented out of ignorance and repeated out of laziness"] (iv)—and utility. The story exhibits "un point de vue très moral" ["a very moral point of view"] (v). Indeed, the preface warns readers that they will hardly know whom to pity more, the victim or the tyrant, since the former at least has the consolations of innocence. Finally, the whole story is a useful lesson about the potential ravages of jealousy.

Genlis's narrative, then, like Cottin's, derives its tension from two levels of discourse and meaning: on the one hand, the morals explicitly proposed both in the preface and in the body of the work and, on the other, a different, more compelling (although not really contradictory) message that derives from a reading of plot. Genlis's reticence about criticizing parental authority and social institutions, her preference for displacing the blame for her heroine's tribulations onto an adolescent oversight, seem to me no less strategic than Cottin's embedding of her heroine's sexuality in sentimental discourse.[4]

Genlis condemns Cottin, like Riccoboni, for violating certain fictional conventions and social prescriptions: virtuous women are never suicidal and adulterous women are not virtuous. For Genlis, the "reasonable" words Cottin puts in Claire's mouth at the end, where she recognizes that her error was "d'avoir coloré le vice des charmes de la vertu" ["to have painted vice with the charms of virtue"] (180–81), are futile inasmuch as the entire work has sought to do precisely that.[5] But Genlis's *Histoire intéressante* exhibits comparable contradictions: unedifying portrayals of contorted passions and shortsighted parents are quaintly adduced by author and editors as a lesson in filial trust and a warning about jealousy.

As Cottin's novel is a decisive chapter in the history of women's efforts to write about sexuality and to reconfigure notions like "virtue," Genlis's reading of Cottin's rhetorical inconsistencies is also instructive. The essay, along with others, had been originally commissioned for a multi-volume publication called *Biographie universelle*. When Genlis learned, however, that among the collaborators were some to whose liberal views she could not subscribe, she withdrew from the project and brought out the articles she had already written as *De l'influence des femmes sur la littérature française*. Its publication in 1811 provoked controversy. *Le journal de l'Empire* published a series of attacks, accusing Genlis of inaccuracies and even specifying, in the kind of condescending commentary that women's writing often elicits, that she lacked the ability to carry on literary and political disputes: "Elle a trop prouvé qu'elle n'avait pas plus que les autres femmes la vigueur et la précision nécessaires pour cette espèce de combat" ["She has proven only too clearly that she does not possess any more than other women do the vigor and precision necessary for this type of combat"] (Broglie 379).

Genlis's attack on Cottin, in particular, scandalized the reviewer for *Le journal de l'Empire* (Broglie 380) and would continue for many years to stimulate interest. In the lengthy unsigned introduction to the 1824 edition of her complete works, for example, there is an extended discussion of Genlis's criticism and the suggestion that despite her highly moral work Genlis was a contentious woman, whereas Cottin at least was generous and self-effacing.[6]

For a recent commentator, Marie-Pierre Le Hir, Genlis and Cottin represent opposing visions of women: the "femme-amour/femme-passion" of Cottin, the "femme-mère/femme-éducatrice" of Genlis (953). If Genlis's criticism does indeed promote this notion, that same critical discourse serves to throw into relief the complexity of her fiction, where heroines may be as impassioned as they are virtuous, and their actions may exhibit both the extravagance and the implausibility that Genlis elsewhere condemned.

Genlis's exhortations to Christian morality and filial disclosure may function in creative tension with the way a coded story "speaks" to readers. What I mean to argue here is that although Genlis's opposition to Cottin is based, as Le Hir has noted, on her interest in exalting woman as mother and educator, her own tales do not advance this agenda exclusively. For novels, even the most moralistic—perhaps especially the most moralistic—almost inevitably contain more than just lessons.

Two other novels by Genlis illustrate the point. *Les voeux téméraires* [Rash vows] (1798)—which she would incidentally accuse Cottin of having plagiarized in *Malvina* (*De l'influence* 358–59)—also treats a virtuous heroine suspected of adultery. A story about marital unhappiness, infidelity, and death, this too is couched as a moral lesson which seems, like the injunction to daughterly candor in *Histoire intéressante,* less compelling than other aspects of the fervent tale of passion and entrapment that it adorns. The first part of the lesson is made explicit in the preface: *sensibilité* without wisdom and moderation is ruinous. The marriage of the English heroine, Constance Lady Clarendon, serves as proof. Her mother has encouraged so exaggerated a notion of *sensibilité* that Constance cannot content herself with the placid love of her husband, who eventually dies as an indirect result of their misunderstandings—including his mistaken belief that she is guilty of adultery with his brother-in-law.

A companion lesson, having to do with precipitate promises or vows, is forecast in the title. In a second phase of the story, the widowed Constance and the French nobleman, Sainville, fall in love. But having sworn never to love again, having even gone so far as to inscribe that promise on her husband's tomb, Constance feels she must reject Sainville. Only when she learns that his despair is ruining his health does she finally announce, after much anguish and with only moderate conviction, that she will marry him despite her vow. Poor Sainville's misery only increases at this news, for he has just been to Malta and taken a vow of celibacy. Constance declares she will stay by his side regardless of what society may think; but they have hardly had a chance to embrace when she has a sudden attack of fever and dies. The novel ends with Sainville being dragged away from her deathbed.

In her dedication to the novel, Genlis, never given to false modesty, called *Les voeux téméraires* "le roman le plus moral que nous ayons dans notre langue" ["the most moral novel that we have in our language"]. If it teaches, as its author would have it, the dangers of the excessive sensibility so much in vogue, Constance's story and her ambivalence about sex and marriage also place her in a tradition of widows. Although hardly a suicide, her precipitate death is willed at some level: it ends her continual persecution by a series of men—her dispirited husband, her wicked brother-in-law, and the importunate Sainville, among others. Genlis's plots, moreover, by no means eschew suicide: the reprehensible brother-in-law in *Les voeux téméraires* kills himself, for example, as does the villain in her historical novel, *Le siège de la Rochelle* (1808). This is apparently a justifiable fictional peripeteia when the suicidal figure is male and criminal.

Her three-volume *Les mères rivales ou la calomnie* (1800), an intricate novel in epistolary form, is likewise framed by its title and the preface to volume 3 as a moral treatise about the ravages of calumny. Much of its interest, however, resides in its depiction of the protagonists' love affairs and of the bizarre union of the two main characters, who are adoptive brother and sister as well as husband and wife (Genlis's work demonstrates her ongoing concern with illegitimate births and adoptions).

"O la charmante petite créature!" ["Oh, the charming
little creature!"]. (Pauline d'Erneville, her maid and the foundling.)
Schumann/Meno Haas. Frontispiece, Félicité de Genlis,
Les mères rivales ou la calomnie, vol. 1 (Berlin: De la Garde, 1800).
Collection of Robert L. Dawson.

Pauline d'Erneville finds a baby girl, Léocadie, in the closet in a Paris inn and lovingly raises her, only to be widely accused of having secretly given birth to the child. Even Pauline's brother-husband, who should know better, doubts her virtue until at the end Léocadie is revealed to be *his* child, conceived in a brief extramarital affair with the beautiful and enigmatic countess of Rosmond. Genlis uses the plot as a vehicle for commentary on moral behavior and various forms of maternal and conjugal love, but as Charrière, that astute reader of word and gesture, put it (she was talking about the literary taste of Frederick William II of Prussia):

Il aurait encore mieux aimé dans les Mères rivales, ce livre si fort d'aventures, la partie romanesque que la partie du raisonnement. Madame de Rosmond et ses amants l'auraient beaucoup moins ennuyé que son jardin moral et allégorique.[7]

[He would have much preferred the romantic part to the reasoning part in *Les mères rivales,* that novel so rife with adventure. Madame de Rosmond and her lovers would have bored him much less than the moral and allegorical garden.]

Histoire intéressante, Les voeux téméraires, and *Les mères rivales* give evidence of Genlis's talents as a storyteller—her powerful imagination, verve, and compelling characterizations—gifts she would deploy, along with her considerable wordiness, in a long succession of novels ranging from the sentimental to the historical to the gothic. The macabre elements that characterize the gothic, much in vogue in the 1780s, are evident in the monstrous husband in *Histoire intéressante,* in his faking his wife's death (he buries a wax figure made to resemble her), and in her imprisonment in the dungeon. In all three of these novels, Genlis effectively uses the conventions of the gothic as Cottin uses those of sensibility, to translate the intersections between imagination and social reality.

The duchess's nocturnal underground existence symbolizes the potential horrors of an arranged marriage. Similarly, in *Les voeux téméraires,* Constance's vow never to remarry and her unexplained death illuminate psychological dimensions of widowhood. And the uneasy fraternal-romantic love between the protagonists of *Les mères rivales,* as well as their plans for intermarrying their own adoptive and birth children, pose questions about the junctions of incestuous arrangements and arranged marriages.

In both Cottin and Genlis, then, partially repressed content sometimes overwhelms enunciated morals. While Genlis counseled against passion and preached values for Christian living—obedience, forgiveness, moderation—at another level her novels, like those of Riccoboni, Charrière, Elie de Beaumont, and Cottin, were criticizing patriarchal arrangements and men's economic and social prerogatives. Her unusually forceful novelistic images of maternity and matriarchy, while they present models intended for imitation, also incorporate veiled protest.[8] Like other feminine sentimental and didactic texts, Genlis's are stories about social realities and about women's relations to the conventions governing parental authority, marriage, biological and surrogate motherhood, and widowhood—the conventions that shaped and circumscribed their lives.

CONCLUSION

Je vous dirai en grand secret (parce que c'est une vérité qu'il n'est pas bon de répandre), que l'amour ne vit qu'autant qu'il est libre; qu'il n'en est point qui puisse résister au mariage.

[I'll tell you in the greatest confidence (because it's a fact that should not be publicized) that love survives only as long as it is free; none can withstand marriage.]—*Amélie Mansfield*

The themes and tensions that structure Félicité de Genlis's stories recall the work of Jeanne Le Prince de Beaumont and bring us full circle. In both cases, there is sustained interest in the education, vindication, and salvation of women; there is also opposition to passion as a basis for marriage, and there are even veiled suggestions of misogamy. A juxtaposition of the two will serve as reminder that although the writings I have examined are arranged in a certain historical sequence (for example, Riccoboni embodied and fostered the anglomania characteristic of the early part of the second half of the century; *Caroline de Lichtfield* reflects the popularity of German motifs a few decades later; Charrière's works implicitly respond to the agenda for a "domestic novel" exemplified by the work of Richardson and Rousseau; Cottin could not have written so explicitly about sex fifty years earlier), these novels may also be considered a vast synchrony of female concerns and literary options and benefit from being read with and against each other.

Indeed, it bears mentioning that the novelists I have discussed, and in particular the ones who lived beyond 1800, were themselves reading and commenting on each other as well as on those who had recently pre-deceased them: Genlis critiqued the manuscript of *Caroline de Lichtfield* for her correspondent Montolieu, admired Le Prince de Beaumont, and, of course, pored painfully over certain novels by Riccoboni and Cottin; Montolieu's friend, General de Montesquiou, supplied her with the complete works of Riccoboni; Souza intensely disliked Genlis whom she accused of lies and ingratitude; Cottin alludes in *Malvina* to Riccoboni's *Juliette Catesby* and waxes lyrical in her correspondence over Charrière's *Caliste;* Charrière proposed marketing *Trois femmes* the way Souza had promoted *Adèle de Sénange,* while Charrière's protagonists read works by Le Prince de Beaumont, Souza, and Genlis.

In 1782, when the last text that I discuss at length, *Histoire intéressante de Madame la duchesse de C***,* first appeared as part of *Adèle et Théodore,* all these novelists were alive, and it is fair to assume that, given the stir caused by its publication, virtually all of them would have read it within a short time. It is true that Sophie Ristaud, future Madame Cottin, was only twelve, but *Adèle et Théodore* was intended for young people. Indeed, as the last born of these novelists, Cottin may be viewed in one sense as belonging to a younger generation than the others. But her death in August 1807 came only twenty months after Charrière's; and Montolieu, Souza, and Genlis all outlived her by over twenty years.

Although half a century separates the appearance of the novel I began with, Le Prince de Beaumont's *Lettres de Madame du Montier* (published in periodical form in 1750–52), from the last, Genlis's *Les mères rivales* (1800), the similarities between these two authors and their work are striking. Like Genlis, Le Prince de Beaumont was a governess, an inveterate pedagogue, a long-term resident of foreign countries, a devoted mother and grandmother, and an indefatigable writer of children's tales and moral stories for adults. There was an explicit conjunction between the work of the two in the 1780s, when Genlis published a play based on *La Belle et la Bête.* Both women, moreover, wrote historical novels and epistolary novels of sentiment, and both linked stories of implausible adventure and suffering to injunctions about Christian morality and proper behavior.

For example, des Essarts, the handsome young fiancé in *Mémoires de Madame la baronne de Batteville,* is literally buried alive during an epidemic of plague, only to rise again from the grave—as Genlis's duchess of C*** does from her underground dungeon—to a still more complete experience of religion. And if Le Prince de Beaumont's Lucie in *Lettres d'Emérance à Lucie* is one of the early characters in fiction to breast-feed her baby, and somewhat ostentatiously at that (2: 145), a minor but exquisite implausibility in the *Histoire intéressante,* also covertly in the service of didacticism, is that the sadistic and otherwise unredeemed duke charmingly waits to imprison his wife until the day after she has weaned their daughter. One senses the presence of Genlis the pedagogue and advocate of Rousseau's theories.

Indeed, women writers frequently incorporated into their novels his insistence on the importance of breast-feeding one's own children. In her "desert" home, nine months after an irregular marriage (undertaken without benefit of the Church), Daubenton's Zélie (*Zélie dans le désert*) gives birth to a son and notes "Je fus bientôt rétablie parce que je nourrissais" ["I was soon well again because I was breast-feeding"] (1: 299). Her aplomb is as exceptional as her marital status and her habitat, however, for episodes relating to breast-feeding usually constitute a source of tension between fictional husbands and their unhappy wives.

Most of the husbands are not nearly so accommodating in this matter as the normally fiendish duke of *Histoire intéressante.* When Emilie, for example, in Louise d'Epinay's *Histoire de Madame de Montbrillant* announces her desire to breast-feed, her husband declares himself unconditionally opposed to such "ridiculousness" (1: 295), revealing his inherent crassness—one more early sign that the marriage that the heroine so wanted will bring her little gratification. The sinister husband in *Alfrede ou le manoir de Warwick* (1794) by Constance de Cazenove d'Arlens (another member of the Constant family) likewise denies his wife permission to nurse their baby, a refusal that helps bring about the wife's illness and death.

When the story of Cottin's *Claire d'Albe* begins, she is already the mother of two children and nursing the younger one. Both the men of the household, however, subtly undermine her, just as they fail to understand her most delicate instincts: her husband says that a baby who has suckled can't tell her mother from her nanny, and Claire's admirer Frédéric complains that the infant reeks of sour milk.

The figure of Mistress Henley is the most poignant of these maternal nurses or aspiring nurses. The husband in this case offends not by *refusing* his wife permission to nurse but by insisting on the importance of doing so. Pregnancy seems initially to give the disheartened Mistress Henley a reason for living, but she is ambivalent about breast-feeding (as she is about so many things), wishing on the one hand to establish a bond with her infant and fearing on the other for the loss of her line. Most of all, she fears what her husband's reaction is likely to be, equally anxious that he will pronounce it indispensable regardless of the potential consequences for her looks and that he will reject it as one of her silly notions. He spares her, as she says, neither humiliation. Breast-feeding, he declares, is the first and most sacred maternal obligation, except in cases where a vice or defect in the mother could harm the child—Mistress Henley's case precisely.

He coolly announces his intention of consulting a doctor to learn whether the mother-to-be's extreme "vivacity" makes it preferable to engage a nurse. Not a word, she says, about *her* health or pleasure; it was a question only of this child "qui n'existait pas encore" ["who didn't yet exist"]. This time, she is undone. "Adieu la joie de ma grossesse," she writes, "adieu toute joie" ["Farewell the joy of pregnancy, farewell all joy"] (8: 120). A little later she notes that she would not deliberately take her own life, but sorrow can kill.

The opening letter of a later novel by Charrière, *Sir Walter Finch et son fils William* (written in 1799; published posthumously in 1806), turns on the refusal of the reasonable Sir Walter's unreasonable pregnant wife to have a nurse stand by in case of need: she seems to feel instinctively and inarticulately that not having an alternate source of milk is a kind of insurance against dying. But she does die shortly after giving birth to

William, and the eminently resourceful Sir Walter, with no nurse in the wings, considers using a goat to do the job.

Reactions of husbands, running the gamut from the dogmatic, to the punitive, to the dismissive, are among the most highly charged gestures in these novels. Indeed, the military skirmishes that are standard fare in many early novels are here transposed not just to the bedrooms but also to the very bodies of women and to their most intimate maternal and womanly attachments. Fatal and near-fatal clashes about the use to which married women may put their breasts and the significance and shape of their maternal bonds may be read as emblematic of a body of literature where traditional military battles tend to be either in the past or the geographical distance.[1]

The struggle of these heroines for self-ownership is carried out in an arena where sexual and often maternal identity as well as generational relations are at stake; in conflicts over breast-feeding come together questions about power, protocols, and conjugal economies. These episodes comment on women's reactions to social pressures and on their struggles with the most brutal and delicate of social and material realities. Thus the issue of breast-feeding represents here, as it often has since, a claim by women to social space and time, specifically to a central role in the formation of a child's identity. It is inherent in patriarchy that the husband would strive to dissipate maternal-physical presence, to impose on the child the "name of the father" exclusively. How better than to use a goat?

The endings of these stories likewise center on maternal loyalties and connections. One particularly vivid theme brings several rather different stories to an end and illustrates another characteristic female gathering of plot. When the heroine of *Histoire intéressante* emerges from her underground prison, she lyrically rediscovers the sounds and sights of nature and the feel of freedom. Since her husband has died, she is both independent and wealthy; she can accept the hand of Belmire, whom she has loved and courageously protected, and who, although believing her dead, has nonetheless remained single. But instead of the conclusion we might expect—their marriage, which would unambiguously reassert her assimilation by society and her subscription to the marital economy as a privileged means of fulfillment—she first declines to marry, then hands Belmire over to her daughter. Here is the duchess relating how she announced her resolution to him:

> Je vous la donne, lui dis-je; elle est à vous, elle vous aime, elle a quinze ans, c'est l'âge où je vous vis pour la première fois: elle vous retrace tout ce que j'étais alors, et par sa figure et par ses sentiments. Le sort vous rend aujourd'hui ce qu'il vous ravit autrefois: et moi, n'étant pas née pour faire votre bonheur, je ne puis m'en consoler qu'en vous voyant heureux par ma fille. (107)

> [I'm giving her to you, I told him; she's yours, she loves you, she's fifteen—my age when I saw you for the first time: her looks and her feelings will remind you of everything I was then. Fate is restoring to you today what it previously took from you; and I, who was not born to bring you happiness, can console myself only by seeing my daughter do so.]

She recalls Le Prince de Beaumont's baroness of Batteville, who also marries an older man though in love with one her own age, and who afterward uses the freedom of widowhood to arrange for her daughter to marry the younger man in her place. And these are not the only stories to conclude with the marriage of a daughter to the man her mother once desired. Benoist's Sophronie does the same when she finally realizes that her own interest in Valzan is hopeless: "Je ne puis être votre amante," she exclaims in the simplistically edifying conclusion, "eh bien! je ferai plus; je veux être votre amie, votre mère" ["I can't be your lover; well, then, I'll be something more: I want to be your friend, your mother"] (48).

In *Alfrede ou le manoir de Warwick,* the title character falls in love with a portrait found in her dead mother's effects; it turns out to be the likeness of Edouard Randall, whom the long-suffering mother had loved. After various peripeteia, Alfrede and Randall plight their troth on her mother's grave, in a sort of posthumous mother-daughter bonding; perhaps we may read it as replacing the nursing bond between the same mother and daughter which the malevolent husband/father had thwarted years earlier.

Whereas Edouard conveniently transfers passion from a dead mother to a living daughter, Le Prince de Beaumont's des Essarts and Genlis's Belmire even more nimbly shift their allegiance (during the very lifetime of the mothers) to the nubile daughters. *La baronne de Batteville,* several times longer than *Histoire intéressante,* comments at greater length on the mother's motivations in proposing this realignment of affections and on the lover's reactions. These widows, with the freedom and wealth to do as they choose, establish their superiority over lovers who obviously have remained at a more primitive stage of emotional and sensual development.

The persistence of this myth and its incarnation in the novels of the two most renowned female educators of the century suggest its vitality as well as its perceived suitability as a vehicle for "moral" lessons. It opens up the very conventionality of these novels to an array of meanings. It implicitly recognizes, of course, the psychological legacies of nightmarish marriages: after all they have been through, these protagonists, like other weary widows of fiction, prefer not to marry again. It gives play, at the same time, to a vision of generational female solidarity that makes it possible to substitute a daughter's sexuality for her mother's. And, of course, it nicely illustrates the empowering of mothers characteristic of novels by women.

The particular act of renunciation and withdrawal embodies the fantasy of ultimate control: power over the marital economy and individual economies, manipulation of masculine and filial sexuality, and the ability to reproduce oneself and rewrite history at will. As the duchess's announcement, with its shifting subject, makes clear—"*I'*m giving her to you . . . *Fate* is restoring to you"—the mature heroine casts herself in the heady role of destiny. Her decree is also, although less obviously, a way of wreaking a unique vengeance on an initially intrusive and finally irrelevant husband: in an act of widowly infidelity, his only offspring is bequeathed to his rival.

Through this drastic gesture, women characters become protagonists of their own creation. Their act of resistance and sublimation is depicted by the didactically inclined authors as maternal, even saintly, a triumph of prudence—precisely the qualities in which Claire d'Albe seems (to Genlis) to be deficient. But this closing scenario also covertly articulates concerns that *are* raised by the conclusion of *Claire d'Albe*—questions about current versions of marriage, rites of sexuality, and conventions regulating women's "happiness" and their relation to "reason."

A simple formulation in the last lines of Diderot's *Sur les femmes* may be applied to novels by women throughout the period: "Ou les femmes se taisent, ou souvent elles ont l'air de n'oser dire ce qu'elles disent" ["Either women keep quiet or often they seem not to dare say what they are saying"] (261). The conclusions of these stories demonstrate once more how women authors of sentimental novels, in language that the *Lettre en réponse à L'année merveilleuse* recognized as discriminating and originary, often said more than they seemed to be saying about the conventions they both used and lived. Perhaps, moreover, they are "daring" in a sense inaccessible to Diderot: with the novel form so strongly defined by women authors, it became a recognizable vehicle of female power. These novels constitute an ongoing conversation among women in which the secret meanings, the points of antagonism and rupture, the seemly sub-versions were, through the transparency of the fictional conventions, probably as legible to the participants as they are becoming once again to us.

FRENCH NOVELS

BY 18TH-CENTURY WOMEN

This list by no means pretends to be exhaustive: only titles mentioned in this study are noted, along with the edition on which references and citations are based. Where pertinent, other modern editions are also listed. The dates on the left are those of the original editions.

Beauharnais, Fanny Mouchard de Chaban, comtesse de

1780   *L'Abailard supposé ou le sentiment à l'épreuve*. Paris: Nilsson, s.d.

1781   *L'aveugle par amour*. Paris and Liège: Lemarié, 1782.

1789   *Les noeuds enchantés ou la bizarrerie des destinées*. 2 vols. Rome: de l'imprimerie papale, 1789.

Beccary, Madame

1769   *Lettres de Milady Bedfort*. Paris: de Hansy, 1769.

1778   *Milord d'Ambi, histoire anglaise*. 2 vols. Paris: Gaugery, 1778.

1781   *Mémoires de Fanny Spingler, histoire anglaise*. 2 vols. Paris: Knapen, 1781.

Bédacier, Catherine Durand

1699   *La comtesse de Mortane*. 2 vols. Paris: Prault, 1736.

Belvo, marquise de

1761   *Quelques lettres écrites en 1743 et 1744 par une jeune veuve au chevalier de Luzeincour*. N.p., 1761.

Benoist, Françoise Albine Puzin de la Martinière

1766   *Célianne ou les amants séduits par leurs vertus*. Amsterdam and Paris: Lacombe, 1766.

1766   *Elisabeth*. 4 vols. Amsterdam: Arkstée and Merkus, 1766.

1767   *Lettres du colonel Talbert*. 4 vols. Amsterdam and Paris: Durand, 1767.

1768   *Agathe et Isidore*. 2 vols. Amsterdam and Paris: Durand, 1768.

1769   *Sophronie ou leçon prétendue d'une mère à sa fille*. London and Paris: Duchesne, 1769.

1770   *L'erreur des désirs*. 2 vols. Paris: Regnard and Demonville; Lyon: Cellier; Rouen: Lucas, 1770.

1781   *Les erreurs d'une jolie femme ou l'Aspasie française*. Brussels and Paris: Duchesne, 1781.

Cazenove d'Arlens, Constance Louise de Constant-Rebecque de

1794   *Alfrede ou le manoir de Warwick*. 2 vols. Lausanne: Luquiens, 1794.

Charrière, Isabella Agneta Elisabeth van Tuyll van Serooskerken (Belle de Zuylen) de

1763   *Le noble*. Amsterdam: G. A. van Oorschot, 1980. In vol.8 of *Oeuvres complètes*. Ed. Jean-Daniel Candaux, C. P. Courtney, Pierre H. Dubois, Simone Dubois-De Bruyn, Patrice Thompson, Jeroom Vercruysse, and Dennis M. Wood. 1979–84.

1784   *Lettres neuchâteloises*. Amsterdam: G. A. van Oorschot, 1980. In vol.8 of *Oeuvres complètes*.

1784   *Lettres de Mistriss Henley publiées par son amie*. Amsterdam: G. A. van Oorschot, 1980. In vol.8 of *Oeuvres complètes*.

1785   *Lettres écrites de Lausanne*. Amsterdam: G. A. van Oorschot, 1980. In vol.8 of *Oeuvres complètes*.

1787   *Caliste ou continuation des Lettres écrites de Lausanne*. Amsterdam: G. A. van Oorschot, 1980. In vol.8 of *Oeuvres complètes*.

1796   *Trois femmes*. Amsterdam: G. A. van Oorschot, 1981. In vol.9 of *Oeuvres complètes*.

1798   *Honorine d'Userche*. Amsterdam: G. A. van Oorschot, 1981. In vol.9 of *Oeuvres complètes*.

1799   *Sainte Anne*. Amsterdam: G. A. van Oorschot, 1981. In vol.9 of *Oeuvres complètes*.

1806   *Sir Walter Finch et son fils William*. Amsterdam: G. A. van Oorschot, 1981. In vol.9 of *Oeuvres complètes*.

Other modern editions:

> *Caliste, Lettres écrites de Lausanne*. Ed. Claudine Herrmann. Paris: Des femmes, 1979.
>
> *Honorine d'Userche*. Toulouse: Editions Ombres, 1992.
>
> *Lettres écrites de Lausanne* (published with *Julie ou la Nouvelle Héloïse*). Ed. Jean Starobinski. 2 vols. [Lausanne]: Editions Rencontre, 1970.
>
> *Lettres neuchâteloises*. Ed. Isabelle and Jean-Louis Vissière. Preface by Christophe Calame. Paris: La différence, 1991.
>
> *Lettres neuchâteloises suivi de Trois femmes*. Postface by Charly Guyot. Lausanne: Bibliothèque romande, 1971.

Cottin, Marie (Sophie) Ristaud

1799   *Claire d'Albe*. Paris: Hiard, 1831.

1801   *Malvina*. Paris: Ménard and Desenne, fils, 1824. In vols. 2–4 of *Oeuvres complètes*.

1803   *Amélie Mansfield*. Paris: Ménard and Desenne, fils, 1824. In vols. 5–7 of *Oeuvres complètes*.

1803   *La prise de Jéricho*. In vol. 12 of *Oeuvres complètes*.

1805   *Mathilde ou mémoires tirés de l'histoire des croisades*. Paris: Ménard and Desenne, fils, 1824. In vols. 8–11 of *Oeuvres complètes*.

1806   *Elisabeth*. Paris: Ménard and Desenne, 1824. In vol. 12 of *Oeuvres complètes*.

Modern edition:

> *Claire d'Albe*. Preface by Jean Gaulmier. Paris: Régine Deforges, 1976.

Dalibard, Françoise Thérèse Aumerle Saint-Phalier

1749   *Le portefeuille rendu ou lettres historiques par Mademoiselle de S****. 2 vols. London: 1750.

Daubenton, Marguerite

1786   *Zélie dans le désert*. 2 vols. London and Paris: Belin, Desenne and Royez, 1786.

Elie de Beaumont, Anne Louise Morin Dumesnil

1764   *Lettres du marquis de Roselle*. London and Paris: Cellot, 1770.

1776   *Anecdotes de la cour et du règne d'Edouard II, roi d'Angleterre*. [Books 1 and 2 are by Tenein, book 3 by Elie de Beaumont.] Paris: Pissot, 1776.

Epinay, Louise Florence Pétronille Tardieu d'Esclavelles, dame de la Live d'
—— *Histoire de Madame de Montbrillant*. Ed. Georges Roth. 3 vols. Paris:
    Gallimard, 1951.

Falques (or Fauques), Marianne Agnès
    1751   *Le triomphe de l'amitié, ouvrage traduit du grec*. 2 vols. London and
        Paris: Bauche fils, 1751.

Fontette de Sommery, Mademoiselle
    1785   *Lettres de Madame la comtesse de L*** à Monsieur le comte de R****.
        Nouvelle édition. Paris: Barrois, 1786.

Genlis, Stéphanie Félicité Ducrest de Saint-Aubin, marquise de Sillery, com-
    tesse de
    1782   *Adèle et Théodore ou lettres sur l'éducation*. 3 vols. Paris: Lambert,
        1785.
    1783   *Histoire intéressante de Madame la duchesse de C****. Lausanne:
        Vincent, 1783. (Geneva and Paris: Slatkine, 1982.) Originally
        appeared as interpolated story in *Adèle et Théodore*, 1782.
    1784   *Les veillées du château ou cours de morale à l'usage des enfants*. 4 vols.
        Maestricht: Dufour and Roux, 1784.
    1798   *Les voeux téméraires ou l'enthousiasme*. 2 vols. Hambourg: Cha-
        teauneuf, and Paris: Bernard, 1798.
    1800   *Les mères rivales ou la calomnie*. 3 vols. Berlin: De la Garde,
        1800.
    1807   *Le siège de la Rochelle*. New York: Lockwood, 1867.

Graffigny, Françoise d'Issembourg d'Happoncourt de
    1747   *Lettres d'une Péruvienne*. Ed. Bernard Bray and Isabelle Landy-
        Houillon. Paris: Garnier-Flammarion, 1983.
    Other modern edition:
        Lettres d'une Péruvienne. Preface by Colette Piau-Gillot. Paris:
        Côté-Femmes, 1990.

Guénard de Méré, Elisabeth
    1800   *Irma ou les malheurs d'une jeune orpheline*. 4 vols. Paris: Delhy, An
        VIII.

La Guesnerie, Charlotte Marie Anne Charbonnier de
    1760   *Mémoires de Miledi B....* 4 vols. Amsterdam and Paris: Cuissart,
        1760.

Le Prince de Beaumont, Jeanne Marie

1748   *Le triomphe de la vérité ou mémoires de M. de la Villette.* 2 vols. Nancy: Thomas, 1748.

1754   *Civan, roi de Bungo, histoire japonaise.* 2 vols. London: Nourse, 1754.

1756   *Lettres de Madame du Montier.* 2 vols. Lyon: Bruyset Ponthus, 1767. (Anthologized in 1753, published separately in 1756.)

1765   *Lettres d'Emérance à Lucie.* 2 vols. Lyon: Bruyset Ponthus, and Paris: Saillant, 1765.

1766   *Mémoires de Madame la baronne de Batteville ou la veuve parfaite.* Lyon: Bruyset Ponthus, 1766.

1767   *La nouvelle Clarice, histoire véritable.* 2 vols. Lyon: Bruyset Ponthus, 1775.

Mérard de Saint-Just, Anne Jeanne Félicité d'Ormoy

1788   *Histoire de la baronne d'Alvigny.* London and Paris: Maradan, 1788.

1788   *Mon journal d'un an ou mémoires de Mademoiselle de Rozadelle-Saint-Ophelle.* Parma and Paris: 1788.

Montolieu, Elisabeth Jeanne Pauline Isabelle Polier de Bottens de Crousaz, baronne de

1786   *Caroline de Lichtfield.* 3 vols. London: Dulau, 1809.

Motte, Mademoiselle

1775   *Célide ou histoire de la marquise de Bliville.* 2 vols. Paris and Liège: Bassompierre, 1776.

Puisieux, Marie Madeleine d'Arsant de

1768   *Mémoires d'un homme de bien.* 3 vols. Paris: Delalain, and Dijon: Coignard de la Pinelle and Frantin, 1768.

Riccoboni, Marie Jeanne de Heurles de Laboras Mézières

1757   *Lettres de Mistriss Fanni Butlerd.* Ed. Joan Hinde Stewart. (Reprint of Paris: Volland, 1786.) Geneva: Droz, 1979.

1758   *Histoire de M. le marquis de Cressy.* Ed. Olga B. Cragg. *Studies on Voltaire and the Eighteenth Century* 266. Oxford: Voltaire Foundation, 1989.

1759   *Lettres de Milady Juliette Catesby à Milady Henriette Campley, son amie.* Preface by Sylvain Menant. Paris: Desjonquères, 1983.

1764   *Histoire de Miss Jenny, écrite et envoyée par elle à Mylady, comtesse de Roscomonde, ambassadrice d'Angleterre à la cour de Dannemark.* Paris: Volland, 1786. In vol.3 of *Oeuvres complètes.* Nouvelle édition.

1765   *Histoire d'Ernestine.* Paris: Volland, 1786. In vol.5 of *Oeuvres complètes.*

1767   *Lettres d'Adélaïde de Dammartin, comtesse de Sancerre, à M. le comte de Nancé, son ami.* Paris: Volland, 1786. In vol.6 of *Oeuvres complètes.*

1772   *Lettres d'Elisabeth-Sophie de Vallière à Louise Hortence de Canteleu, son amie.* Paris: Volland, 1786. In vol.4 of *Oeuvres complètes.*

1777   *Lettres de Mylord Rivers à Sir Charles Cardigan.* Paris: Volland, 1786. In vol.6 of *Oeuvres complètes.*

       Other modern editions:

       Histoire d'Ernestine. Preface by Colette Piau-Gillot. Paris: Côté-femmes, 1991.

       L'histoire du marquis de Cressy. Ed. Alix S. Deguise. Paris: Des femmes, 1987.

       Les lettres de Mylord Rivers. Ed. Olga B. Cragg. Geneva: Droz, 1993.

Robert, Marie-Anne de Roumier

1763   *La voix de la nature ou les aventures de Madame la marquise de* * * *. 5 vols. Amsterdam: Compagnie, 1770.

1767   *Nicole de Beauvais ou l'amour vaincu par la reconnaissance.* 2 vols. The Hague and Paris: Desaint et al., 1767.

Souza, Adélaïde Marie Emilie Filleul, comtesse de Flahaut, marquise de

1794   *Adèle de Sénange ou lettres de Lord Sydenham.* In *Oeuvres de Madame de Souza.* Nouvelle édition. Preface by Sainte-Beuve. Paris: Charpentier, 1840.

1799   *Emilie et Alphonse.* In *Oeuvres de Madame de Souza.* Paris: Garnier (Bibliothèque amusante), 1865.

1801   *Charles et Marie.* In *Oeuvres de Madame de Souza.* Nouvelle édition. Preface by Sainte-Beuve. Paris: Charpentier, 1840.

1808   *Eugène de Rothelin.* In *Oeuvres de Madame de Souza.* Nouvelle édition. Preface by Sainte-Beuve. Paris: Charpentier, 1840.

Tencin, Claudine Alexandrine Guérin de

1735   *Mémoires du comte de Comminge.* Preface by Michel Delon. Paris: Desjonquères, 1985.

1739   *Le siège de Calais.* Preface by Pierre-Jean Rémy. Paris: Desjonquères, 1983.

1776   *Anecdotes de la cour et du règne d'Edouard II, roi d'Angleterre.* [Books 1 and 2 are by Tencin, book 3 by Elie de Beaumont.] Paris: Pissot, 1776.

Vasse, Cornélie Pétronille Bénédicte Wouters, baronne de

1782   *Les aveux d'une femme galante ou lettres de Madame la marquise de ***à Myladi Fanny Stapleton.* London and Paris: Balard, 1782.

Villeneuve, Gabrielle Suzanne Barbot de Gallon de

1753   *La jardinière de Vincennes.* 5 vols. London and Frankfort: Bassompierre, 1778.

NOTES

CHAPTER I: VOCATION AND PROVOCATION

1   *Les gynographes* was originally published as a sequel to *Le pornographe* and *La mimographe* in a didactic series entitled *Idées singulières*.

2   Restif's retrogressive insistence on the importance of keeping women in their place is part of a controversy about the nature of women and their proper role which had been going on for centuries. One need not look far for other eighteenth-century examples of misogynist views. A broadside published by the Abbé Gabriel François Coyer in 1748, to which I shall return in my next chapter, is a wittier illustration than Restif's of both misology and misogyny. On the other hand, the eighteenth century also saw innumerable treatises that set out in one way or another to defend women's intellectual and moral qualities, from *Les femmes savantes ou bibliothèque des dames* [Women scholars or a ladies' library] (1718), to Legouvé, *Le mérite des femmes* (1800).

3   Cf. Nancy K. Miller, who speaks of "Laclos's and Sade's closural moves of putting the woman in her place" (*Displacements* 47).

4   Letter to Mr. Thicknesse, quoted in La Harpe, *Oeuvres* 15: 527. Elisabeth Guénard de Méré was sufficiently vexed by the problem of pirated editions that on the reverse of the title page of *Irma ou les malheurs d'une jeune orpheline* [Irma or the misfortunes of a young orphan] (1800), she placed a note threatening counterfeiters with a lawsuit and offering a reward for the identification of anyone involved in the production, distribution, or sale of counterfeit editions.

5   Shirley Jones 211. My readings likewise call into question Jones's gener-

alization that "such novels as are known to have been written by women during the eighteenth century are all, without exception, characterized by rigorous moral conservatism" (211).

6 A character in Restif's *La paysanne pervertie* nonetheless recommends this as Benoist's most outstanding work (392).

7 For information about Madeleine de Puisieux, see Alice M. Laborde, *Diderot et Madame de Puisieux* (Saratoga, CA: Anma Libri, 1984).

8 Cf. the Goncourts, who cite a description from *Les nouvelles femmes* (Geneva, 1761) of the fateful moment when the bride "prononçait un *oui* dont elle ne sentait ni la force ni les obligations" ["pronounced a *yes* of which she felt neither the force nor the obligations"] (65).

9 Novels by women did not, of course, uniformly urge the love match. The very title of Benoist's *L'erreur des désirs* (1770) announces a different slant: Léonice brings a lifetime of troubles upon herself when she rejects her mother's intuitions about the man Léonice wants to marry. And Charrière's *Lettres de Mistriss Henley*, which I shall discuss in chapter 5, poignantly ironizes about an independent woman's ability to choose a spouse.

10 In *Tender Geographies* Joan DeJean notes that the mid-eighteenth century in France, like the 1670s, was characterized by "intense debate" about marriage (150), and discusses in particular the contract theory of marriage as it appears in the work of Pothier. For Pothier, as she concludes, "marriage was an affair of property" (152). DeJean's important book, which makes arguments sometimes analogous to mine for women writers of the seventeenth century, appeared as I was doing the final revisions for this study.

11 Plots of countless novels reflect women's vulnerability to virtual imprisonment in convents. For reasons of morality or convenience, women characters are often forced by husbands or families either to live in convents as boarders or to take the veil. A character in a short interpolated story in Françoise Dalibard's *Le portefeuille rendu* [The wallet returned] (1749), for example, is forced into a convent after her husband discovers she is having an affair (1: 26). Madame d'Her ... in the same novel recounts how her father put her in a convent at the age of seventeen because she refused to marry the fifty-five-year-old suitor he had selected for her; the father then announced he was giving her the choice of

capitulating or taking the veil (1: 108). Indeed, a 1756 novel by de Carné, *Histoire de Madame la comtesse de Monglas,* is subtitled *consolation pour les religieuses qui le sont malgré elles* [consolation for those who are nuns in spite of themselves]. The title character of Mérard de Saint-Just's *Histoire de la baronne d'Alvigny* (1788) is finally locked away in a convent by a husband who loses patience with her gambling.

12 Françoise de Graffigny's Zilia in *Lettres d'une Péruvienne* (1747) comments on the injustice of laws that allow a man to punish severely the least appearance of infidelity in his wife while conducting his own affairs with impunity. The wedding ceremony, she adds, is the only instant of equality in marriage: afterward it seems that the wife alone is bound by the ties of marriage (345). Graffigny knew what she was talking about, having vividly experienced the inequalities of marriage and the difficulties of separating from a brutal husband.

13 In a similar vein, the young heroine of *Histoire de Madame de Montbrillant* describes the reading of the marriage contract in the presence of her fiancé and herself: "mon oncle qui en fit la lecture semblait craindre, par la rapidité avec laquelle il lisait, que nous n'en retinssions, ou même en entendissions, un mot" ["my uncle, who did the reading, seemed to fear, to judge by the rapidity with which he read, that we might remember, or even understand, a word of it"] (1: 226).

14 Edmée de la Rochefoucauld, *Femmes d'hier et d'aujourd'hui* (Paris: Grasset, 1966).

15 Cf. DeJean's comments in the introduction to *Tender Geographies* on "the early woman writer's complex relation to the *nom d'auteur*" and on the code by which women writers are today known only as "Madame de" or "Mademoiselle de."

16 The inconsistencies of the typesetting of the first edition of her major novel parallel this oscillation in the spelling of her name: Fanny Spingler's confidante is called "Corali" until page 52, after which she is "Coraly"; on page 53, "Ladi" Malgarde likewise becomes "Lady" Malgarde, and a character called "Jenny" becomes "Janny."

17 Cf. DeJean (*Tender Geographies*) and Miller (*Subject to Change*).

18 For more details on Riccoboni's names, see Flaux 8–9. Cf. also English Showalter's illuminating comments on the variant spellings of the name of the author of *Lettres d'une Péruvienne.* She was baptized Françoise

d'Happoncourt, but she and her husband took the name of a property that is variously spelled in contemporary legal documents and editions of her work as "Graffigny," "Grafigny," "Grafigni," "Graffigni," and even "Graphigni." Does it matter now? Showalter asks: "Only to the degree that it is yet another sign of marginalization; and like the ambiguous hommage of 'Madame' instead of 'Françoise' and the use of her husband's 'Graf(f)igny' instead of her own 'Hap(p)oncour(t),' the deference to her whimsical orthography instead of standard spelling effectively problematizes her name. One way or the other, the problem would have been resolved long ago for a canonical author" (Review of *Vierge du soleil/fille des lumières: la "Péruvienne," de Mme de Grafigny et ses "suites,"* in *Eighteenth-Century Studies* 24, no. 1 [Fall 1990]: 134–35).

19   Nancy K. Miller notes, in a similar vein, that René Etiemble's 1966 Pléïade anthology, *Romanciers du dix-huitième siècle*, includes no women authors (*Displacements* 39–40). I would add that since even this anthology (with its limitations), on which teachers of the eighteenth-century novel counted for so long, is currently unavailable, the time is right for an alternative anthology that would include novels like those of Riccoboni and Charrière.

20   I am grateful to English Showalter for pointing this out to me.

21   Of Adélaïde de Souza, whose personality and work he clearly admired, the baron de Maricourt remarked in his 1907 study, "Femme, elle n'eut point une logique sans défaut" ["As a woman, her logic was by no means faultless"] (174). A few pages earlier, he explained that her best-known novel, *Adèle de Sénange*, is "une autobiographie tracée en termes flatteurs" ["an autobiography written in flattering terms"] (170).

22   Yves Benot, *Diderot de l'athéisme à l'anticolonialisme* (Paris: Maspéro, 1981), 104.

CHAPTER 2: SPEECH AND SAINTLINESS

1   For information about Le Prince de Beaumont's life and publications, see Patricia A. Clancy.

2   Originally published in England in 1757 as *Young Misses Magazine*.

3   J. Q. C. Mackrell, *The Attack on "Feudalism" in Eighteenth-Century France* (London: Rutledge, 1973), 85.

4   Jonathan Swift, *Annus Mirabilis*, in *Works* (Edinburgh: Archibald Con-

stable and Co., 1824), 13: 133. For a discussion of the debt that the *Bagatelles morales* owes the English, see Louise Elsoffer-Kamins, "Un imitateur original de Jonathan Swift: L'abbé Coyer et ses *Bagatelles morales* (1754)," *Revue de Littérature Comparée* 23 (1949): 469–81.

5 *Lettres sur quelques écrits de ce temps* (no title page) 1: 135.

6 For example, the "prosopopée de Fabricius" in the *Discours sur les sciences et les arts* (1750) protests the feminization of masculine behavior, and in *Emile* (1762), there is an allusion to the failure of modern culture to maintain sexual identity (3: 14; 4: 746).

7 For a bibliographical description of this and other items in the debate between Coyer and Le Prince de Beaumont, see Dawson's *Additions*. Let me add that M. A. Reynaud, in a typographically and organizationally confusing 1972 typescript which I consulted at the Library of Congress, cites (but gives no source for) a "carnet intime" ["personal notebook"] of 1745 in which Le Prince de Beaumont seems to have originally drafted remarks appearing in the *Lettre en réponse*. Even if the issue was discussed as early as 1745, it was not until 1748 that the quarrel took on broad importance.

8 This argument for the excellence of women's writing style is related to a traditional feminist emphasis on woman's gift for grasping meaning: quoting the seventeenth-century feminist Gabriel Gilbert's *Panégyrique des dames*, Carolyn C. Lougee explains that women were said to possess a sort of intuition by which "they acquire by birth what men acquire only by work and by years" (*Le paradis des femmes: Women, Salons and Social Stratification in Seventeenth-Century France* [Princeton: Princeton University Press, 1976], 31–32).

9 Robert Dawson lent me his copy of this publication, which is not listed in major libraries or bibliographies.

10 Still other pieces appeared in the polemic between Coyer and Le Prince de Beaumont, including his *Lettre à une jeune dame nouvellement mariée* [Letter to a young lady, newly married] (inspired by Swift) and her *Réponse d'une jeune femme nouvellement mariée à Paris* [Response of a young woman newly married in Paris].

11 For a discussion of *Civan* and its sources, see Fernand Baldensperger, "Un roman exotique de Mme Le Prince de Beaumont," *Revue de littérature comparée* 26, no.1 (January-March 1952): 45–53.

12 *Madame du Montier* was published in periodical form between 1750 and
1752, then included in *Lettres sérieuses et amusantes* (1753), a multi-
volume collection of works by various authors, and issued separately in
1756. It was reedited at least ten times before the end of the century. *La
baronne de Batteville* was reedited at least four times after its original
1766 publication (Martin, Mylne, and Frautschi 21–22, 112). The volume by Angus Martin, Vivienne G. Mylne, and Richard Frautschi, *Bibliographie du genre romanesque en France (1751–1800)*, has been an indispensable reference work for me throughout this project.

13 Trans. Stamper Richardson, 2 vols. (London: Noble, 1758).

14 A similar idea appears in Jean-Jacques Rousseau's *Julie ou la nouvelle
Héloïse* (1761): "Les romans sont peut-être la dernière instruction qu'il
reste à donner à un peuple assez corrompu pour que toute autre lui soit
inutile" ["Novels are perhaps the final lesson that remains to be given to
a society so corrupt that any other lesson would be useless"] (2: 277).

15 For example, Emérance to Lucie: "Nous étions destinées vous et moi à
éprouver des aventures si extraordinaires qu'elles sont vraies sans être
vraisemblables" ["You and I were destined to have adventures so extraordinary that they are true although they seem unreal"] (2: 260).

16 Comparable plot elements, of course, occur with variations in other
novels. When Madame D. M. in Dalibard's *Le portefeuille rendu* becomes
an invalid, she marries off her suitor to her sixteen-year-old daughter. In
this case, the unhappy bride pines away three years after the marriage. In
Balzac's *Le lys dans la vallée*, a dying Madame de Mortsauf encourages
Félix de Vandenesse to marry her daughter. But, like Julie (and unlike Le
Prince de Beaumont's heroines), she attempts this because she herself is
unavailable—and like Julie she fails. The relation between Eugène de
Rastignac and Delphine de Nucingen, lovers in *Le père Goriot*, is radically
modified when she gives him her daughter in marriage (*Le député
d'Arcis*); but Delphine, of course, is all the while married to the baron de
Nucingen.

17 Le Prince de Beaumont was apparently fond of this formulation. It
appears again in *La nouvelle Clarice*: "J'ai lu quelque part que si l'on
faisait un noviciat dans le mariage, il y aurait peu de professes" ["I read
somewhere that if there were a novitiate in marriage, few would enter
the order"] (1: 15).

18 Erich Auerbach, *Mimesis*, trans. Willard R. Trask (Princeton: Princeton University Press, 1973) 359–94.

19 *Conversations d'Emilie* (Paris: Pissot, 1776) 106, quoted in Alice Parker, "Louise d'Epinay's Account of Female Epistemology and Sexual Politics," *French Review* 55, no.1 (October 1981): 45.

CHAPTER 3: DOXAL VIRTUE

1 The date of composition of *Jacques le fataliste et son maître* is not easily pinpointed. Diderot probably began working on it around 1765 and continued to do so off and on for about nineteen years (cf. ed. Yvon Belaval, pp.7–8).

2 The others are Richardson's *Clarissa* (1747–48), Graffigny's *Lettres d'une Péruvienne* (1747), Riccoboni's *Lettres de Milady Juliette Catesby* (1758), Rousseau's *Julie ou la Nouvelle Héloïse* (1761), and Crébillon's *Lettres de la marquise de* *** *au comte de* *** (1732).

3 Much later in the century, Isabelle de Charrière would publish *Sainte Anne* (1799), about a nobleman in love, to the horror of his haughty mother, with the granddaughter of a gardener, a young woman who has never even learned to read. But in a manner characteristic of Charrière's understated plots and endings, things are resolved without startling revelations. Young Monsieur de Sainte Anne marries Babet d'Estival, and both are exactly what they seemed to be.

4 For an analysis of this scene, see Alice M. Laborde, 86–92.

CHAPTER 4: REMARRYING

1 She seems to allude obliquely to repercussions of this when she complains in a letter of 1772 to David Garrick that when she was six, a lawsuit stripped her of her father and her property (*Letters*, ed. James C. Nicholls, 227). In a provocative paper delivered at the 1991 meeting of the International Society for Eighteenth-Century Studies, "Fallacies of Literary History: The Myth of Authenticity in the Reception of *Fanni Butlerd*," Aurora Wolfgang comes to the conclusion, as I had on reflection, that the passage in question, about an event that altered what should have been Riccoboni's "fate," refers in fact to this childhood trauma and not, as I suggested in my introduction to *Lettres de Mistriss Fanni Butlerd*, to a later love affair.

2   That Fanni's letters were themselves inspired by an unhappy love affair of Riccoboni's cannot be proven with certainty, but is plausible. I have recently learned from Mireille Flaux that Michèle Servien (both Flaux and Servien have written French doctoral dissertations on Riccoboni) concludes from her research that, although we cannot be sure, there is nothing to contradict the hypothesis identifying Alfred with the real comte de Maillebois. I am grateful to Mireille Flaux whose letters to me have suggested useful insights into Riccoboni's work.

3   Colette Piau, in a June 1989 radio broadcast on France Culture, *La chaste Madame Riccoboni: Les folies de l'amour au dix-huitième siècle.*

4   For additional information on Riccoboni's life, see especially Emily Crosby, Michèle Servien, the James C. Nicholls edition of her letters, and the Olga Cragg edition of *Histoire de M. le marquis de Cressy.* For a recent full-length study, including reflection abbout Riccoboni's life, see the thesis of Mireille Flaux, *Madame Riccoboni: Une idée du bonheur au féminin au siècle des lumières* (Lille: Université de Lille III, Atelier national de reproduction des thèses, 1991), which reached me as my book was going to press.

5   Madame M. 197. The commentator is referring, apparently among others, to Charles Palissot de Montenoy who in *La dunciade* taunted

> . . . cette Rubiconi,
> Qui n'a point fait le *Marquis de Cressy,*
> Qui n'a point fait les *Lettres de Fanny,*
> Qui n'a point fait *Juliette Catesby.*

[that "Rubiconi" who didn't write the *Marquis de Cressy,* who didn't write the *Letters of Fanny,* who didn't write *Juliette Catesby*] (88).

6   The February 1786 review in the *Correspondance littéraire* of Fontette de Sommery's *Lettres de Madame la comtesse de L*** à Monsieur le comte de R**** (1785) notes that this novel, too, was suspected of being the work of Riccoboni, then of Genlis—and adds that such suspicion in itself constitutes rather high praise (part 3, 3: 447).

7   For an incisive reading of the exchange between Riccoboni and Laclos, see Susan K. Jackson, "In Search of a Female Voice: *Les liaisons dangereuses.*"

8   My references are to the excellent Olga Cragg edition, which appeared in

a 1989 issue of *Studies on Voltaire and the Eighteenth Century* and has an outstanding critical apparatus.

9 For example, Arlette André, "Le féminisme chez madame Riccoboni"; Colette Cazenobe, "Le féminisme paradoxal de Madame Riccoboni"; Colette Piau, "L'écriture féminine? A propos de Marie-Jeanne Riccoboni"; Andrée Demay, *Marie-Jeanne Riccoboni ou de la pensée féministe chez une romancière du XVIIIe siècle*. Cook notes the limitations of both what she calls the "biographicalist" criticism of Riccoboni and a preoccupation with the "feminist 'content'" of her novels (33).

10 Demay, for instance, specifies that Riccoboni, being neither "Rousseau nor Laclos," does not belong with the greatest novelists of her century (7–8).

11 Cf. André Monglond on Riccoboni: "Pour la première fois, la femme soulève le problème de sa destinée" ["For the first time, woman raises the question of her destiny"] (*Histoire intérieure* 229).

12 See, for example, Cook and my *The Novels of Mme Riccoboni*.

13 Lest my reader be confused by the repetition of names, let me note that a good many of the century's heroines were called Adèle or Adélaïde: in addition to Riccoboni's Adélaïde de Sancerre and Adélaïde du Bugei, we shall encounter still another Adélaïde in this chapter (a heroine of Marie-Anne Robert), and, briefly, another Adelle (in a novel by Benoist). There was also, I might add, a profusion of Sophies and Emilies, and (especially in the years following Rousseau's *Julie ou la nouvelle Héloïse* [1761]) of Julies and Claires, while "English" heroines of French novels seem to be almost always Jenny or Fanny (often spelled Fanni).

14 Sarah Simmons observes that women characters in the eighteenth-century novel tend to be remarkable mostly for their "pallor" and "mediocrity" and adds that not even the "heroines" among them can compare with their male companions in the influence exerted on other characters and events (1918). Simmons's article makes no mention of novels written by women.

15 Fréron complains in *L'année littéraire* that Fanny shows no "restraint" (6: 54 [1757]). For Félicité de Genlis, Fanny is too impassioned and utterly lacking in "decency and charm" (*De l'influence* 280–81). Nineteenth-century novelist-critic Julia Kavanagh finds her "a great deal too free in act and speech" (1: 304).

16 *De l'influence* 280. Fréron, on the other hand, reasoned that so gentle and tender a creature might be more likely than another to fall prey to the kind of inconsolable grief that leads to suicide (4: 128 [1758]).

17 André is also one of the rare critics to speculate, even briefly, about why Riccoboni did not use her own career as material for her novels: perhaps because a novelist-actress was hardly considered worthy of commendation, she suggests, and Riccoboni did not want to frighten away her public (1993).

18 And when Emilie realizes that her brother has carried off their sister in hopes of marrying her, she asks, in almost the same words: "Quelle est donc la force du sang? Ces mouvements sont-ils si semblables à l'amour qu'on puisse s'y tromper?" ["What, then, is the power of blood? Are its impulses so similar to love that we can be mistaken about them?"] (4: 25).

19 Ruth P. Thomas reaches a similar conclusion about five fictional widows (including Juliette Catesby): "The widow is doubly a victim, first of a society that forces her into an unhappy or unsatisfying marriage, and then of herself. Knowingly or not, she adopts at least some of the modes and values of the society that oppresses her, and she seals her own fate" (449).

CHAPTER 5: MAPPING THE QUOTIDIAN

1 In one of the earliest important articles to appear on Charrière, "Les *Lettres écrites de Lausanne* de Madame de Charrière: inhibition psychique et interdit social," which was published in 1970, Jean Starobinski notes that in her fiction "almost imperceptible" incidents play a major role (130). My reading of Charrière and especially of *Lettres écrites de Lausanne* owes a constant debt to Starobinski's interpretation.

2 A good source of information on the life of Charrière remains Philippe Godet's 1906 biography, *Madame de Charrière et ses amis*.

3 Cf. Riccoboni who in an April 1782 letter to Laclos qualified as "bagatelles" her own collected works, which included, of course, some of the century's most popular novels (*Laclos* 759). *Le mari sentimental* itself recalls a short interpolated story in Riccoboni's *Lettres de Mylord Rivers* (1776). A middle-aged Frenchman marries a woman he has known and admired for years, and the day after the wedding he is stunned to discover that, charming as she is from 6 P.M. to midnight, she can be "a

fury in the morning" and spend the rest of the day persecuting those unfortunate enough to have to deal with her (402).

4   The novels of Charrière, and none more so than *Lettres de Mistriss Henley*, may be read as a chapter in the history of the detail from the mid-eighteenth century which Naomi Schor astutely sets out in *Reading in Detail*. With its emphasis on ornamentation (the rouge, plumes, and artificial flowers of which Mr. Henley disapproves for his wife and daughter; the bedroom furnishings and wall hangings) and the everyday (domestic life and family and social obligations in Hollowpark), Mistress Henley's story participates in the "semantic network" of the detail that Schor delineates, giving play to an oppressive set of culturally determined "sexual hierarchies" (4).

5   The unfortunate heroes, respectively, of Prévost's *Le philosophe anglais ou histoire de Monsieur Cleveland* (1731–39) and Baculard d'Arnaud's *Les époux malheureux* (1746).

6   Susan S. Lanser uses Janine Rossard's "Le désir de mort romantique dans *Caliste*" as the point of departure for a shrewd study of *Lettres de Mistriss Henley*, reading "in the light of gender the phenomena that Rossard's 1972 essay associates with a more general *mal du siècle*," and emphasizing especially the gestures by which Charrière "challenges the linguistic and moral coupling of 'reason' and 'right'" ("Courting Death" 49, 51).

7   Two excellent studies of closure in Charrière's work are Susan K. Jackson, "The Novels of Isabelle de Charrière, or, A Woman's Work Is Never Done," and Elizabeth J. MacArthur, "Devious Narratives: Refusal of Closure in Two Eighteenth-Century Epistolary Novels."

8   In Laclos's *Les liaisons dangereuses* (1782), on the other hand, the absence of meaningful mother-daughter communication allows Madame de Merteuil to persuade Cécile Volanges of the compatibility of the observation of the proprieties and certain illicit gratifications. In Genlis's *Histoire intéressante de la duchesse de C**** (which I shall discuss in chapter 10), which first appeared the same year as *Les liaisons dangereuses*, the heroine's tribulations are also ascribed to failures of mother-daughter communication.

9   For Starobinski, it's the "dramatized version" (133).

10 At the time of her marriage, however, she is designated as "Maria Sophia ***" (214).

11 As Paul Pelckmans notes in "La fausse emphase de la 'mort de toi,'" a marriage between William and Caliste would hardly have raised a general outcry, for apart from William's father, everyone is astonished rather at his failure to marry Caliste (506). Her chambermaid reports to William that people feel that he "should" marry Caliste (205); the uncle of Caliste's first lover calls William an "imbecile" for not daring to marry her (209); and Caliste's husband himself expresses astonishment in a letter to William after Caliste's death that, loving William as she did, she was unable or unwilling to bring him to marry her (232).

12 For Starobinski, *Lettres écrites de Lausanne* describes a world "où nul ne sait accomplir les gestes décisifs qui rompraient le mauvais charme" ["where no one is able to carry out the decisive gestures that would break the evil spell"] (147), a peaceful world in which there nonetheless reigns a noiseless "moral terror" (150).

CHAPTER 6: ECONOMIES

1 Robert L. Dawson, *Additions* 307. There were also later editions, translations, imitations, and adaptations. The playwright Mabille, for example, produced an insipid three-act comedy version, where the heroine, no longer a widow, loses the autonomy so essential to the Riccoboni story; Frances Moore Brooke translated the novel into English. An index of the work's continuing popularity might be seen in the fact that a woman writing letter-novels ten to twenty years later gave her characters names similar to that of Juliette's confidante, Milady Henriette Campley: in Beccary's *Lettres de Milady Bedfort* (1769), supposedly translated from the English, there is a "Lady Camplé," while her *Milord d'Ambi, histoire anglaise* (1778) has a character named "Miss Henriette Camplei."

2 Janet Altman's chapter "Of Confidence and Confidants" contains insights into the role of the confessional letter in *Juliette Catesby* and other novels.

3 D'Ossery's second brother dies from a "fall," while hunting.

4 Elsewhere I have argued for a reading of the scene as a rape and have examined the conventions of the epistolary genre that are enlisted in palliating this form of violence ("La lettre et l'interdit").

5 It's perhaps worth mentioning that if Charrière's working girl, Julianne, is a bit slovenly in act and dress ("mal mise" and "de mauvaise façon" [66], according to Marianne de la Prise), Riccoboni's is romanticized: Sara and the other flower sellers are neatly dressed, carry nicely arranged baskets, and wear large, straw hats that make them look even prettier.

CHAPTER 7: WEDDING NIGHTS

1 In confirmation of this tradition, the heroine of Marguerite Daubenton's *Zélie dans le désert* writes near the end of her story: "Si nous avions écrit un roman, l'histoire de mon amie et la mienne finiraient à l'époque de notre mariage. Mais comme ce n'est pas une fiction, je vais en donner la suite" ["If we had written a novel, my story and my friend's would end at the time of our marriage. But since it's not a fiction, I'm going to continue it"] (2: 309).

2 The monumental, canonical male authors, of course, also allude to wedding nights, but their tone tends to be different, ranging from the satirical to the scientific. Here is Diderot's Jacques le fataliste commenting on the grotesque marriage masterminded by Madame de la Pommeraye between the marquis des Arcis and a young whore: "Délivrez-moi du souci de la première nuit des noces, et jusqu'à présent je n'y vois pas un grand mal" ["Release me from the anxiety of the wedding night, and for the present I see no great harm in it"] (190–91). Madame de Merteuil reminisces more solemnly but with comparable detachment about her own experience as a virgin bride: she made an effort to appear embarrassed and fearful, but felt in fact only a scientific interest in the events of the wedding night (172).

3 Similarly, eighteenth-century art sometimes represents the bride's *coucher*, but does not depict what happens behind the bed curtains. Over two centuries later, Colette would use a comparable narrative pattern in evoking her own apocalyptic experience. In *Noces*, the account of her life with her awesome first husband, Willy, she describes in lavish detail the decor in which she was wed, the guests, her dress, and even the eating of the ritual cake of nougat and ice cream. But three *points de suspension* alone represent what happens next, and then begins a new paragraph: "Le lendemain, mille lieues, des abîmes, des découvertes, des métamorphoses sans remède me séparaient de la veille" ["The next day, a thou-

sand leagues, abysses, metamorphoses for which there was no help separated me from the day before"] (*Oeuvres complètes* 7 [Paris: Flammarion, 1949], 251). The three dots strategically interrupt her story at the point of a literally unspeakable divide; like Madame de Mortane, Colette continues with a leap to "the next day."

4   The opening paragraph of the *Le canapé couleur de feu* (1714) by Fougeret de Montbron recounts the courtship and wedding of a rich old prosecutor and a young widow after his money. They leave the wedding celebration and retire to her room to consummate the marriage, but the groom proves impotent: after an hour of "sweating blood," he has to give up (7). Is this the male version of wedding-night anxiety?

5   Not infrequently, of course, the consummation of a marriage was postponed because of the bride's youth. This is the case, for example, for Riccoboni's Madame de Sancerre, whose mother judges her "delicate and unformed," and for a protagonist in Charrière's *Honorine d'Userche* (1798), whose husband joins his regiment directly after the wedding ceremony, leaving her alone for a year—with disastrous consequences.

6   "Ce roman," commented the *Correspondance littéraire* in an article dated February 1786, "commence par où les autres finissent, par le mariage de l'héroïne" ["This novel begins where the others leave off, with the heroine's marriage"] (part 3, 3: 450).

7   For biographical information, I am indebted to Monsieur and Madame William Sévery, *La vie de société dans le pays de Vaud à la fin du dix-huitième siècle*, and especially to Dorette Berthoud, *Le général et la romancière*.

8   Wall's story also appeared in a French translation the year Montolieu's novel was published: *Albertine* by Nicolas de Bonneville was included in his *Choix de petits romans imitées de l'allemand* [Selection of short novels based on the German].

9   Quoted in Dawson, *Baculard* 2: 676, from a manuscript at the Bibliothèque Nationale (n.a.f. 6851, *f.* 14).

10   A.-A. Barbier and N. L. M. Desessart, *Nouvelle bibliothèque d'un homme de goût, entièrement refondue, corrigée et augmentée*, 5 vols. (Paris: Duminil-Lesueur, 1808–10), 5: 76.

11   Among French novels by women, Staël also extols Lafayette's *La prin-*

cesse de Clèves, Tencin's *Mémoires du comte de Comminge*, Charrière's *Cal-iste* and the works of Riccoboni (1: 71).

12 For example, *Raison et sensibilité*, freely adapted from Jane Austen, *Le Robinson suisse*, adapted from the novel of Johann David Wyss, and a translation of Schiller, *Le nécromancien*.

13 The 1809 London Dulau edition of the novel includes a center fold-out bearing the words and music of Caroline's song.

14 Chénier concedes in the letter cited earlier: "ce n'est pas très bien écrit" ["it's not very well written"].

15 For further discussion of the novel's use of irony, see my "Sensibility with Irony: Madame de Montolieu at the End of an Era."

CHAPTER 8: GILDED CAGES

1 For biography, see the baron de Maricourt; for Souza's letters to the comtesse d'Albany, see Saint-René Taillandy. For a consideration of the relation between the French novel and the events of the 1780s and 1790s in France, see Henri Coulet, "Quelques aspects du roman anti-révolutionnaire sous la Révolution," and my next chapter. I am grateful to Marie-José Fassiotto for helping me track down some biographical detail.

2 *Eugène de Rothelin* in particular resembles *Adèle de Sénange*. Eugène falls in love with his cousin Athénaïs, whose family is estranged from his own branch, and who moreover is already joined to another man in an uncon-summated *mariage de raison*. In the end, the husband agrees to an annul-ment and Eugène and Athénaïs marry. A number of other characters traditional in the eighteenth-century novel also have counterparts in *Adèle de Sénange*, including a cherished grandparent, a young woman saved from the convent by an arranged marriage, and a cruel parent who wants the entire family inheritance to go to the eldest son. In the 1820s and 1830s, Souza published more novels, including *Mademoiselle de Tournon*, *La comtesse de Farge*, and *La duchesse de Guise*, but they do not equal her earlier works.

3 The baron de Maricourt also uses almost the same words as Chénier to describe Souza's work, lauding the purity and good taste of her lan-guage: "la correction du langage et la mesure du bon ton" (171–72).

4 They are wont, moreover, to regard Souza's work as a document about a

certain exquisite pre-Revolutionary mentality and "established social order," or as a late example of eighteenth-century literary charm. Cf. Elizabeth Fox-Genovese on certain nineteenth-century commentators: "Many of [the Goncourts'] predecessors and successors—the scholars and men of letters who edited innumerable volumes of women's letters and memoirs and wrote of the salons and the lives of eighteenth-century French women—explicitly identified their work as an attempt to recapture the sweetness of life in that final flowering of aristocratic society before the Revolutionary holocaust destroyed everything worth living for" (Intro. to Spencer, 2).

5   In the last line of Souza's next novel, *Charles et Marie*, the hero apostrophizes the heroine in terms that can equally describe Sydenham's history with Adèle: "je voulais vous dominer, votre douceur m'a soumis" ["I wanted to control you; your sweetness conquered me"] (285).

6   My discussion here and in the pages that follow is obviously much indebted to Tanner.

7   The Goncourts stress the affectionate feelings that many women had for the convents where they were raised. They portray the eighteenth-century convent as typically a cheerful place to which women might later return, as Adèle does, during bereavement, or simply in order to relive for brief periods the "happiness of childhood" (58–59).

8   The cautionary tale of the nun is reminiscent of a similar one in Marivaux's *La vie de Marianne*, and the nun's escape from her convent only to be miserable in society is a version of Diderot's *La religieuse*.

9   Here again, I am using Tanner's notions of the functions of "city" and "field."

10   Charrière's *Trois femmes* (1796) contains a scene where the young lovers, Emilie and Théobald, sit by a fire on a winter's night reading aloud the recently published *Adèle de Sénange*; at the dance scene, Théobald becomes furious (9: 77). Years later, Souza herself was to include in *Eugène de Rothelin* an episode about jealousy similar to the scene in *Adèle de Sénange*.

CHAPTER 9: BRAZEN DESIRE

1   For an assessment of the novel's debt to Rousseau, Richardson, Ricoboni, and others, as well as for biography and extensive selections from Cottin's correspondence, see L. C. Sykes.

2 The original edition is dated "an VII" ["year VII"]. According to Monglond, its publication was recorded on "10 thermidor an VII" (*La France révolutionnaire* 4: cols. 1113–14): this would correspond approximately to July 1799.

3 Cf. Kavanagh, who observes that the little we know of Cottin's life "reads a striking lesson on the mysterious difference which there is between an author and an author's works." She comments specifically on the dichotomy in *Claire d'Albe* between fictional content and biographical truth: "The subject—a young, lovely, but guilty wife—was a strange one to be chosen by the widow of a husband both fond and beloved" (2: 174, 176).

4 Cf. Fauchery, who notes that spring has a tendency to become the ritual moment of a heroine's sentimental unrest (726).

5 For example, Colette Cazenobe, "Une préromantique méconnue, Madame Cottin," Janine Rossard, *Pudeur et romantisme*, and Jean Gaulmier, "Sophie et ses malheurs ou le romantisme du pathétique."

6 If Gaulmier takes heed of the extraordinary tension and the violent scenes that contemporaries found, as he says, "indefensibly audacious" (6), Cazenobe surprisingly remarks that nothing in Cottin's novels could shock the reader, that she made a point of observing "all the proprieties" ("Une préromantique méconnue" 190).

7 Cottin's *Amélie Mansfield* (1803), another melancholy story of ill-starred passion and destruction, likewise features a hero whose sentimentality and devotion go hand in hand with a certain brutality of instinct and action. Of this novel, Constance de Cazenove d'Arlens, a novelist and a friend and admirer of Staël and Montolieu (as well as first cousin to Benjamin Constant), wrote in the year of its publication that it was "aussi invraisemblable, aussi dangereux que possible" ["as hard to believe, as dangerous as possible"] (*Journal* 53).

8 Cf. also André Monglond: "En pleine Terreur, à deux pas de l'échafaud, en littérature le goût Louis XVI continue de régner" ["In the middle of the Terror, two steps from the scaffold, Louis XVI taste continues to reign in literature"] (*Histoire intérieure* 1: 103).

9 For Coulet, *Claire d'Albe* specifically demonstrates that "l'héroïsme sentimental de *La nouvelle Héloïse* et l'alliance de la vertu et du bonheur recherchée par les bourgeois de la Révolution sont également impossi-

bles à une époque de réaction qui rétablit l'autorité absolue de l'homme, du patron, du mari, qui tient dans la dépendance et le dénuement les paysans et les ouvriers et qui confond réussite professionnelle et financière avec devoir moral" ["the sentimental heroism of *La nouvelle Héloïse* and the alliance of virtue and happiness sought by the bourgeois of the Revolution are equally impossible in a time of reaction which reestablishes the absolute authority of man, master, husband, who keeps peasants and workers in dependence and destitution and who confuses professional and financial success with moral duty"] ("Quelques aspects" 39–40).

10 Or, as Rossard puts it, of "passion" and "pudeur" (*Pudeur et romantisme* 16).

CHAPTER 10: MORALS

1 *De l'influence des femmes sur la littérature française* is another chapter in the history of canon formation that Joan DeJean sets out for the period from the late seventeenth to the late eighteenth century (*Tender Geographies*). It bears noting that Genlis's book is an authentically alternative literary history: in the last lines of the preface, implicitly underscoring her mainstream view of women's role, Genlis describes her work as a sketch not of "French literature" *by women*, but simply of "French literature."

2 For additional biographical information, see Gabriel de Broglie.

3 Witness, for example, the fifteen-page appendix setting out Adèle's "course of reading" from the age of six to twenty-two. In fact, *Adèle et Théodore* is mentioned in Charrière's *Lettres écrites de Lausanne*, published three years later, as the very standard of pedagogical fiction: Charrière's letter-writing narrator expands on the principles that guided her in educating her daughter, but also reminds her correspondent that allowance must be made for real-life factors, for she and her daughter are not "un roman comme Adèle et sa mère" ["a novel like Adèle and her mother"] (149).

4 Despite having grown up with an irresponsible mother and a fiscally incompetent father, Genlis the educator never stopped insisting that children owe their parents blind obedience.

5 Claire's story may end in dishonor, but it exudes, as Julia Kavanagh confirms, "a seductive charm in every step" leading to ruin (II: 176).

6 Cottin, *Oeuvres complètes* (Ménard et Desenne, 1824). Another nineteenth-century critic, Pauline de Meulan Guizot, also commented perceptively on both Cottin and Genlis, noting that it was senseless to try to judge the former's writing until the emotions it aroused had disappeared—and these emotions, she added, last a long time. Guizot characterized Genlis's own style with this lapidary phrase: it is "toujours bien et jamais mieux" ["always good and never better"] (quoted in Sainte-Beuve's preface to Guizot, *Le temps passé* 55).

7 *Mes souvenirs sur Berlin, Potsdam et Sans Souci ou supplément à l'ouvrage de M. de Ségur l'Aîné* (Charrière, *Oeuvres complètes* 10: 306).

8 For an excellent discussion of Genlis's pedagogy and her portrayal of matriarchy, especially in *Adèle et Théodore* and *Les veillées du château* [*Tales of the Castle*] (1784), see Ellen Moers 217–31.

CONCLUSION

1 The action of Riccoboni's *Histoire de M. le marquis de Cressy*, for example, begins when the title character returns from the war with Spain. And the departure of Fanni Butlerd's lover for the army is important not because of any fighting he might do but because his absence motivates her letters. Genlis's *Les veillées du château* has its point of departure even more exactly in the leave-taking of the marquis de Clémire when he goes to the army. Military service was an expensive proposition for a man, so his wife, mother-in-law, and two children simultaneously leave Paris for their château in Burgundy in order to reduce household expenses while he is away; in this "domain of absolute matriarchy" (Moers 222), they spend their evenings telling the moral tales that make up the volume.

SELECTED BIBLIOGRAPHY

Altman, Janet Gurkin. *Epistolarity: Approaches to a Form*. Columbus: Ohio State University Press, 1982.

André, Arlette. "Le féminisme chez Madame Riccoboni." Transactions of the Fifth International Congress on the Enlightenment. In *Studies on Voltaire and the Eighteenth Century* 193: 1988–95. Oxford: Voltaire Foundation, 1980.

Barchillon, Jacques. *Le conte merveilleux français de 1690 à 1790*. Paris: Honoré Champion, 1975.

Bearne, Catherine Mary. *Four Fascinating Frenchwomen*. London and Leipzig: T. Fisher Unwin, 1910.

Berthoud, Dorette. *Le général et la romancière, 1792–1798: épisodes de l'émigration française en Suisse, d'après les lettres du général de Montesquiou à Mme de Montolieu*. Neuchâtel: La Baconnière, 1959.

Bettelheim, Bruno. *The Uses of Enchantment*. New York: Knopf, 1977.

Bonneville, Nicolas de. *Albertine: anecdote tirée de l'histoire secrète de la cour de ****. In *Choix de petits romans imités de l'allemand*. Paris: Barrois and Royes, 1786. 19–63.

Boudier de Villemert, Pierre Joseph. *L'ami des femmes ou morale du sexe*. Paris: Royez, 1788.

Boutet de Monvel. *L'amant bourru*. Nouvelle édition. Paris: Duchesne, 1778.

Broglie, Gabriel de. *Madame de Genlis*. Paris: Perrin, 1985.

Carné, de. *Histoire de Madame la comtesse de Monglas ou consolation pour les religieuses qui le sont malgré elles.* 2 vols. Amsterdam and Paris: Hochereau, 1756.

Cazenobe, Colette. "Le féminisme paradoxal de Madame Riccoboni." *Revue d'histoire littéraire de la France* 88, no.1 (January-February 1988): 23–45.

———. "Une préromantique méconnue, Madame Cottin." *Travaux de littérature* 1 (1985): 175–202.

Cazenove d'Arlens, Constance de. *Deux mois à Paris et à Lyon sous le Consulat:journal de Mme de Cazenove d'Arlens [fév.-avril 1803].* Paris: Picard, 1903.

La chaste Madame Riccoboni: les folies de l'amour au dix-huitième siècle. Radio program by Régis Labourdette. Prod. Arlette Dave. With participants Colette Cazenobe, Mireille Flaux, Colette Piau, and Joan Hinde Stewart. France Culture. June 1989.

Chénier, Marie Joseph. *Tableau historique de l'état et des progrès de la littérature française depuis 1789.* Paris: Maradan, 1816.

Cioranescu, Alexandre. *Bibliographie de la littérature française du dix-huitième siècle.* 3 vols. Paris: Centre National de la Recherche Scientifique, 1969.

Clancy, Patricia A. "A French Writer and Educator in England: Mme Le Prince de Beaumont." *Studies on Voltaire and the Eighteenth Century* 201: 195–208. Oxford: Voltaire Foundation, 1982.

Constant, Samuel de. *Le mari sentimental ou le mariage comme il y en a quelques-uns.* Ed. Giovanni Riccioli. Milan: Cisalpino-Goliardica, 1975.

Cook, Elizabeth Heckendorn. "Going Public: The Letter and the Contract in *Fanni Butlerd." Eighteenth-Century Studies* 24, no.1 (Fall 1990): 21–45.

Coulet, Henri. "Quelques aspects du roman antirévolutionnaire sous la Révolution." *Revue de l'Université d'Ottawa/University of Ottawa Quarterly* 54, no.3 (1984): 27–47.

———. "Le thème de la 'Madeleine repentie' chez Robert Challe, Prévost et Diderot." *Saggi e ricerche di letteratura francesa* 14: 287–304. Paris: Bulzoni, 1975.

Coyer, Gabriel François. *L'année merveilleuse.* In *Bagatelles morales et dissertations.* Nouvelle édition. London and Frankfort: Knoch and Eslinger, 1755.

Crosby, Emily. *Une romancière oubliée: Madame Riccoboni.* Paris: Rieder, 1924.

Selected Bibliography

Darrow, Margaret H. "French Noblewomen and the New Domesticity: 1750–1850." *Feminist Studies* 5, no.1 (Spring 1979): 41–65.

Dawson, Robert L. *Additions to the Bibliographies of French Prose Fiction, 1618–1806. Studies on Voltaire and the Eighteenth Century* 236. Oxford: Voltaire Foundation, 1985.

———. *Baculard d'Arnaud: Life and Prose Fiction. Studies on Voltaire and the Eighteenth Century* 141–42. Oxford: Voltaire Foundation, 1976.

———. *The French Booktrade and the "Permission Simple" of 1777: Copyright and the Public Domain, with an edition of the permit registers. Studies on Voltaire and the Eighteenth Century* 301. Oxford: Voltaire Foundation, 1992.

DeJean, Joan. *Tender Geographies: Women and the Origins of the Novel in France.* New York: Columbia University Press, 1991.

Demay, Andrée. *Marie-Jeanne Riccoboni ou de la pensée féministe chez une romancière du XVIIIe siècle.* Paris: La Pensée Universelle, 1977.

Desfontaines, François Georges Fouques. *Lettres de Sophie et du Chevalier de ***, pour servir de supplément aux Lettres du marquis de Roselle.* 2 vols. London and Paris: L'Esclapart, 1765.

Diderot, Denis. *Jacques le fataliste et son maître.* Ed. Yvon Belaval. Paris: Gallimard Folio, 1973.

———. "Sur les femmes." In *Oeuvres complètes.* Ed. J. Assézat. 20 vols. 2: 251–62. Paris: Garnier, 1875.

Dorat, Claude Joseph. *Lettres en vers et oeuvres mêlées de M. D***.* Paris: Sébastien Jorry, 1767.

Eliot, George. "Woman in France: Madame de Sablé." In *Essays and Reviews of George Eliot.* Intro. Mrs. S. B. Herrick. Boston: Aldine, 1887. 58–90.

Etienne, Servais. *Le genre romanesque en France depuis l'apparition de la "Nouvelle Héloïse" jusqu'aux approches de la Révolution.* Brussels: Lamertin, 1922.

Fauchery, Pierre. *La destinée féminine dans le roman européen du dix-huitième siècle: 1713–1807: Essai de gynécomythie romanesque.* Paris: Armand Colin, 1972.

Les femmes savantes ou bibliothèque des dames, par Monsieur N. C. Amsterdam: Michel Charles Le Cene, 1718.

Fink, Beatrice, ed. *Isabelle de Charrière/Belle Van Zuylen.* Spec. issue of *Eighteenth-Century Life* 13, no.1 (February 1989).

Flaux, Mireille. *Madame Riccoboni: Une idée du bonheur au féminin au siècle des lumières*. Lille: Université de Lille III, Atelier National de Reproduction des Thèses, 1991.

Fletcher, Dennis. "Restif de la Bretonne and Woman's Estate." In *Woman and Society in Eighteenth-Century France*. Ed. Eva Jacobs et al. London: Athlone, 1979, 9b–109.

Fontenay, Elisabeth de. *Diderot ou le matérialisme enchanté*. Paris: Grasset, 1981.

Fougeret de Montbrun. *Le canapé couleur de feu*. Paris: Bernard Laville (Erotika Biblion), 1970.

Fournel, *Traité de l'adultère*. 2d ed. Paris: Demonville, 1783.

Fréron, Elie Catherine. *L'année littéraire*. 292 vols. Paris: Mérigot, 1754–90.

Gacon-Dufour, Marie Armande Jeanne d'Humières. *Mémoire pour le sexe féminin, contre le sexe masculin*. London and Paris: Royez, 1787.

Galien de Chateau Thiery, Madame. *Apologie des femmes appuyée sur l'histoire*. Paris: Didot, 1748.

Gaulmier, Jean. "Sophie et ses malheurs ou le romantisme du pathétique." *Romantisme* 3 (1972): 3–16.

Gay, Jules. *Bibliographie des ouvrages relatifs à l'amour, aux femmes, au mariage, et des livres facétieux pantagruéliques, scatalogiques, satiriques, etc.* 4th ed. 4 vols. Paris: Lemonnyer, 1894.

Genlis, Stéphanie Félicité de. *De l'influence des femmes sur la littérature française*. Paris: Maradan, 1811.

Ginisty, Paul. "Les souvenirs sentimentaux de Mme Riccoboni." In *Mémoires et souvenirs de comédiennes (XVIIIe siècle)*. Paris: Louis Michaud, 1914.

Godet, Philippe. *Madame de Charrière et ses amis*. 2 vols. Geneva: A. Jullien, 1906.

Goncourt, Edmond and Jules. *La femme au dix-huitième siècle*. Preface by Elisabeth Badinter. Paris: Flammarion, 1982.

Grente, Georges (Cardinal), ed. *Dictionnaire des lettres françaises. Le dix-huitième siècle*. 2 vols. Paris: Fayard, 1960.

Grimm, Melchior. *Correspondance littéraire, philosophique et critique . . .*, 6 vols. Paris: Longchamps and Buisson, 1812–13.

Guizot, François Pierre Guillaume and Elisabeth Charlotte Pauline de Meulan Guizot. *Le temps passé*. 2 vols. Paris: Perrin, 1887.

Hearne, Betsy. *Beauty and the Beast: Visions and Revisions of an Old Tale.* Chicago and London: University of Chicago Press, 1989.

Hesse, Carla. "Reading Signatures: Female Authorship and Revolutionary Law in France, 1750–1850." *Eighteenth-Century Studies* 22, no.3 (Spring 1989): 469–87.

Hoffman, Paul. *La femme dans la pensée des lumières.* Paris: Orphrys, 1977.

Jackson, Susan K. "In Search of a Female Voice: *Les Liaisons dangereuses.*" In *Writing the Female Voice: Essays on Epistolary Literature.* Ed. Elizabeth C. Goldsmith. Boston: Northeastern University Press, 1989. 154–71.

———. "The Novels of Isabelle de Charrière, or, A Woman's Work Is Never Done." *Studies in Eighteenth-Century Culture* 14 (1985): 299–306.

Jones, Shirley. "Madame de Tencin: an Eighteenth-Century Woman Novelist." In *Woman and Society in Eighteenth-Century France.* Ed. Eva Jacobs et al. London: Athlone, 1979. 207–17.

Kavanagh, Julia. *French Women of Letters: Biographical Sketches.* 2 vols. London: Hurst and Blackett, 1862.

Kelly, Joan. "Early Feminist Theory and the Querelle des Femmes, 1400–1789." *Signs* 8, no.1 (1982): 4–8.

Laborde, Alice M. *Diderot et l'amour.* Saratoga, CA: Anma Libri, 1979.

Laclos, Choderlos de. *Oeuvres complètes.* Ed. Laurent Versini. Paris: Gallimard Pléiade, 1979.

Lacroix, Jean François de. *Dictionnaire historique portatif des femmes célèbres.* 2 vols. Paris: Cellot, 1769.

Laden, Marie-Paule. " 'Quel aimable et cruel petit livre': Madame de Charrière's *Mistriss Henley.*" *French Forum* 11, no.3 (September 1986): 289–99.

Lafayette, Marie-Madeleine Pioche de la Vergne. *Romans et nouvelles.* Ed. Emile Magne and Alain Niderst. Paris: Garnier, 1970.

La Harpe, Jean François de. *Cours de littérature.* Paris: Hiard, 1834. 23 vols.

———. *Letters to the Shuvalovs.* Ed. Christopher Todd. *Studies on Voltaire and the Eighteenth Century* 108. Oxford: Voltaire Foundation, 1973.

———. *Oeuvres.* 16 vols. Vols. 14–15: *Littérature et critique.* Paris: Verdière, 1821.

Lanser, Susan S. "Courting Death: *Roman, romantisme,* and *Mistress Henley's* Narrative Practices." *Eighteenth-Century Life* 13, no.1 (February 1989): 49–59.

————. "Plot, Voice, and Narrative *Oubli: Juliette Catesby*'s Twice-Told Tale." In *Eighteenth-Century Women and the Arts*. Ed. Frederick M. Keener and Susan E. Lorsch. NY: Greenwood, 1988. 129–39.

Larnac, Jean. *Histoire de la littérature féminine en France*. 4th ed. Paris: Kra, 1929.

Legouvé. *Le mérite des femmes*. Paris: Pougin, 1835.

Le Hir, Marie-Pierre. "Le mélodrame de Mme Hadot, ou le poison de la différence." *French Review* 63, no.6 (May 1990): 950–58.

Le Prince de Beaumont, Jeanne Marie. *Arrêt solemnel de la nature, par lequel le grand événement de l'année 1748 est sursis jusqu'au premier août 1749.* [Paris, 1748].

————. *La Belle et la Bête*. In *Le magasin des enfants*. 2d ed. Ed. Eugénie Foa. Leipzig: F. A. Brockhaus, 1851.

————. *Lettre en réponse à l'Année merveilleuse, par Mad. Leprince D. B.* Nancy: Thomas, Henry and Bertheau, n.d.

Leutrat, Jean Louis. "L'histoire de Madame de la Pommeraye et le thème de la jeune veuve." *Diderot Studies* 18:121–37. Ed. Otis Fellows and Diana Guiragossian. Geneva: Droz, 1975.

M., Madame. "Mme Riccoboni." *Revue de Paris* (1841) 35: 184–208.

Mabille. *Cécile*. Paris: Ballard, 1780.

MacArthur, Elizabeth J. "Devious Narratives: Refusal of Closure in Two Eighteenth-Century Epistolary Novels." *Eighteenth-Century Studies* 21, no.1 (Fall 1987): 1–20.

Maricourt, Baron André de. *Madame de Souza et sa famille*. 2d ed. Paris: Emile-Paul, 1907.

Martin, Angus, Vivienne G. Mylne, and Richard Frautschi. *Bibliographie du genre romanesque français 1751–1800*. London: Mansell, and Paris: France Expansion, 1977.

————. "Romans et romanciers à succès de 1751 à la Révolution d'après les rééditions." *Revue des Sciences humaines* 35, no.139 (1970): 383–89.

Mauzi, Robert. *L'idée du bonheur dans la littérature et la pensée françaises au dix-huitième siècle*. Paris: Armand Colin, 1960.

————. "Les maladies de l'âme au XVIIIe siècle." *Revue des sciences humaines*, fasc. 100 (October-December 1960): 459–93.

May, Georges. *Le dilemme du roman au XVIIIe siècle*. New Haven: Yale University Press, and Paris: Presses Universitaires de France, 1963.

Mercier, Michel. *Le roman féminin*. Paris: Presses Universitaires de France, 1976.

Merlant, Joachim. *Le roman personnel de Rousseau à Fromentin*. Paris: Hachette, 1905.

Michaud, Joseph François. *Bibliographie universelle, ancienne et moderne*. Nouvelle édition. 45 vols. Paris: Desplaces, 1854–65.

Miller, Nancy K. "Men's Reading, Women's Writing: Gender and the Rise of the Novel." In *Displacements*, ed. Joan DeJean and Nancy K. Miller. Baltimore: Johns Hopkins University Press, 1991. 37–54.

———. *Subject to Change: Reading Feminist Writing*. New York: Columbia University Press, 1988.

Moers, Ellen. *Literary Women*. New York: Doubleday, 1976.

Monglond, André. *La France révolutionnaire et impériale: annales de bibliographie méthodique et description des livres illustrés*. 9 vols. Paris: Arthaud, 1935.

———. *Histoire intérieure du préromantisme français de l'abbé Prévost à Joubert*. 2 vols. Grenoble: Arthaud, 1929.

Mooij, Anne Louis Anton. *Caractères principaux et tendances des romans psychologiques chez quelques femmes-auteurs, de Mme Riccoboni à Mme de Souza (1757–1826)*. Drukkerij de Waal: Groningen, 1949.

Mornet, Daniel. "Les enseignements des bibliothèques privées (1750–1780)." *Revue d'histoire littéraire de la France* 17 (1910): 449–96.

Ouellet, Réal. "La théorie du roman épistolaire en France au XVIIIe siècle." *Studies on Voltaire and the Eighteenth Century* 89: 1209–27. Oxford: Voltaire Foundation, 1972.

Palissot de Montenoy, Charles. *La dunciade ou la guerre des sots*. Chelsea, 1764.

Pelckmans, Paul. "La fausse emphase de la 'mort de toi.'" *Neophilologus* 72 (1988): 499–515.

Piau, Colette. "L'écriture féminine? A propos de Marie Jeanne Riccoboni." *Dix-huitième siècle* 16 (1984): 369–86.

Portemer, Jean. "Le statut de la femme en France depuis la réformation des coutumes jusqu'à la rédaction du code civil." In *La femme*. Recueil de la Société Jean Bodin, part 2: 447–97. Brussels: Editions de la librairie encyclopédique, 1962.

Pothier, Robert Joseph. *Traité de la communauté, auquel on a joint un traité de la puissance du mari sur la personne et les biens de la femme*. 2 vols. Paris: Debure, and Orleans: Rouzeau-Montaut, 1770.

Prudhomme, L. *Biographie universelle et historique des femmes célèbres, mortes ou vivantes*. 4 vols. Paris: Lebigre, 1830.

Quérard, Joseph Marie. *La France littéraire, ou dictionnaire bibliographique*. 12 vols. Paris: Firmin Didot, 1827–64.

———, and Bourquelot, Louis Félix. *La littérature française contemporaine* (continuation of preceding title). 6 vols. Paris: Daguin, 1842–57.

Restif de la Bretonne, Nicolas. *Oeuvres*. 9 vols. Ed. Henri Bachelin. Geneva: Slatkine, 1971 (reprint of the ed. of Paris, 1930–32).

———. *La paysanne pervertie*. Chronology and preface by Béatrice Didier. Paris: Garnier-Flammarion, 1972.

Reynaud, M. A. *Madame Leprince de Beaumont: vie et oeuvre d'une éducatrice*. 2 vols. Lyon: [1972; typescript, Library of Congress].

Riccoboni, Marie Jeanne. *Mme Riccoboni's Letters to David Hume, David Garrick and Sir Robert Liston: 1764–1783*. Ed. James C. Nicholls. *Studies on Voltaire and the Eighteenth Century* 149. Oxford: Voltaire Foundation, 1976.

Rossard, Janine. "Le désir de mort romantique dans *Caliste*." *PMLA* 87, no.3 (May 1972): 492–98.

———. *Pudeur et romantisme*. Paris: Nizet, 1982.

Rousseau, Jean-Jacques. *Oeuvres complètes*. Ed. Bernard Gagnebin and Marcel Raymond. 4 vols. Paris: Pléiade, 1959–69.

Rowe, Karen. "Feminism and Fairy Tales." *Women's Studies* 6, no.3 (1979): 237–57.

Sabatier de Castres, Antoine. *Les trois siècles de la littérature française*. 5th ed. 4 vols. The Hague and Paris: Moutard, 1781.

Sade. *Idée sur les romans*. Bordeaux: Ducros, 1970.

Sainte-Beuve, Charles Augustin. *Portraits de femmes*. Nouvelle édition. Paris: Garnier, 1882.

Saint-René Taillandier, ed. *Lettres inédites de J. C. I. de Sismondi, de M. de Bonstetten, de Madame de Staël et de Madame de Souza à Madame la comtesse d'Albany*. Paris: Michel Lévy, 1863.

Schor, Naomi. *Reading in Detail: Aesthetics and the Feminine*. New York and London: Routledge, 1987.

Servien, Michèle. "Madame Riccoboni, vie et oeuvre." 2 vols. Thesis, Université de Paris IV, 1973.

Sévery, Monsieur and Madame William de. *La vie de société dans le pays de Vaud à la fin du dix-huitième siècle.* 2 vols. Lausanne: Bridel, and Paris: Fischbacher, 1911.

Simmons, Sarah. "Héroïne ou figurante? La femme dans le roman du XVIIIe siècle en France." Transactions of the Fifth International Congress on the Enlightenment, *Studies on Voltaire and the Eighteenth Century* 193: 1918–24. Oxford: Voltaire Foundation, 1980.

Spencer, Samia I., ed. *French Women and the Age of Enlightenment.* Intro. by Elizabeth Fox Genovese. Bloomington: Indiana University Press, 1984.

Staël, Germaine de. *Essai sur les fictions,* in *Oeuvres complètes de Madame la baronne de Staël-Holstein,* 2 vols. Paris: Firmin Didot, 1861. Vol. 1: 62–72.

Starobinski, Jean. "Les *Lettres écrites de Lausanne* de Madame de Charrière: inhibition psychique et interdit social." *Roman et lumières au XVIIIe siècle.* Paris: Editions sociales, 1970. 130–51.

Stewart, Joan Hinde. "Aimer à soixante ans: les lettres de Madame Riccoboni à Sir Robert Liston," *Actes du Colloque International "Aimer en France: 1760–1860."* Publications de la Faculté des Lettres de Clermont-Ferrand, 1980. 1: 181–89.

———. "Designing Women." *A New History of French Literature.* Ed. Denis Hollier. Cambridge and London: Harvard University Press, 1989. 553–58.

———. "La lettre et l'interdit." *Romanic Review* 80, no.4 (November 1989): 521–28.

———. *The Novels of Madame Riccoboni.* Chapel Hill: North Carolina Studies in the Romance Languages and Literatures, 1976.

———. "Sensibility with Irony: Madame de Montolieu at the End of an Era." *Kentucky Romance Quarterly* 25, no.4 (1978): 481–89.

Sykes, L. C. *Madame Cottin.* Oxford: Basil Blackwell, 1949.

Tanner, Tony. *Adultery in the Novel.* Baltimore and London: Johns Hopkins University Press, 1979.

Testud, Pierre. *Rétif de la Bretonne et la création littéraire.* Geneva: Droz, 1977.

Thomas, Ruth P. "Twice Victims: Virtuous Widows in the Eighteenth-

Century French Novel." *Studies on Voltaire and the Eighteenth Century* 266: 433–49. Oxford: Voltaire Foundation, 1989.

Traer, James F. *Marriage and the Family in Eighteenth-Century France.* Ithaca and London: Cornell University Press, 1980.

Varga, A. Kibédi. "Romans d'amour, romans de femmes à l'époque classique." *Revue des sciences humaines* 44, no.168 (1977): 517–24.

Versini, Laurent. *Laclos et la tradition.* Paris: Klincksieck, 1968.

———. *Le roman épistolaire.* Paris: Presses Universitaires de France, 1979.

Whatley, Janet. "Isabelle de Charrière." In *French Women Writers: A Bio-Bibliographical Source Book.* Ed. Eva Martin Sartori and Dorothy Wynne Zimmerman. New York, Westport, CT, London: Greenwood, 1991. 35–46.

INDEX